S0-BLX-504

THE SOUTHWEST HISTORICAL SERIES

EDITED BY

RALPH P. BIEBER

III

Stephen Watts Kearny
From an oil painting

JOURNAL OF A SOLDIER UNDER KEARNY AND DONIPHAN

1846-1847

by

GEORGE RUTLEDGE GIBSON

edited by

RALPH P. BIEBER

Associate Professor of History, Washington University, St. Louis

PORCUPINE PRESS
Philadelphia
1974

First edition 1935
(Glendale: The Arthur H. Clark Co., 1935)

Reprinted 1974 by
PORCUPINE PRESS, INC.
Philadelphia, Pennsylvania 19107

Library of Congress Cataloging in Publication Data

Gibson, George Rutledge, 1810 (ca.)-1885.
Journal of a soldier under Kearny and Doniphan, 1846-1847.

(The Southwest historical series, 3)
Reprint of the 1935 ed. published by A. H. Clark Co., Glendale, Calif.
1. United States--History--War with Mexico--1845-1848--Personal narratives. 2. Gibson, George Rutledge, 1810 (ca.)-1885. I. Title.
F786.S752 vol. 3 [E411] 917.9'03'2s [973.6'23'0924]
ISBN 0-87991-303-7 [B] 74-7157

Manufactured in the United States of America

CONTENTS

ILLUSTRATIONS

PREFACE

PREFACE

In 1873, George Rutledge Gibson, of Mattoon, Illinois, sent his Mexican war journal to his brother, Charles, in St. Louis, with instructions to present it to the Missouri Historical Society. When Charles Gibson delivered the manuscript to the society, he wrote: "I have read it through and find it in some respects most interesting – so much so that I have at times thought it ought to be published." Although this evaluation was made over sixty years ago, the editor is in entire agreement with it. Indeed, Gibson's journal of military service under Kearny and Doniphan is one of the best and most detailed accounts of its type thus far located.

The editor has reproduced the original manuscript with some alterations. He has corrected its spelling, punctuation, and paragraphing, and has changed its capitalization to conform to the format of the publisher. He has also occasionally altered its grammar and word order; but such changes have been made only when they were necessary to avoid a very awkward expression or to clarify the meaning of the author. All additions, with the exception of chapter headings, have been enclosed in brackets.

The editor wishes to thank the Missouri Historical Society for permission to publish the manuscript. For aid given in the preparation of this work, he is also grateful to Miss Stella M. Drumm, librarian, Mrs. Nettie Harney Beauregard, archivist, and Miss Anne Kinnaird, assistant archivist, Missouri Historical Society; Mrs. Richard E. Perry, Mrs. Kenneth G. Carpenter, Miss Marion Perry, and Mr. Gerolt Gibson, St. Louis; Colonel Easton R. Gibson, Monterey, California; Mr. William McCord Harris, New York City; Miss Blanche Gray, librarian, Mattoon Public Library, Mattoon, Illinois; and Professors Richard Jente and George B. Marsh, Washington University. For valuable assistance in preparing the manuscript for publication, the editor is indebted to his wife, Ida Parker Bieber.

RALPH P. BIEBER

Washington University
St. Louis, Missouri
June 27, 1934

INTRODUCTION

INTRODUCTION

Kearny's occupation of New Mexico and Doniphan's conquest of Chihuahua were the most adventurous and colorful military campaigns in the Southwest during the Mexican war. Leaving Fort Leavenworth with about seventeen hundred troops in the early summer of 1846, Colonel Kearny marched rapidly westward over the Santa Fé trail, and following a hot and toilsome journey across nearly nine hundred miles of uninhabited plains, took possession of New Mexico without firing a gun. He soon departed for California with a portion of his forces, leaving orders for Colonel Doniphan, who had accompanied him from Fort Leavenworth, to join Brigadier-general Wool in Chihuahua. After leading an expedition against the Navajo Indians, Doniphan proceeded south with about nine hundred men, crossed over a country devoid of much subsistence for man or beast, successfully engaged the Mexicans in the battles of Bracito and Sacramento, and early in March, 1847, entered the city of Chihuahua, approximately six hundred miles south of Santa Fé. George Rutledge Gibson, a Missouri volunteer who saw service under both Kearny and Doniphan, kept a daily journal of his experiences from Fort Leavenworth to Chihuahua and return. This journal,[1] which is here published for the first time, makes available much new information on the campaigns of these famous military leaders.

George Rutledge Gibson, the eldest of a family of

[1] Gibson presented his journal to the Missouri Historical Society in 1873.

seven sons and one daughter, was born in Christiansburg, Montgomery county, Virginia, about 1810.[2] His parents were Hugh Gibson, a native of Pennsylvania, and Elizabeth Brown Rutledge Gibson, a native of Virginia. His paternal grandfather, John Gibson, and his maternal grandfather, George Rutledge, a descendant of the Rutledges of South Carolina, had been soldiers in the American Revolution; and his father, Hugh Gibson, fought in the War of 1812.[3] George Rutledge Gibson spent the early years of his life in Christiansburg, which was situated on a broad summit of a mountain range in one of the most beautiful parts of southwestern Virginia. "There the long slopes of the Alleghenies lie covered with evergreens interspersed with glades, rivulets, and water-falls; there the dense undergrowth of green laurel is ablaze in June with millions of white flowers; there the dark blue of distant mountains holds the eye and the memory."[4] The environment of his boyhood was in sharp contrast to the dry, treeless plains over which he was to march during the exciting days of the Mexican war.

Gibson received an elementary education in his native town, and afterward studied law and was admitted to the bar. Later he migrated west to Vincennes, Indiana, where he began to practice law in 1834. Vincennes was then a "Creole French village, sprinkled with Americans, but still interesting as one of the French posts."[5] In the later thirties he fell in love with Amelia Electa

---

[2] Charles Gibson, Autobiography (Easton Rutledge Gibson, ed.), MS., Easton Rutledge Gibson, Monterey, California; E. W. Morgan (Director of Pensions, Veterans Administration, Washington, D.C.) to the editor, Aug. 1, 1932.

[3] Genealogy of the Gibson Family, MS., William McCord Harris, New York City; Charles Gibson, Autobiography, MS.

[4] Charles Gibson, Autobiography, MS.

[5] *Ibid.*

Hillebert, an attractive girl of eighteen who was attending the St. Rose Academy in Vincennes. She was a native of York, Clark county, Illinois, her father being one of the prominent pioneers of the Wabash valley in eastern Illinois. Gibson and Miss Hillebert were married at York on August 13, 1839, and returned to Vincennes to reside. Their first child, James H. Gibson, was born on April 19, 1843. How long they continued to live in Vincennes has not been determined, but by 1844 they had moved west to Independence, Missouri.[6]

Founded on the edge of the frontier in 1827, Independence shortly thereafter became the main starting and outfitting point for those who traveled across the plains and mountains of the Far West. On Gibson's arrival it was still a small town of about seven hundred inhabitants, but it could boast of one newspaper, the *Western Expositor;* four churches; two taverns, the Washington Hotel and the Independence House; nine blacksmith shops, some operating four or five forges; seven wagonwright establishments, which made wagons for prairie travel; four saddleries; one tinsmith shop; one gunsmith shop; and about a dozen general stores. Most of the business centered around the public square. Though a few brick buildings were being erected, the majority of the houses were frame. The most conspicuous building in the town was the Jackson county courthouse, a brick structure built in 1838. Independence was a very busy place during the spring and summer, when its merchants sold outfits and supplies to numerous caravans bound for New Mexico, California, or Oregon. Among

[6] Tombstone Inscription, James H. Gibson, Dodge Grove Cemetery, Mattoon, Ill.; *Daily Journal-Gazette* (Mattoon, Ill.), May 12, 1906; *Mattoon Commercial* (Mattoon, Ill.), May 17, 1906; *Independence Journal* (Independence, Mo.), Sept. 12, 1844; E. W. Morgan to the editor, Aug. 1, 1932.

the crowd moving to and fro around its public square were Santa Fé traders with broadbrimmed hats, Indians, dark-skinned Mexicans, and a few long-haired trappers in buckskin. Long trains of mules or oxen pulling huge covered wagons wended their way through the dusty streets, urged on by vociferous drivers cracking their whips and making a great noise.[7]

Soon after coming to this busy frontier town, Gibson decided to publish a newspaper, of which he became both owner and editor. He called it the *Independence Journal*. It was a weekly paper, appearing every Thursday morning, and the subscription price was $2.50 a year. The first number was published on September 12, 1844, when the policy of the editor was announced. Gibson declared that he would be a "zealous advocate" of the Whig platform and of the election of Henry Clay, that he would promote the commercial and agricultural interests of western Missouri, and that he would print the latest and most authentic news from the Mexican provinces, the Oregon country, California, and the Rocky mountains.[8] The journal had a good circulation and appeared regularly until the election of James K. Polk, when its strong Whig bias forced it to cease publication.[9]

---

[7] *Independence Journal,* Sept. 12, 19, 1844; *Weston Journal* (Weston, Mo.), Feb. 15, Mar. 1, 1845; *Lexington Express* (Lexington, Mo.), Feb. 18, 1845; *Daily Missouri Republican* (St. Louis), Apr. 28, 1845; *History of Jackson County, Missouri* (Union Historical Co., Kansas City, 1881), 636; Edwin Bryant, *What I Saw in California* (New York, 1848), 13-14; Josiah Gregg, *Commerce of the Prairies,* in *Early Western Travels, 1748-1846* (Reuben G. Thwaites, ed., Cleveland, 1905), XIX, 189-193. Hereafter this edition of Gregg will be cited in the footnotes.

[8] *Independence Journal,* Sept. 12, 1844.

[9] George Rutledge Gibson to Charles Gibson, Oct. 22, 1873, MS., Missouri Historical Society (hereafter cited as M.H.S.). The last number of the *Independence Journal* in the newspaper files of the Missouri Historical Society is dated October 31, 1844. Gibson presented the *Independence Journal* to the society in 1874.

During the latter part of 1844, Gibson moved to the neighboring town of Weston, where, early in the following year, he established another newspaper, the *Weston Journal*. Like its predecessor, it was a weekly paper, the first number appearing on January 4, 1845. This time Gibson declared that he had undertaken the publication of a journal not "purely political" in character, but one devoted to the "agricultural, commercial, and mechanical interests of the country, as well as [to] the political movements of the day." He stated that he would advocate the annexation of Texas "without dishonor, and by common consent"; the occupation of the Oregon country; the erection of a chain of posts from Missouri to the Rocky mountains to protect emigrants; and federal aid to open and improve the navigation of the Missouri river and other streams of national importance. He also asserted his intention of printing the proceedings of the state and national governments, and of giving special attention to news about Independence and the Santa Fé trade.[10] The *Weston Journal* was one of the best papers published on the western frontier, but in a few months it ceased to exist because of inadequate financial support.[11] Gibson was then forced to return to the practice of law for a livelihood, in which profession he was eking out an existence in Weston on the outbreak of the Mexican war.

The strained relations between the United States and Mexico which had existed ever since Texas declared its independence in 1836, reached a crisis in the spring of 1846, when the military forces of Major-general Zachary Taylor and General Mariano Arista clashed on

[10] *Weston Journal,* Jan. 4, 1845.

[11] The last number of the *Weston Journal* in the newspaper files of the Missouri Historical Society is dated April 19, 1845. Gibson presented the *Weston Journal* to the society in 1874.

disputed territory east of the Río Grande. On May 11, President Polk sent a message to congress stating that Mexican troops had passed our boundary and had "shed American blood upon the American soil." He declared that war existed "by the act of Mexico herself," and called upon the people "to vindicate with decision the honor, the rights, and the interests" of their country. He asked congress for authority to call into the public service a large body of volunteers to serve for not less than six or twelve months unless discharged sooner, since, in his opinion, volunteer troops were unquestionably "more efficient than any other description of citizen soldiers." He also recommended that liberal provision be made to sustain our entire military force.[12] Congress responded with alacrity and on May 13 passed a law providing for the prosecution of the "existing war" between the United States and Mexico. To enable the government to bring the conflict to a speedy and successful termination, the act authorized the president to use the army, navy, and militia, and "to call for and accept the services of any number of volunteers not exceeding fifty thousand, who may offer their services, either as cavalry, artillery, infantry, or riflemen, to serve twelve months after they shall have arrived at the place of rendezvous, or to the end of the war, unless sooner discharged, according to the time for which they shall have been mustered into service." The volunteers were to be subject to the rules and articles of war, were to have the same organization and pay as the regular army, and were to be accepted by the president in companies, battalions, squadrons, and regiments, with officers appointed in the manner prescribed by law in the several states and territories from which the volunteers

[12] James D. Richardson, *A Compilation of the Messages and Papers of the Presidents, 1789-1897* (Washington, 1899), IV, 437-443.

came. Ten million dollars was appropriated to carry the act into effect.[13] Congress passed another law on the same day empowering the president to increase by voluntary enlistment the number of privates in each company of the regular army from sixty-four to any number not exceeding one hundred.[14] Polk also issued a proclamation on May 13 announcing the existence of a state of war and calling on all the people to support any measures the government might take to obtain "a speedy, a just, and an honorable peace." [15]

The occupation of New Mexico was an important part of the first campaign decided upon after the formal opening of the conflict. Polk had long been anxious to acquire this province by peaceable means; so when the war with Mexico began he was naturally very much interested in taking it as soon as possible.[16] Besides, Senator Thomas Hart Benton, of Missouri, representing the views of his constituents, urged immediate action in this direction.[17] On the very day when the president proclaimed the existence of hostilities, the War Department took steps to send an expedition to Santa Fé. William L. Marcy, Secretary of War, sent Polk's proclamation to Stephen W. Kearny, colonel of the First regiment of dragoons, whose headquarters were then at Fort Leavenworth.[18] Brigadier-general Roger Jones,

[13] United States, *Statutes at Large,* IX, 9-10; Justin H. Smith, *The War with Mexico* (New York, 1919), I, 190; George Lockhart Rives, *The United States and Mexico, 1821-1848* (New York, 1913), II, 160-161.

[14] United States, *Statutes at Large,* IX, 11; Smith, *The War with Mexico,* I, 190.

[15] Richardson, *Messages and Papers of the Presidents, 1789-1897,* IV, 470.

[16] *The Diary of James K. Polk* (Milo M. Quaife, ed., Chicago, 1910), I, 396, 400, 403-404; *St. Louis Daily New Era,* May 22, 1846.

[17] *The People's Daily Organ* (St. Louis), May 14, 1846; *St. Louis Daily New Era,* May 12, 14, 22, 25, 26, 29, 1846.

[18] Marcy to Kearny, May 13, 1846, Military Book, XXVI, MSS., Old Records Division, Adjutant-general's Office, War Department (hereafter cited as

the adjutant-general, informed Kearny that the War Department had decided to organize a body of fifteen hundred mounted volunteers to assemble without delay at the most convenient place on the frontier, in order to protect the property of Santa Fé traders and take possession of Santa Fé. He told the colonel that this force would include, among other organizations, two companies of artillery, that two companies of the First dragoons should be consolidated with the volunteers, and that he (Kearny) would probably be assigned to command the entire expedition.[19] On the same day – May 13 – the Secretary of War requested John C. Edwards, governor of Missouri, to organize "at the earliest practicable period" one regiment of eight companies of mounted volunteers and two companies of volunteer light artillery for a movement against New Mexico over the Santa Fé trail. He asked the governor to designate Fort Leavenworth as the place of rendezvous, where the men were to be enrolled in the service of the United States. Should the commander of the expedition deem a smaller or larger number of Missouri volunteers necessary, or should he prefer to have a portion serve as infantry, that officer would be authorized to signify his desires to the governor and to make known to the latter "the wishes of the government thereon." Since it was of the highest importance that the troops reach Santa Fé before Mexico could send its forces there, Marcy urged Edwards to use "all possible dispatch" to have the men organized and sent toward New Mexico. He also reminded the executive of "the extreme importance" to the honor of Missouri and of the United States that officers

O.R.D., A.G.O.); Kearny to Jones, June 29, 1846, Letters Received, MSS., Old Files Section, Adjutant-general's Office, War Department (hereafter cited as O.F.S., A.G.O.).

[19] Jones to Kearny, May 13, 1846, Letters Sent, XXII, MSS., O.F.S., A.G.O.

be "judiciously selected." Marcy concluded: "Please to consider the destination of the above force confidential and use proper precautions to prevent its becoming known." [20]

During the next few weeks the War Department issued a number of orders to Colonel Kearny relating to the occupation of New Mexico. On May 14 he was definitely placed in command of the Santa Fé expedition. At the same time he was directed to send a good supply of stores to Bent's Fort ahead of the troops, and to provide himself with goods suitable for presents to the Indian tribes which might be encountered in the course of the march.[21] On May 27 the Secretary of War wrote him that President Polk had made arrangements to have "a person of high character and good repute in the Roman Catholic church" accompany the expedition, who would induce the Mexicans to confide in the assurance Kearny would make that their religious institutions would be respected.[22] Four days later Winfield Scott, commanding general of the army, advised him to add to his force "valuable men at or about Bent's Fort," and American citizens residing or trading in New Mexico – suggestions which were probably prompted by the press and residents of St. Louis.[23] On June 3, Marcy gave him instructions, which were originally drafted by the president,[24] to establish a temporary civil government in New Mexico after its occupation; to abolish all arbitrary restrictions that might exist there, "so far as it may be done with safety"; and to assure the people that the

[20] Marcy to Edwards, May 13, 1846, Military Book, XXVI, MSS., O.R.D., A.G.O.

[21] Jones to Kearny, May 14, 1846, Letters Sent, XXII, MSS., O.F.S., A.G.O.

[22] *House Ex. Docs.*, 31 cong., 1 sess., no. 17, p. 236.

[23] Scott to Kearny, May 31, 1846, Letters Sent, XXII, MSS., O.F.S., A.G.O.; Penn to Marcy, May 19, 1846, William L. Marcy MSS., Library of Congress; *St. Louis Daily New Era,* May 14, 19, 1846.

[24] Polk to Marcy, June 2, 1846, William L. Marcy MSS., Library of Congress.

United States desired to give them a free government, similar to that which existed in our territories, with the least possible delay. "It is foreseen," continued Marcy, "that what relates to the civil government will be a difficult and unpleasant part of your duty, and much must necessarily be left to your own discretion. In your whole conduct you will act in such a manner as best to conciliate the inhabitants, and render them friendly to the United States."[25] On June 13 the adjutant-general wrote Kearny that Brigadier-general Wool, acting under orders from Major-general Taylor, would advance from San Antonio de Béxar to the city of Chihuahua, which he would probably reach not long after the occupation of Santa Fé. Jones therefore suggested that it might be desirable for the colonel on arriving in New Mexico to communicate with Wool, so that each commander might learn of the position and success of the other, and both might "act in concert, should an extreme case make it necessary."[26]

Although the War Department made immediate and thorough preparations to take possession of New Mexico by force of arms, Polk sincerely hoped that the troops could occupy that province without fighting. Senator Benton, who was in close touch with the president, stated the aims of the administration in a letter dated Washington, D.C., May 14, 1846, extracts from which were first published in St. Louis about a week later. He wrote: "Our first care in this sudden change in our relations with that country [Mexico] was to try and take care of our Santa Fé trade. For this purpose, it will be proposed to the people of New Mexico, Chihuahua and the other internal provinces, that they remain quiet and

[25] *House Ex. Docs.*, 30 cong., 1 sess., no. 60, pp. 154-155.

[26] Jones to Kearny, June 13, 1846, Letters Sent, XXII, MSS., O.F.S., A.G.O.

continue trading with us as usual, upon which condition they shall be protected in all their rights and be treated as friends." The military movement toward Santa Fé, he asserted, was "to make sure of the main object, to wit: peace and trade, to be secured peaceably if possible, forcibly if necessary. For unless they accept these conditions, the country will have to be taken possession of as a conquest. This, however, we hope will not be necessary, as it will be so obviously to the interest of the inhabitants of that part of Mexico (too far off from the Central Government to have any effect in general hostilities) to enjoy the benefits of peace and trade, with the full protection of all their rights of person, property, and religion." [27] That Colonel Kearny was fully aware of the desires of the administration is evidenced by his proclamation to the people of New Mexico on July 31, 1846,[28] and by his letters to Governor Armijo and Adjutant-general Jones on the following day,[29] all of which embodied the ideas contained in Benton's letter. Moreover, in 1849, Henry S. Turner, Kearny's chief of staff during the Mexican war, wrote that the occupation of New Mexico "without bloodshed, or resistance on the part of the inhabitants" was the object of the Santa Fé expedition and was "much desired by our Government at the time." [30]

The War Department was eager to give prompt notice of the formal opening of hostilities to American citizens in or on the way to New Mexico. As early as February 9, 1846, Manuel Álvarez, United States consul in Santa

27 *Daily Missouri Republican,* May 22, 1846.

28 *House Ex. Docs.,* 30 cong., 1 sess., no. 60, p. 168.

29 Kearny to Armijo, Aug. 1, 1846, Kearny to Jones, Aug. 1, 1846, Letters Received, MSS., O.F.S., A.G.O.

30 Turner to Magoffin, Jan. 14, 1849, Magoffin MSS., General Accounting Office, Washington, D. C.

Fé, had written to the State Department that the lives and property of Americans were in danger there.[31] Marcy had probably seen this communication, for on May 13 he appointed George Thomas Howard, of Texas, a member of the Texan-Santa Fé expedition in 1841, to proceed immediately on a "delicate mission" to Santa Fé. Howard was ordered to carry the news of the existence of war to the American caravans which had left western Missouri for New Mexico during the early part of May, "so as to prevent them from falling into the hands of the enemy," and then to impart the same information to our citizens in Santa Fé and its vicinity, whose persons and property might be endangered unless they were warned of the commencement of hostilities before the government of New Mexico could learn of it. He was told that the mission would require him to exercise great discretion, especially after he reached Santa Fé, since the utmost prudence would then be necessary to carry out his instructions without revealing them to the governor of New Mexico. He was urged to make his journey "with the greatest possible dispatch," for the delay of a single day might "prove disastrous" to our citizens.[32]

Making his preparations for departure as quickly as possible, Howard soon left Washington, D.C., for the West. He reached St. Louis on May 21, and on the following day boarded a Missouri river steamer for Fort Leavenworth.[33] At that post Colonel Kearny, in accordance with instructions from the Secretary of War, provided him with a small escort of dragoons, who were

[31] Álvarez to Buchanan, Feb. 9, 1846, Consular Reports, Santa Fé, MSS., State Department.

[32] Marcy to Howard, May 13, 1846, Military Book, XXVI, MSS., O.R.D., A.G.O.; *The Diary of James K. Polk* (Quaife, ed.), I, 396.

[33] *Weekly Reveille* (St. Louis), May 25, 1846.

ordered to accompany him to Bent's Fort or as far as he might desire them.[34] About June 1 he began his prairie journey and hastened westward over the Santa Fé trail. But he was unable to overtake the caravans which had left western Missouri during the early part of May, because they had traveled to New Mexico by forced marches after learning of the outbreak of hostilities, anxious to dispose of their merchandise at war prices and under no apprehension that their goods would be confiscated by the Mexican authorities.[35] Upon reaching the Arkansas crossing, Howard decided to intrust the rest of his mission to two of his men, whom he sent ahead to Santa Fé and Taos. He himself journeyed more leisurely to some ranches near the Rayado and Ponil creeks, about fifty miles east of Taos, where he planned to await their return. His messengers arrived in Santa Fé about June 24 but learned that the news of the declaration of war had already reached there and that the lives and property of American citizens were in no danger. Having narrowly escaped capture as spies, they returned to Howard, who immediately departed for the East to report to the Secretary of War.[36]

Meanwhile Colonel Kearny was organizing a military force at Fort Leavenworth in compliance with instructions from the War Department. On May 26 he received information of the declaration of war and of his appointment to command the Santa Fé expedition.[37] Well quali-

[34] Kearny to Marcy, May 28, 1846, Letters Received, MSS., O.F.S., A.G.O.; *House Ex. Docs.*, 31 cong., 1 sess., no. 17, p. 235.

[35] *St. Louis Daily New Era,* June 25, 1846; *Daily Missouri Republican,* July 3, 1846; *Southwest Historical Series,* I, 179-181.

[36] Kearny to Jones, July 17, 1846, Letters Received, MSS., O.F.S., A.G.O.; Howard to Marcy, Aug. 13, 1846, Index to Letters Received, Secretary of War's Files, MSS., O.R.D., A.G.O.; *Daily Missouri Republican,* July 3, Sept. 7, 1846; *Weekly Reveille,* Aug. 10, 1846, Jan. 18, 1847.

[37] Kearny to Jones, May 28, 1846, Kearny Letter Book, MS., M.H.S.

fied for his task by over a quarter century of service in various parts of the Far West,[38] he made immediate preparations to concentrate troops and supplies for a rapid march to New Mexico. On the day when he learned of the existence of hostilities he anticipated the wishes of the president by sending a message to Archbishop Kenrick, of St. Louis, asking him to appoint a priest to accompany the army to Santa Fé.[39] The following day he dispatched Lieutenant Henry S. Turner, of the First dragoons, to Jefferson City, Missouri, to ascertain what measures Governor Edwards had taken to raise volunteers and when they might be expected at Fort Leavenworth. Under the authority granted to him by the Secretary of War, he ordered the lieutenant to make a requisition upon the governor for two companies of volunteer infantry, in addition to the eight companies of mounted men and the battalion of artillery already called for by Marcy. Kearny likewise directed Turner to proceed to St. Louis "to obtain from the heads of the several departments there, all that will be necessary for the volunteers on this expedition." [40] On May 31 he wrote to Brigadier-general George M. Brooke, of St. Louis, commander of the Third military department, requesting him to order two companies of the First dragoons then stationed at Forts Atkinson and Crawford to repair immediately to Fort Leavenworth, where they were to join three companies of the same regiment and march with the Missouri volunteers to New Mexico.[41] Four days later the colonel appointed An-

[38] *Southwest Historical Series,* I, 185.

[39] Kearny to Marcy, June 15, 1846, Kearny Letter Book, MS., M.H.S. Archbishop Kenrick declined to appoint a priest to accompany Kearny. *Daily Missouri Republican,* Sept. 7, 1846.

[40] Kearny to Jones, May 28, 1846, Kearny Letter Book, MS., M.H.S. See also Kearny to Edwards, May 27, 1846, *ibid.*

[41] Kearny to Brooke, May 31, 1846, *ibid.*

toine Robidou, of St. Joseph, Missouri, an interpreter for the expedition.[42] Expecting to meet "many and various" Indian tribes on the way to Santa Fé, he wrote a letter dated June 20 to the United States Indian agent at Westport, Missouri, asking him to furnish a mounted party of about fifty Shawnee and Delaware Indians to join the army as soon as possible.[43] Besides, Kearny made a number of requisitions upon the St. Louis Arsenal and the Liberty Arsenal for muskets, rifles, carbines, dragoon pistols, howitzers, cavalry sabres, cartridges, and ammunition.[44] He also advertised in the newspapers for horses, mules, oxen, and wagons to transport supplies to New Mexico.[45]

The state of Missouri coöperated with Colonel Kearny and promptly called out all the volunteers he and the War Department desired. About April 10, 1846, Governor John C. Edwards left Jefferson City to visit some of the larger cities of the country in order to sell state bonds. On arriving in New Orleans early in May, he learned of the clash between the forces of Taylor and Arista and decided that actual hostilities were imminent. About May 4, anticipating that the War Department would call upon Missouri for troops to march to Santa Fé, he ordered G. A. Parsons, adjutant-general of the state, to comply with any such requisition without waiting for further instructions. He left New Orleans shortly afterward and reached Washington, D.C., on May 14, when he had an audience with the president. Polk informed him that on the previous day the Secre-

42 Kearny to Robidou, June 4, 1846, *ibid.*

43 Turner to Cummings, June 20, 1846, Letters Received, MSS., O.F.S., A.G.O. The editor has found no evidence that these Indians accompanied Kearny.

44 Kearny to Leonard, June 4, 1846, Turner to Bell, June 20, 25, 26, 1846, Kearny Letter Book, MS., M.H.S.

45 *Missouri Statesman* (Columbia), June 12, 1846; Martha R. Barnidge, Missouri in the Mexican War, MS., M.A. thesis, Washington University.

tary of War had made a requisition upon the state of Missouri for a regiment of volunteer cavalry and artillery for service in New Mexico. Immediately after the interview the governor forwarded an order to the adjutant-general of Missouri requiring him to recruit the regiment demanded.[46] But about May 24, before this order reached Jefferson City, Parsons acted under the authority granted to him by Edwards from New Orleans and called out the requisite number of volunteers from St. Louis and various counties bordering on the Missouri river. No man was to be accepted who was under eighteen or over forty-five years of age, or who was not in good physical condition. The volunteers were to proceed with all possible dispatch to Fort Leavenworth, where they were to report "by their officers" to the commandant at that post. They would then be organized into "regiments of cavalry, mounted men, or light artillery, and be mustered into the service of the United States." This call was signed: "By order of the commander-in-chief. G. A. Parsons, adjutant-general, Missouri militia."[47] Lieutenant-governor Young arrived in Jefferson City on May 30 and exercised the powers of governor until Edwards's return on June 20.[48]

The people of Missouri responded with enthusiasm to the call for volunteers to serve under Kearny. "The war feeling is precisely what it should be here," wrote Shadrach Penn, Jr., editor of the St. Louis *Missouri Reporter,* to the Secretary of War as early as May 19.[49]

---

46 Missouri, *House Journal,* 14 Gen. Assem., 1 sess., pp. 179-182.

47 *Ibid.,* p. 182; *The People's Daily Organ,* May 27, 1846; *Daily Missouri Republican,* May 28, 1846.

48 Missouri, *House Journal,* 14 Gen. Assem., 1 sess., p. 182; *Daily Missouri Republican,* June 1, 6, 1846; *Jefferson Inquirer* (Jefferson City, Mo.), June 3, 1846; *Boonville Commercial Bulletin* (Boonville, Mo.), June 27, 1846.

49 Penn to Marcy, May 19, 1846, William L. Marcy MSS., Library of Congress.

After learning of Marcy's requisition upon the state, the *Daily Missouri Republican*[50] declared: "The only difficulty which presents itself to us, is, that the number ordered in the requisition bears no proportion to the number who really want to go. Several thousand can be readily raised – indeed, there will be difficulty in restraining them, rather than to fill up the ranks." "A much larger body of men will offer than can be received," asserted the *St. Louis Daily New Era*,[51] "and the object should be to select the most effective men, and those that will most promptly equip and march to the scene of action." The *Missouri Reporter* observed: "The military expedition ordered by the War Department to proceed to the northern provinces of Mexico, we regard as one of vast importance; and we rejoice that it has been entrusted to the command of so able, experienced and gallant an officer as Col. Kearny. There is no man in the regular army under whom Missouri volunteers would more readily serve." [52]

The St. Louis newspapers were busy offering advice to the prospective volunteers, as well as to Colonel Kearny. The expedition's success, they declared, depended upon the promptness with which it started, the qualifications and conduct of its officers, the ability to transport sufficient supplies over about nine hundred miles of uninhabited plains, and the enlistment of an adequate number of troops. They asserted that the soldiers must possess certain qualities, such as subordination, bravery, patience, and endurance. Warning the volunteers not to expect a holiday or a pleasure trip, they advised them to prepare for fatigue, hunger, thirst,

[50] May 22, 1846.

[51] May 26, 1846.

[52] *Missouri Reporter* (St. Louis), May 29, 1846.

violent storms, hot suns, and hard fighting.[53] The *Weekly Reveille* [54] stated that the troops "must have, at times, stomachs which can not only digest any kind of food presented, but which can submit to 'short allowance' when necessary. . . Going to Santa Fé is going to endure a toilsome march on limited supplies, with precarious means of subsistence when there, and on the return. Hence let none undertake the trip who have not soldiers' hearts, and, we may add, soldiers' bodies and soldiers' stomachs." The *Missouri Reporter* [55] predicted: "The march is to be a long and tedious one – almost unequalled in modern history."

Whether these suggestions were fully appreciated by all the prospective volunteers cannot be stated definitely, but it is certain that nothing cooled the ardor of those who were eager to enlist. Many craved fame and adventure, and the expedition to Santa Fé promised to provide both abundantly. During the latter part of May and the early part of June zealous recruits offered their services in such numbers that the quota was quickly filled. Young, athletic, adventurous, and full of enthusiasm, most of the men came from good families.[56] The city of St. Louis contributed one company of mounted volunteers [57] and

[53] *St. Louis Daily New Era,* May 26, 27, 1846; *Missouri Reporter,* May 29, June 5, 1846; *Weekly Reveille,* June 1, 1846; *Daily Missouri Republican,* June 3, 1846.

[54] June 1, 1846.

[55] May 29, 1846.

[56] John T. Hughes, *Doniphan's Expedition* (Cincinnati, 1848), 25; *Weekly Tribune* (Liberty, Mo.), June 13, 27, 1846; *Jefferson Inquirer,* June 17, 1846; *Missouri Reporter,* June 1, 1846; *Daily Missouri Republican,* June 8, 9, 1846.

[57] The Laclede Rangers. On May 24, 1846, the adjutant-general of Missouri issued a call for four hundred mounted men from the city and county of St. Louis. Four companies were quickly organized, one of which was called the "Laclede Rangers." But early in June, Lieutenant-governor Young countermanded this call and ordered that two companies of artillery be recruited in the city of St. Louis. The Laclede Rangers refused to be disbanded and on June 7 departed by boat for Fort Leavenworth. On the following day they

two companies of light artillery; the rest of the mounted volunteers came from the counties of Clay, Jackson, Lafayette, Saline, Cole, Howard, Callaway, and Franklin. Besides, Cole and Platte counties each furnished one company of infantry. Among the recruits from Platte was George Rutledge Gibson, who, at the age of thirty-six, had decided to leave his meager law practice in Weston for an opportunity to serve his country. After the required number of men had been obtained in each community, officers were elected, a company was organized, and the volunteers were drilled, activities which were followed with deep interest by admiring friends, relatives, and citizens generally. In most cases a silk flag or guidon made by the women of the community was presented to the company with appropriate ceremonies. The day of departure for Fort Leavenworth was long to be remembered. Crowds filled the streets, the company paraded in its best style amid fervent applause, and the last farewells were said.[58] Eight companies marched overland, while five proceeded up the Missouri river by steamboat.[59] The feelings of the people who remained behind were well expressed by the Liberty *Weekly*

stopped at Jefferson City, where they received a letter from the lieutenant-governor to Colonel Kearny asking that officer to muster them into the service of the United States. Kearny complied with the request on June 10, immediately after the company arrived at Fort Leavenworth. On June 27, after the eight companies of mounted volunteers reached the fort, the colonel ordered that the Laclede Rangers, who had hitherto been doing duty with the mounted volunteers, be assigned to duty with the companies of the First regiment of dragoons. Kearny, Order No. 4, June 27, 1846, Letters Received, MSS., O.F.S., A.G.O.; *The People's Daily Organ,* May 27, 1846; *Daily Missouri Republican,* June 6, 1846; *Weekly Reveille,* June 8, 15, 1846; *Jefferson Inquirer,* June 10, 1846.

58 Richard Smith Elliott, *Notes Taken in Sixty Years* (St. Louis, 1883), 217-219; William Elsey Connelley, *Doniphan's Expedition* (Topeka, 1907), 530-580; *Glasgow News* (Glasgow, Mo.), June 4, 11, 1846; *Weekly Reveille,* June 1, 8, 1846; *Jefferson Inquirer,* June 10, 1846; *Weekly Tribune,* June 6, 1846.

59 Companies from the following counties marched overland to Fort Leaven-

Tribune,[60] which made the following comment after the departure of the Clay county volunteers for Fort Leavenworth: "This gallant band have taken their leave, but they carry with them the prayers of this people, that they may arrive safely at their journeys end, and then, if they have to fight, may success attend them; and may they win for themselves a name that will stand out on the pages of history long after they shall have passed away."

As early as June 6, about two weeks after Missouri's call for troops, three volunteer companies[61] arrived at Fort Leavenworth; and thereafter they continued to reach the post at intervals until June 27, when the last company came.[62] On the latter date the Platte county infantry, in which Gibson had enlisted, marched into the fort. Gibson had been elected second lieutenant. Shortly after arriving, the companies were mustered into the service of the United States, inspected, and supplied with quarters, forage, mess kits, rations, sabres, guns, and ammunition. They also received a year's allowance of money for clothing – the last cash which most of them were destined to be paid until the end of their period of enlistment. Each company was drilled by an officer of the First dragoons, who found the men enthusi-

worth: Clay, Jackson, Saline, Cole (mounted company), Howard, Callaway, Franklin, and Platte. The three companies from St. Louis, the infantry company from Cole county, and the mounted company from Lafayette county reached Fort Leavenworth by boat.

60 June 6, 1846.

61 Kearny to Edwards, June 7, 1846, Kearny Letter Book, MS., M.H.S.

62 The following is a list of Missouri volunteer companies and the dates of their arrival at Fort Leavenworth: Clay, Jackson, and Lafayette county companies, June 6; Saline county company, June 9; Laclede Rangers (St. Louis), June 10; Cole county company (mounted), Cole county company (infantry), and Howard county company, June 15; artillery company A (St. Louis), June 18; artillery company B (St. Louis), June 20; Callaway county company, June 23; Franklin county company, June 26; and Platte county company (infantry), June 27.

astic for the service though somewhat reluctant to conform entirely to the discipline of the regular army. In spite of the rigors of military life, the volunteers were usually cheerful. Only occasionally, when they were short of food because they had consumed their rations too quickly, did they lose their good humor and create a disturbance in camp; but this disaffection quickly disappeared upon the issuance of additional provisions. Camp kettles, mess pans, and tents were slow in arriving; hence the troops were ordered to make up in part for this temporary deficiency by constructing their own tents and by purchasing some kettles and pans from the general stores in the neighboring towns in Missouri. A German company of artillerists from St. Louis at times entertained and inspired the rest by marching about the fort singing the songs of their fatherland. Colonel Kearny had the confidence of the volunteers, all of whom admired his military ability. Unruffled by infractions of discipline, and exercising considerable patience, tact, and skill, he gradually molded the raw recruits into the semblance of an army.[63]

As soon as seven companies of mounted volunteers had reached the fort, Kearny decided to organize them into a regiment without waiting for the arrival of the eighth company, which was expected soon. He ordered that field officers for the regiment be chosen on the morning of June 18, and asked Major-general Ward, of the Missouri militia, to preside at the election.[64] The voting took place on the parade ground at the appointed

[63] Kearny to Jones, June 16, 1846, Kearny Letter Book, MS., M.H.S.; *Täglicher Anzeiger des Westens* (St. Louis), July 6, 1846; *Weekly Reveille,* June 15, 22, 29, July 6, 1846; *Weekly Tribune,* June 20, 1846; *Jefferson Inquirer,* July 1, 1846; *St. Louis Daily New Era,* June 20, 1846; Elliott, *Notes Taken in Sixty Years,* 222; Hughes, *Doniphan's Expedition,* 25-26.

[64] Kearny to Minor, June 17, 1846, Kearny Letter Book, MS., M.H.S.

time, when the various candidates made speeches. "One promised," declared an eyewitness, "that he would 'particularly guard the command from the imposition of high prices on sugar, coffee, etc., by the Sutler – they must have such things at fair prices whenever they want – no selling at two dollars a cupfull, all must be cheap – 10 or 12 cents a pound.' Another was to be the 'father of the command,' while another engaged to be 'both father and mother' – and all were agreed in sharing the privations, dangers, beds and all the *et ceteras* of the soldier – to be the first to lead to, and the last to leave, the battle field."[65] After the aspirants for each office had presented their views, a poll was taken by having the volunteers form in line behind their choice, thus eliminating any possibility of fraud.[66] Alexander W. Doniphan, of Clay county, brigadier-general of the Missouri militia, and John W. Price, of Howard county, were the candidates for colonel of the regiment; the former was chosen by an overwhelming majority. The other officers selected were: Charles F. Ruff, of Clay county, lieutenant-colonel, and William Gilpin, of Jackson county, major.[67] Kearny immediately sent a list of the successful candidates to the governor of Missouri, who issued their commissions.[68] On June 19, Kearny ordered that the officers elected should enter upon their duties at once, and should be obeyed and respected accordingly. At the same time he urged both officers and men to be prompt and energetic in the performance of their tasks, and warned them not to lose a moment in preparing themselves for the arduous march across the

65 *Daily Missouri Republican,* June 22, 1846.

66 Marcellus B. Edwards, A Journal of an Expedition to New Mexico and the Southern Provinces, MS., M.H.S.; Elliott, *Notes Taken in Sixty Years,* 221.

67 Connelley, *Doniphan's Expedition,* 133.

68 Kearny to Minor, June 18, 1846, Kearny Letter Book, MS., M.H.S.

plains.[69] The organization thus effected, which finally consisted of eight companies and over eight hundred men, was called the "First regiment of Missouri mounted volunteers." [70]

The rest of the Missouri volunteers, as well as the companies of the First dragoons assigned to the expedition, were organized by Colonel Kearny into squadrons and battalions. Early in June, Captain Moore was directed to lead a squadron of two companies of the First dragoons.[71] The two companies of volunteer artillery from St. Louis were formed into a battalion, and on June 27, Captain Fischer, being the senior officer, was placed in temporary command. But about two weeks later while the troops were on the march, Major Clark, who had just arrived, superseded Fischer.[72] The Laclede Rangers, a mounted company of volunteers from St. Louis which had been a part of Doniphan's regiment, were ordered to do duty with the First dragoons on and after June 27.[73] Two days afterward Captain Angney, the senior officer, was put in charge of a battalion of two companies of volunteer infantry, in one of which Gibson was serving.[74] A squadron of two companies of the First dragoons from Forts Atkinson and Crawford, which arrived at Fort Leavenworth after Kearny's departure and marched from there on July 6, was in command of Captain Sumner.[75] The total number of troops

69 Kearny, Order No. 1, June 19, 1846, Letters Received, MSS., O.F.S., A.G.O.

70 Connelley, *Doniphan's Expedition*, 438, 529.

71 Kearny to Moore, June 5, 1846, Kearny to Noble, June 12, 1846, Kearny Letter Book, MS., M.H.S.

72 Kearny, Order No. 4, June 27, 1846, Order No. 8, July 10, 1846, Letters Received, MSS., O.F.S., A.G.O.

73 Kearny, Order No. 4, June 27, 1846, *ibid.*

74 Kearny, Order No. 5, June 29, 1846, *ibid.*

75 Sumner to Jones, July 4, 1846, *ibid.;* P. St. Geo. Cooke, *The Conquest of New Mexico and California* (New York, 1878), 2-3.

organized by Colonel Kearny for the Santa Fé expedition, including the various companies of the First regiment of dragoons and all the Missouri volunteers, was about seventeen hundred.[76] This force was called the "Army of the West."[77]

One of Kearny's greatest problems was to obtain and transport an adequate amount of supplies for an army marching nine hundred miles or more from its base of operations. Profiting by his experience during the previous year when he commanded an expedition of First dragoons from Fort Leavenworth to the South pass, he issued orders for the concentration of the kind of stores which he had found indispensable in prairie travel. Even though his directions were not always executed at once, and occasionally not executed at all, he received the coöperation of the chief ordnance officer, the quartermaster, and the commissary, in St. Louis, who sent him provisions, ordnance, military equipment, and wagons.[78] In western Missouri he purchased additional food and wagons, as well as thousands of oxen, mules, and horses. Besides, he hired many teamsters and wagon masters. Early in June, before the departure of the main body of troops, he began to dispatch trains of prairie schooners laden with stores to Bent's Fort; so that by the sixteenth of that month about a hundred wagons were on their way.[79] Continuing to depart at intervals during the rest

[76] Kearny to Jones, June 29, 1846, Letters Received, MSS., O.F.S., A.G.O.; *Weekly Reveille,* July 27, 1846; Hughes, *Doniphan's Expedition,* 27.

[77] Kearny to Allen, June 19, 1846, Kearny Letter Book, MS., M.H.S.; *Weekly Reveille,* July 6, 1846.

[78] Kearny to Jones, June 16, 1846, Kearny Letter Book, MS., M.H.S.; *St. Louis Daily New Era,* June 9, 15, 22, 25, 1846; *Weekly Reveille,* June 22, 29, 1846; *Daily Missouri Republican,* June 3, 1846.

[79] *Senate Ex. Docs.,* 30 cong., 1 sess., no. 1, pp. 544-545; *Daily Missouri Republican,* June 23, 25, 1846; *Weekly Reveille,* June 22, 1846; *Weekly Tribune,* June 20, 1846.

of the summer, these caravans were strung along the whole length of the Santa Fé trail, forming a constantly-moving chain of supplies from "the States" to New Mexico. Despite the exertions of Kearny and his staff, the troops were not always furnished with sufficient food and equipment – a fact which the volunteers frequently mentioned in their letters to friends and relatives at home.[80]

The Army of the West, like its trains of supplies, left Fort Leavenworth in separate sections, the first companies marching from the post on June 5 and the last on July 6. The first detachment was dispatched because of a letter of June 3 which Colonel Kearny received from George T. Howard, who was then seventy miles west of Independence on his way to Santa Fé and Taos. Howard wrote that a quantity of arms and ammunition was being transported to New Mexico by the trading caravans of Armijo and Speyer,[81] which were

[80] *St. Louis Daily New Era,* July 4, 14, Sept. 7, 1846; *Daily Missouri Republican,* July 15, 22, 1846; *Weekly Tribune,* Aug. 1, Sept. 5, 1846; *Weekly Reveille,* July 20, 1846; Rives, *The United States and Mexico,* II, 214.

[81] Albert Speyer's train, consisting of about twenty-five wagons, was loaded with a large amount of merchandise for the Mexican trade, which was purchased prior to the outbreak of hostilities. Two of the wagons contained arms and ammunition, which the governor of Chihuahua had ordered from Speyer in 1845. Speyer's haste to enter Santa Fé ahead of Kearny was not only to prevent the capture of his arms and ammunition by the dragoons, but also to obtain a *guía,* or custom-house permit, from Governor Armijo, which would enable him to sell his goods in any part of Mexico. Since that country's seaports were blockaded by the United States navy, Speyer anticipated that merchandise would be scarce and consequently command high prices. Other traders who made forced marches to Santa Fé ahead of Kearny in order to obtain *guías* and dispose of their merchandise at war prices were: Colburn, McKnight, Aubry, Rallston, Hill, Webb, Doan, Weick, Blummer, Pruett, Mayer, and Turley. *Daily Missouri Republican,* June 1, 25, July 3, Aug. 20, 24, 1846, May 18, 1847; *Weekly Reveille,* July 6, Aug. 31, 1846; *St. Louis Daily New Era,* June 25, July 3, 1846; *Southwest Historical Series,* I, 179-181. Manuel Armijo's train of wagons was in charge of one of the governor's trusted employees, and contained some arms and ammunition. It entered

then hastening westward over the Santa Fé trail, and that two companies of Mexican cavalry would be sent to escort them to Santa Fé.[82] Upon receiving this information on the evening of June 4, Kearny immediately directed Howard to catch up with the caravans and detain them until the arrival of two companies of the First dragoons which would be dispatched from Fort Leavenworth on the following day.[83] On June 5, Kearny ordered Captain Benjamin D. Moore to command a squadron of companies C and G of the First dragoons and proceed at once to overtake the wagons containing the arms and ammunition. He also directed the captain to take along two twelve-pounder mountain howitzers, to stop the progress of all Santa Fé traders, and in case he met any Mexican cavalry, to capture those whom he was unable to kill.[84] The next day Kearny wrote Moore that Captain Waldo, of the Missouri mounted volunteers, had informed him that Governor Armijo had about seventy thousand dollars' worth of merchandise in his caravan, and that in case these goods could be detained, "we hold the governor as our friend and ally." Kearny therefore ordered Moore, who had already left Fort Leavenworth, to select one hundred of his most efficient men and horses and proceed ahead by forced marches to overtake the governor's wagons. "It is an object of the greatest importance," continued Kearny, "that we get possession of Governor Armijo's goods (ammunition, arms, etc.), and I rely upon you and your command to do it. Tell the Mexicans that we

---

Santa Fé about June 30. *St. Louis Daily New Era,* June 25, 1846; *Daily Missouri Republican,* June 25, 1846; *Täglicher Anzeiger des Westens,* Aug. 25, 27, 1846; *Southwest Historical Series,* I, 179, 181.

[82] Kearny to Jones, June 5, 1846, Letters Received, MSS., O.F.S., A.G.O.

[83] Kearny to Howard, June 4, 1846, Kearny Letter Book, MS., M.H.S.

[84] Kearny to Moore, June 5, 1846, *ibid.*

do not intend to deprive them of their property but to stop its progress for the present." [85] Two additional detachments left the fort to reinforce Moore during the next few weeks: fifty men of Captain Allen's company I, First dragoons, under the command of Lieutenant Noble, on June 12, and companies A and D, First regiment of Missouri mounted volunteers, under the command of Captain Waldo, on June 22.[86]

Despite forced marches neither Howard nor Moore caught up with the caravans of Armijo and Speyer. Nor did they overtake the rest of the Santa Fé traders who had left Independence early in May and who were hurrying westward to dispose of their goods in Mexico at war prices. Howard reached the Arkansas crossing on June 16, and failing to capture the wagons loaded with arms and ammunition, traveled at a more leisurely pace.[87] Captain Moore, leaving the Kansas river on June 7, made forced marches for eleven and a half days, averaging about thirty-five miles a day, and arrived at the Arkansas crossing on June 19.[88] But by that time the trains of Armijo and Speyer, as well as of the other early Santa Fé traders, were over two hundred miles ahead, having reached a point which is now in the northeastern part of New Mexico.[89] Failing to overtake the caravans and discovering no signs of Mexican cavalry, Moore abandoned the pursuit and returned to Pawnee Fork, where he halted the progress of all the later Santa

85 Kearny to Moore, June 6, 1846, *ibid.*

86 Kearny to Noble, June 12, 1846, *ibid.;* Kearny, Special Orders No. 1, June 22, 1846, Letters Received, MSS., O.F.S., A.G.O.

87 *Daily Missouri Republican,* July 3, 1846.

88 *Weekly Reveille,* Aug. 17, 1846.

89 A. Wislizenus, *Memoir of a Tour to Northern Mexico, Connected with Col. Doniphan's Expedition, in 1846 and 1847* (Washington, 1848), 11, 15; *Southwest Historical Series,* I, 179-181; *Daily Missouri Republican,* July 3, 1846.

Fé traders. At that place he was reinforced by the troops under Lieutenant Noble and Captain Waldo. On July 11 his enlarged command, accompanied by about one hundred and fifty merchant wagons with their teamsters and proprietors, started for Bent's Fort, which they reached eleven days later. There he encamped until the arrival of Colonel Kearny with the remainder of the Army of the West.[90]

Meanwhile the major part of that army was advancing from Fort Leavenworth. On June 25, Kearny issued orders for companies B, C, F, and G, First regiment of Missouri mounted volunteers, to begin their march under the command of Lieutenant-colonel Charles F. Ruff. Departing from the post on June 26 and 27, these companies proceeded a short distance and on June 29 organized themselves into a battalion.[91] On June 27, Kearny directed Doniphan to start companies E and H – the rest of the volunteer regiment – with Major William Gilpin as commander. This order was executed two days later, when Gilpin and his troops, as well as Colonel Doniphan, left the fort.[92] On the same day – June 29 – two other detachments marched from Fort Leavenworth: the Laclede Rangers, Thomas B. Hudson, captain, an independent company of mounted volunteers from St. Louis; and companies A and B, infantry battalion, Missouri volunteers, in command of Captain

90 Edwards, Journal, July 10-22, 1846, MS., M.H.S.; *Weekly Reveille,* Aug. 17, 1846; *Daily Missouri Republican,* Aug. 3, 1846; Susan Shelby Magoffin, *Down the Santa Fé Trail and into Mexico* (Stella M. Drumm, ed., New Haven, 1926), 42-59; Jacob S. Robinson, *A Journal of the Santa Fé Expedition under Colonel Doniphan* (Carl L. Cannon, ed., Princeton, 1932), 13-19.

91 Charles F. Ruff, Notes of the Expedition to Santa Fé, June 25-29, 1846, MS., M.H.S.; *Daily Missouri Republican,* July 3, 1846.

92 Kearny, Order No. 4, June 27, 1846, Letters Received, MSS., O.F.S., A.G.O.; *Weekly Reveille,* July 20, 1846.

William Z. Angney.[93] Gibson was a member of infantry company B. On June 30 companies A and B, light artillery battalion, Missouri volunteers, in charge of Captain Woldemar Fischer, started for Santa Fé.[94] Colonel Kearny, accompanied by his staff, a small detachment of First dragoons, and some recruits, also departed on the same day.[95] The last part of the Army of the West did not leave Fort Leavenworth until July 6, when Captain Edwin V. Sumner, commanding a squadron of companies B and K, First dragoons, advanced from the post.[96] "The march of the 'Army of the West,'" recorded Hughes, "as it entered upon the great prairies, presented a scene of the most intense and thrilling interest. . . The boundless plains, lying in ridges of wavy green not unlike the ocean, seemed to unite with the heavens in the distant horizon. As far as vision could penetrate, the long files of cavalry, the gay fluttering of banners, and the canvas-covered wagons of the merchant train glistening like banks of snow in the distance, might be seen winding their tortuous way over the undulating surface of the prairies." [97]

A small detachment of topographical engineers accompanied the Army of the West. On June 5, 1846, Colonel J. J. Abert, chief of the corps of topographical engineers, ordered Lieutenant W. H. Emory, with Lieutenants Warner, Peck, and J. W. Abert, to proceed immediately to Fort Leavenworth, where they were to report to Colonel Kearny as field and topographical

93 *Weekly Reveille,* July 20, 1846; *Jefferson Inquirer,* July 15, 1846; *Daily Missouri Republican,* July 3, 1846.

94 *Daily Missouri Republican,* Aug. 6, 1846.

95 Henry S. Turner, Diary, June 30, 1846, MS., M.H.S.

96 Cooke, *Conquest of New Mexico and California,* 3.

97 Hughes, *Doniphan's Expedition,* 30.

engineers of his command. Abert directed them not only to act in this capacity but also to perform any military duty assigned them by Kearny. Anticipating that the expedition would advance through unexplored regions, Abert likewise ordered Emory and his associates to collect data which would provide the government with information about the country traversed.[98] Leaving Washington, D.C., on June 6, the officers crossed the Alleghenies by stage and reached St. Louis a week later. There they made elaborate astronomical observations, checked their instruments, hired ten voyageurs as assistants, and purchased mules, horses, provisions, and a carriage to convey their instruments. They left St. Louis by boat on June 16 and arrived at Fort Leavenworth shortly afterward.[99] On June 23, Kearny ordered them to enter upon their respective duties; but two days later he detached Lieutenant Warner from this service and appointed him ordnance officer of the Santa Fé expedition.[100] Emory, Abert, Peck, and their assistants left the fort early on the morning of June 27.[101]

The various sections of the Army of the West marched from Fort Leavenworth to Bent's Fort, a distance of about 565 miles,[102] in approximately thirty days, averaging nearly twenty miles a day. Making forced marches under orders from Colonel Kearny, they were strung along the Santa Fé trail for many miles. Although each detachment had its own peculiar adventures, all companies proceeded under the same general conditions,

98 *House Ex. Docs.*, 30 cong., 1 sess., no. 41, p. 7.

99 *Ibid.*, pp. 7-8; *Weekly American* (St. Louis), June 19, 1846; *Weekly Reveille*, June 22, 1846.

100 Kearny, Order No. 2, June 23, 1846, Order No. 3, June 25, 1846, Letters Received, MSS., O.F.S., A.G.O.

101 *House Ex. Docs.*, 30 cong., 1 sess., no. 41, p. 386; *Weekly Reveille*, July 6, 1846.

102 *House Ex. Docs.*, 30 cong., 1 sess., no. 41, p. 176.

experiencing similar pleasures and hardships. Some wagons broke down, and a number of horses and oxen died or were left exhausted on the prairies because of the strain of constant traveling. The recruits were thrilled at the first sight of the Great Plains but finally grew very tired of the same monotonous landscape day after day. Swarms of gnats, flies, mosquitoes, and other insects alternately harassed them. Many wolves and rattlesnakes were seen, but they proved to be more annoying than dangerous. Rains, no matter how heavy, seldom halted the progress of the army, for the soldiers marched, ate, and slept when drenched to the skin. One day Gibson's feet were so swollen from marching in the rain that he had to cut his boots off. The heat of the sun, entirely unobstructed on the treeless plains, was frequently excessive, and at such times the winds which swept across the parched country felt like blasts from a furnace, scorching the faces of the troops. Occasionally the winds developed into sand storms which, raging for hours at a time, nearly blinded and choked them. When water became scarce, as it sometimes did, they suffered terribly, their tongues and lips swelling and their mouths getting slimy. The battalion of infantry kept pace with and frequently marched ahead of the mounted troops, but as a result many had sore feet.[103] "Their feet were blis-

[103] Kearny to Jones, July 10, Aug. 1, 1846, Letters Received, MSS., O.F.S., A.G.O.; Turner, Diary, July 3, 11, 12, 13, 14, 23, 25, 1846, MS., M.H.S.; Ruff, Notes, July 1, 9, 10, 21, 1846, MS., *ibid.;* Abraham R. Johnston, Journal of the March of the Army of the West, July 4, 9, 11, 12, 13, 19, 26, 1846, Letters Received, MSS., O.F.S., A.G.O.; *Saint Louis Daily Union,* Sept. 7, 1846; *Weekly Tribune,* July 4, Aug. 1, Sept. 5, 1846; *Jefferson Inquirer,* Aug. 4, 11, Sept. 15, 1846; *Täglicher Anzeiger des Westens,* July 23, Sept. 5, 1846; *Weekly Reveille,* July 27, 1846; *Daily Missouri Republican,* Aug. 6, 1846; *Missouri Democrat* (Fayette), Sept. 2, 9, 1846; Frank S. Edwards, *A Campaign in New Mexico with Colonel Doniphan* (Philadelphia, 1847), 24-26, 30-32, 35; Hughes, *Doniphan's Expedition,* 34, 41, 43-44, 46-47, 50, 55; Smith, *The War with Mexico,* I, 288-289.

tered by their long, and almost incredible marches," wrote Hughes. "The ground was often marked with blood in their foot-prints; yet with Roman fortitude they endured the toils of the campaign."[104] Nor was the army as a whole entirely healthy, since dysentery, measles, and other diseases spread rapidly, forcing many to ride in the jolting supply wagons. At one time about half of Gibson's company was on the sick list. Moreover, the scarcity and occasional absence of provisions were a disappointment to all.[105] "To make a war the first thing to do is to be certain of filling your soldiers' bellies," recorded Captain Abraham R. Johnston in his diary on July 23, 1846.[106]

But the Army of the West overcame most handicaps, for the troops were chiefly young, vigorous, persevering, care-free, and anxious to fight the Mexicans. Despite the difficulties encountered, they had a number of diversions and derived enjoyment from the journey itself. Playing cards, singing, and telling stories served as pastimes after the day's march. Fishing and bathing in the streams along the way were recreation for many; hunting buffaloes, antelopes, elk, deer, and jack rabbits were thrilling sports for the mounted troops. The Fourth of July seemed to inspire the men with new life and cheerfulness, for it was celebrated in most companies by resting, drinking healths, hurrahing, playing Yankee Doodle, and firing guns.[107] But Lieutenant-colonel Ruff marched his command twenty-seven miles on that day, discouraging much celebration; "for this," wrote

104 Hughes, *Doniphan's Expedition,* 50.

105 Ruff, Notes, June 28, July 9, 1846, MS., M.H.S.; *Weekly Tribune,* Aug. 1, 1846; *Jefferson Inquirer,* July 15, Aug. 4, 1846; Hughes, *Doniphan's Expedition,* 41-45, 49, 52.

106 Johnston, Journal, July 23, 1846, Letters Received, MSS., O.F.S., A.G.O.

107 *Weekly Tribune,* July 4, 1846; Hughes, *Doniphan's Expedition,* 32, 35-36, 39-40, 47-48, 51, 53.

Hughes, "he was blessed with curses." [108] Prairie travel did not affect most of the troops adversely. Indeed, constant exertion in the open air whetted their appetites, so that even the monotonous daily fare of bread, black coffee, salted pork, and occasional fresh meat tasted good. Some of the volunteers who were sickly before leaving Missouri improved in health as they marched along. One of them was Frank S. Edwards, who wrote: "But, oh, the breath of the prairies! When the breeze, which always rises at sundown, fans your cheek after a hot day's ride, you sink quietly to sleep, feeling that that soft delicious air is bringing health and strength to your weary body." [109] Nor were the men so exhausted that they were unable to recognize the picturesque character of their march. On June 30, Hughes recorded: "This morning the troops moved off majestically over the green prairie, presenting the most animating sight. The long files stretch over miles of level plain, or wind over the beautifully undulating hills, with gun and sabre glittering in the morning sunbeams and pinnon [pennon] proudly streaming in the breeze, while the American Eagle spreads his broad pinions and westward bears the principles of Republican Government." [110] About two weeks later Lieutenant Kribben wrote: "The prairie desert at this place [Pawnee Fork] has the appearance, when viewed at a distance, of a beautiful country town, and our white tents pitched in regular form along the shore of the river – the numberless horses grazing in the distance of several miles around the camp – the many bright fires burning in every direc-

108 *Weekly Tribune*, Aug. 1, 1846. See also Hughes, *Doniphan's Expedition*, 40.

109 Edwards, *A Campaign in New Mexico with Colonel Doniphan*, 26.

110 *Weekly Tribune*, Aug. 1, 1846. See also Hughes, *Doniphan's Expedition*, 37.

tion – the men running and parading about, their arms glittering in the bright rays of the sun – form, altogether, a scene as picturesque as it is original and pleasing to behold." [111]

The several detachments of the Army of the West came to Bent's Fort and vicinity between July 22, when Captain Moore's command reached there, and July 31, when Captain Sumner and his squadron of First dragoons arrived. This adobe trading post, the largest in the Rocky mountain region, was the property of Bent, St. Vrain and Company, who were extensively engaged in the Indian trade, trapping, and the Santa Fé trade. There and in the immediate neighborhood the troops rested, recruited their animals, and made the necessary preparations to resume their march to New Mexico. Gibson and his comrades used some of their leisure to visit various parts of the fort, which they found very interesting. The whole army was now concentrated for the first time and after a few days of inactivity was ready to advance upon Santa Fé.[112]

Before leaving Fort Leavenworth and during his stay at Bent's Fort, Colonel Kearny took steps to occupy New Mexico peaceably, in accordance with the wishes of President Polk. Kearny spread peace propaganda, attempting to convince the Mexicans that it would be to their interest to surrender without fighting. As early as the latter part of May, when George T. Howard was visiting Fort Leavenworth on his way to Santa Fé, Kearny apparently instructed him to inform the inhabitants of New Mexico that in case they laid down their arms and took the oath of allegiance to the United States,

111 *Daily Missouri Republican,* Aug. 6, 1846.

112 Kearny to Jones, Aug. 1, 1846, Letters Received, MSS., O.F.S., A.G.O.; *Jefferson Inquirer,* Sept. 15, 1846; Hughes, *Doniphan's Expedition,* 58.

they would receive the same protection and enjoy the same liberties as other American citizens.[113] It also seems that he dispatched a similar message to the New Mexicans by an express which left Independence for Santa Fé on June 20.[114] When Kearny arrived at Bent's Fort, he found that three Mexican spies had been captured by the troops. He had the spies conducted through the whole camp, gave them permission to see everything, and then talked to them as follows through an interpreter: "You can go home tomorrow and tell your countrymen all that you have seen. To General Armijo you may say that I shall cross the river day after tomorrow and advance with my army on the great trail to Santa Fé. Tell him that we are not coming at night, secretly, or through the mountain passes like an enemy, but in broad daylight; that, like people who are not ashamed of their intentions, we are ready to regard the citizens of New

[113] Hughes, *Doniphan's Expedition,* 50-51; *Daily Missouri Republican,* Sept. 7, 1846.

[114] On June 20, 1846, the *Western Expositor,* of Independence, Missouri, published the following news item: "An express messenger leaves here to day for Santa Fé. He expects to go out at least in 15 days. He takes dispatches with him from the traders and expects to return again immediately. Col. Kearney at the Fort has provided him with a passport so that he will meet with no delay. Our friendly intentions and pacific relations will be made known to the Government through him while at the same time he goes out on other business for the traders in whose employ he is." The preceding quotation is taken from a reprint in the *Boonville Commercial Bulletin,* July 4, 1846. On July 11, 1846, Lieutenant Kribben, who was in close touch with Colonel Kearny, wrote: "Col. Kearney has already begun to make peace overtures to Gen. Armijo, from which he seems to expect much, and an express is three or four weeks ahead for this purpose. Kearney does not believe that New Mexico will offer strong resistance; [he] even intends to subjugate the entire province without striking a blow and to introduce American laws and courts there immediately." *Täglicher Anzeiger des Westens,* July 23, 1846. In mentioning Kearny's express, Lieutenant Kribben does not state whether he refers to Howard, to the messenger who left Independence on June 20, or to another dispatch bearer. See also *Daily Missouri Republican,* June 23, 1846.

Mexico as American citizens and treat them as our equals. Tell General Armijo that we shall take and occupy Santa Fé and all the other cities of New Mexico, and if anyone places an obstacle in our way, we shall remove it immediately. We shall respect all the rights of the citizens, and protect their property as well as their persons. If your countrymen have food for men and animals which they might be inclined to sell us, tell them that they might bring them to us, and we shall give gold and silver for them. Furthermore, be assured that if any one of our soldiers does an injury to the lowliest among you, I shall punish that soldier severely; at the same time, however, be assured that I shall also treat you in a similar manner if you injure any one of us. For all this protection which I thus offer you, your property, and your persons, I only demand that you pay your taxes to me and submit to the laws of the United States." [115]

Before resuming his march from Bent's Fort, Colonel Kearny decided to take further action to secure New Mexico without fighting. On July 31 he issued a proclamation to the citizens of New Mexico declaring that, under instructions from the United States government, he was entering that province with a large military force "for the purpose of seeking union with and ameliorating the condition of its inhabitants." He urged that the people remain at home and follow their usual vocations, and promised that all who should pursue this course would not be molested by the American army but would be protected and respected in their civil and religious rights. However, he warned those who took up arms or

---

[115] Lieutenant Kribben's record of Kearny's speech. *Täglicher Anzeiger des Westens,* Sept. 5, 1846. See also Turner, Diary, July 30, 1846, MS., M.H.S.; Johnston, Journal, July 30, 31, 1846, Letters Received, MSS., O.F.S., A.G.O.; *Weekly Reveille,* Sept. 14, 1846; Hughes, *Doniphan's Expedition,* 56.

encouraged resistance against the United States that he would regard them as enemies and treat them accordingly.[116] He gave a copy of this proclamation to the Mexican spies, who left Bent's Fort for Santa Fé immediately.[117] On the same day he also ordered Eugene Leitensdorfer, a Santa Fé trader who had volunteered his services, to proceed "in the direction of Taos" with two Pueblo Indians and an escort of a subaltern and twenty mounted volunteers, in order to distribute copies of the proclamation in that region and make friendly overtures to the Pueblo.[118]

Anxious to utilize every means at his command to effect a peaceable occupation of New Mexico, Kearny wrote a letter directly to Governor Manuel Armijo on August 1, 1846, the day before the departure of the Army of the West from Bent's Fort. In it Kearny asserted that when the American government annexed Texas, the Río Grande became the boundary between the United States and Mexico. He therefore declared that he was coming to take possession of territory over a part of which Armijo was governor. "I come as a friend," wrote Kearny, "and with the disposition, and intention, to consider all Mexicans and others as friends who will remain peaceably at their homes and attend to their own affairs." The property, the persons, and the religion of such individuals would not be molested by the American army. He stated that he was coming "to this part of the United States" with a strong military force, that a larger body of troops was following in his

116 *House Ex. Docs.*, 30 cong., 1 sess., no. 60, p. 168; Smith, *The War with Mexico*, I, 290; Connelley, *Doniphan's Expedition*, 181.

117 Turner, Diary, July 30, 1846, MS., M.H.S.; Johnston, Journal, July 31, 1846, Letters Received, MSS., O.F.S., A.G.O.

118 Kearny, Special Orders No. 2, July 31, 1846, Letters Received, MSS., O.F.S., A.G.O.; Johnston, Journal, July 31, 1846, *ibid.*; *Daily Union* (Washington, D. C.), Oct. 22, 1846.

rear, and that he had many more men than Armijo could possibly mobilize. "I therefore," urged Kearny, "for the sake of humanity, call upon you to submit to fate and to meet me with the same feelings of Peace and Friendship which I now entertain for and offer to you and to all those over whom you are Governor." For Armijo to yield without resistance, Kearny argued, would be to the governor's interest and to the advantage of all New Mexicans, who would bless their chief executive for the decision he had made. However, if Armijo determined to oppose the advance of the American army, the governor would have to shoulder full responsibility for the blood which would be shed and for the suffering and misery which would ensue; and instead of obtaining the blessings of his countrymen, he would receive their curses. Kearny concluded by issuing a warning that he would consider as enemies all those whom Armijo would lead in arms against him.[119]

This letter was intrusted to the care of Captain Philip St. George Cooke, who, in command of twelve men of the First dragoons, was ordered to proceed to Santa Fé ahead of the army and deliver it to Governor Armijo.[120] Accompanying Cooke were James Wiley Magoffin and José Gonzáles, Chihuahua traders.[121] On August 1, after writing the letter to Armijo, Kearny reported to Adjutant-general Jones: "It is impossible for me to tell what opposition will be made to our entering New Mexico, but I, at this time, feel confident that our force is sufficient to overcome any that may be offered. I have

119 Kearny to Armijo, Aug. 1, 1846, Letters Received, MSS., O.F.S., A.G.O. See also Benjamin M. Read, *Illustrated History of New Mexico* (Santa Fé, 1912), 434-435; Connelley, *Doniphan's Expedition,* 181-182.

120 Cooke, *Conquest of New Mexico and California,* 6, 28; Kearny to Armijo, Aug. 1, 1846, Letters Received, MSS., O.F.S., A.G.O.

121 Cooke, *Conquest of New Mexico and California,* 6.

done all in my power to obtain possession of the Country quietly & peaceably, and I hope to succeed in it." [122]

James Wiley Magoffin, who traveled with Cooke to Santa Fé, was a native of Kentucky and had been a merchant in Mexico for about twenty years.[123] On March 3, 1825, he was appointed United States consul at Saltillo,[124] but sometime afterward moved his business to the city of Chihuahua, where he married a Mexican woman. In 1844 he removed with his family to a farm near Independence, Missouri, but continued to trade with Santa Fé and Chihuahua by the overland route. While on a trip to the East to purchase goods in 1845, he met Senator Benton in Washington.[125] During the spring of the following year, shortly after Magoffin had returned to western Missouri from a trading venture to Chihuahua and Santa Fé, he received a letter from Benton asking him to come to Washington as soon as possible. Magoffin hurried to the national capital, where, at the senator's suggestion, he agreed to accompany the Army of the West to Mexico.[126] On the evening of June 15, 1846, Benton introduced Magoffin to President Polk. In Benton's presence, the president talked with Magoffin for an hour, and obtained much valuable information from him about the northern provinces of Mexico and the "means of conducting a campaign in them." [127] Two

122 Kearny to Jones, Aug. 1, 1846, Letters Received, MSS., O.F.S., A.G.O.

123 Connelley, *Doniphan's Expedition,* 196-197; *The Diary of James K. Polk* (Quaife, ed.), I, 472.

124 Adams to Magoffin, Mar. 3, 1825, Dispatches to Consuls, Mexico, MSS., State Department.

125 Connelley, *Doniphan's Expedition,* 197; Magoffin, *Down the Santa Fé Trail and into Mexico* (Drumm, ed.), xix.

126 Thomas Hart Benton, *Thirty Years' View* (New York, 1858), II, 683; *Daily Missouri Republican,* May 18, 21, 30, 1846; Connelley, *Doniphan's Expedition,* 197; Magoffin, *Down the Santa Fé Trail and into Mexico* (Drumm, ed.), xviii.

127 *The Diary of James K. Polk* (Quaife, ed.), I, 472.

days later Polk had another interview with him, this time in the presence of the Secretary of War. The president and Marcy held a long conversation with Magoffin, who gave them "much valuable information." The latter declared that he was still an American citizen, and "tendered his services to the Government of the U.S. in any way in which he could be useful." Impressed with his character and intelligence, Polk and the Secretary of War "concluded that he could be useful in furnishing supplies for the army, and conciliating the people of the Northern Provinces of Mexico to the U.S." [128]

On the next day – June 18 – Marcy, at the request of the president, wrote Magoffin a letter of introduction to Colonel Kearny. He stated that Magoffin was well acquainted with the people of Santa Fé, Chihuahua, and the intermediate country, that he had been introduced to the president by Senator Benton, and that Polk had had several interviews with him and was favorably impressed with his character, intelligence, and "disposition to the cause of the United States." Marcy continued: "His knowledge of the country and of the people is such as induces the President to believe that he may render important services to you in regard to your military movements in New Mexico. . . Considering his intelligence, his credit with the people, and his business capacity, it is believed that he will give important information and make arrangements to furnish your troops with abundant supplies in New Mexico. Should you apprehend difficulties of this nature, it is recommended to you to avail yourself in this respect, and others, of his services, for which he will, as a matter of course, be entitled to a fair consideration." [129] On the

[128] *Ibid.*, I, 474-475.

[129] *House Ex. Docs.*, 31 cong., 1 sess., no. 17, pp. 240-241. See also Magoffin, *Down the Santa Fé Trail and into Mexico* (Drumm, ed.), 263-264.

same day Marcy wrote a similar letter introducing Magoffin to the commanding officer of the expedition to Chihuahua.[130]

Magoffin left Washington at once and traveled to western Missouri as quickly as possible. Accompanied by José Gonzáles, a Chihuahua merchant, he departed from Independence in a buggy about July 15, and after a rapid journey over the Santa Fé trail arrived at Bent's Fort on July 31.[131] He immediately presented his letter of introduction to Colonel Kearny, who received him in a cordial manner. Indeed, the colonel gladly availed himself of the services of one who was well acquainted with Governor Armijo, and therefore directed Magoffin to accompany Captain Cooke to Santa Fé.[132] On August 1, Kearny wrote to Adjutant-general Jones that he had received the Secretary of War's letter of June 18, and promised to do his utmost to execute Marcy's instructions and the desires of the president.[133]

On August 1 and 2 the Army of the West left Bent's Fort and vicinity and resumed its march to Santa Fé, which was still over three hundred miles distant. Thomas Fitzpatrick, a famous mountaineer, was the guide, and William W. Bent, founder of Bent's Fort, was in command of a small party of spies. Crossing to the south side of the Arkansas river near the site of the present city of La Junta, Colorado, the troops, accompanied by several hundred wagons of the later Santa Fé

130 *House Ex. Docs.*, 31 cong., 1 sess., no. 17, p. 241.

131 Turner, Diary, July 31, 1846, MS., M.H.S.; *Weekly Reveille*, Sept. 14, 1846; William E. Connelley, *A Standard History of Kansas and Kansans* (Chicago and New York, 1918), I, 126.

132 Connelley, *A Standard History of Kansas and Kansans*, I, 124-125, 128; Benton, *Thirty Years' View*, II, 683. See also Ralph E. Twitchell, *The Story of the Conquest of Santa Fé, New Mexico, and the Building of Old Fort Marcy, A. D. 1846*, Historical Society of New Mexico, *Publications*, no. 24, pp. 43, 46, 51.

133 Kearny to Jones, Aug. 1, 1846, Letters Received, MSS., O.F.S., A.G.O.

traders, left the river not far from that point and journeyed to the southwest, following, in a general way, the route now taken by the Atchison, Topeka, and Santa Fé railroad. During the first few days they advanced in several sections and at times by slightly different trails, in order to utilize the scanty water and grass. Indeed, the march of about ninety miles from Bent's Fort to the crossing of the Purgatoire river was the most difficult one on the way to Santa Fé, for the desert nature of the country exposed both man and beast to severe hardships. The heat was intense, causing sore eyes, nosebleed, and general exhaustion among the troops. Gibson and a number of others became sick and were forced to ride in the wagons. A hot southwest wind of great velocity drove clouds of sand into the faces of the weary soldiers, almost blinding and choking them. Some tried to protect themselves from the suffocating effect of these blasts by tying handkerchiefs over their faces, but without much success. The scanty supply of good water caused the men to suffer terribly from thirst. Moreover, many horses and some oxen perished on account of the scarcity of water and grass and the exertion involved in making their way across the deep sand. Soon after an animal died, its carcass provided a feast for wolves and vultures. Due to an inadequate supply of provisions, the army was placed on reduced rations, a hardship which aggravated a situation already almost unendurable.[134]

Both regulars and volunteers were naturally exasper-

[134] Turner, Diary, Aug. 2-5, 1846, MS., M.H.S.; Edwards, Journal, Aug. 2-4, 1846, MS., *ibid.;* Robinson, *A Journal of the Santa Fé Expedition* (Cannon, ed.), 19-21; Hughes, *Doniphan's Expedition,* 61-63; *Täglicher Anzeiger des Westens,* Sept. 24, 1846; *Daily Missouri Republican,* Sept. 25, 1846; Smith, *The War with Mexico,* I, 291; Hubert H. Bancroft, *History of Arizona and New Mexico, 1530-1888* (*Works of H. H. Bancroft,* XVII, San Francisco, 1889), 415.

ated with the many obstacles which they had to encounter. Referring to this dreary march, Lieutenant Elliott wrote: " 'Our army swore terribly in Flanders,' said Uncle Toby; but he never heard the Army of the West." [135] On August 5, Lieutenant Turner recorded in his journal: "The volunteers are beginning to discover that they have made an egregious mistake & their complaints are long & loud. The St. Louis companies bear up tolerably well, but Col. Doniphan's Regt. to a man is sick & tired of the business. . . But for the example set by the regulars, I verily believe the volunteers would not reach Santa Fé." [136] Hughes stated that the parched earth "appeared as though it had not been refreshed by a shower since the days of Noah's flood," and that "dreary, sultry, desolate, boundless solitude reigned as far as the eye could reach." [137] On August 5, Lieutenant Emory wrote: "Passed the rear wagons of the infantry – the horses almost done. Trotting in their rear were three wolves. Many a horse of the army of the west, must this night, I think, give up the ghost." [138] Even Samuel C. Owens, a Santa Fé trader who had made many trips across the prairies, stated that the journey was tedious, the road very bad, and the weather "not only warm but absolutely hot; and at the same time the water very bad and what little there was, being scanty, made the journey any thing but agreeable." [139]

After crossing the Purgatoire river near the present site of Trinidad, Colorado, the troops found more water and grass, but they continued on reduced rations, and

135 Elliott, *Notes Taken in Sixty Years,* 225.

136 Henry S. Turner, Journal, Aug. 5, 1846, MS., M.H.S.

137 Hughes, *Doniphan's Expedition,* 62.

138 *Daily Union,* Oct. 22, 1846.

139 Owens to his wife, Aug. 24, 1846, Owens MSS., Jacksonville, Fla.

the weather was still very warm. The country now became more mountainous, and the scenery was beautiful. To the right of the line of march were the Spanish Peaks, capped with snow; to the left were the Great Plains, stretching to the east as far as the eye could reach; and in front loomed high mountains with precipitous cliffs, across which led the Ratón pass. Traveling through the pass was an arduous task for both men and animals, and many horses and mules perished along the way. Rough roads and rocky hills were the principal obstacles; and the wagons were often hauled up the abrupt mountain spurs by ropes and let down in the same way on the other side. Although the view from the summit of the pass was magnificent, most of the troops were too fatigued and hungry to enjoy it. Within a week after crossing the Ratón, the Army of the West reached the outlying settlements of New Mexico.[140]

While marching from Bent's Fort to Santa Fé, Colonel Kearny continued to spread peace propaganda, taking advantage of every opportunity to inform the New Mexicans of his pacific intentions. On August 10, when the army reached a point near the present town of Cimarrón, New Mexico, a Mexican came into camp from Bent's Fort. The colonel permitted him to travel westward to Taos, about sixty miles away, and gave him copies of the proclamation issued at Bent's Fort on July 31, as well as letters to the alcalde and the padre.[141] On the same day two groups of Mexican spies were captured. Next morning – August 11 – Kearny showed them his army, made them a speech, and then ordered

140 *Täglicher Anzeiger des Westens,* Sept. 24, 1846; Hughes, *Doniphan's Expedition,* 63-67, 70; Elliott, *Notes Taken in Sixty Years,* 225-226; Smith, *The War with Mexico,* I, 291.

141 *Daily Union,* Oct. 22, 1846; *House Ex. Docs.,* 30 cong., 1 sess., no. 41, p. 21.

them to be released after the rear guard had passed. In his speech the colonel declared that he considered New Mexico a part of the United States; that he intended to extend American laws over it, and to substitute laws for the arbitrary will of one man; and that he came as a friend of the people, desirous of protecting their property and religion, and of defending the weak against the strong and the poor against the rich. The speech brightened their faces, which expressed good nature "but almost idiocy." They were mounted on burros, which they guided with clubs instead of bridles; and their whole appearance contrasted sharply with the well-mounted First dragoons. Turning to Emory, Colonel Kearny remarked: "Emory, if I have to fire a round of grape into such men, I shall think of it with remorse all my life." [142] That night two Mexicans from the town of Mora rode into camp, declaring that they had faith in the Americans and therefore approached without hesitation. Kearny, "with great quickness," ordered them to shake hands with him, and then gave them practically the same speech which he had delivered in the morning. He did not release them immediately, for he suspected that they were spies. But on the following day – August 12 – he dismissed the elder Mexican, giving him two copies of the proclamation of July 31 – one for the alcalde of Mora and the other for the people of the town.[143]

In the meantime, conditions in New Mexico favored the Army of the West. Although racially and historically an integral part of the Mexican nation, New Mexico was geographically isolated from the rest of the country.

142 *Daily Union,* Oct. 22, 1846. See also Johnston, Journal, Aug. 10, 11, 1846, Letters Received, MSS., O.F.S., A.G.O.; Turner, Journal, Aug. 11, 1846, MS., M.H.S.; *House Ex. Docs.,* 30 cong., 1 sess., no. 41, pp. 21-23.

143 *Daily Union,* Oct. 22, 1846; Turner, Journal, Aug. 12, 1846, MS., M.H.S.; *House Ex. Docs.,* 30 cong., 1 sess., no. 41, p. 23.

She took little part in national affairs and considered herself an unimportant member of the Mexican republic. Her people, who were mostly poor and ignorant, received no adequate federal protection from the frequent depredations of the Apache, Comanche, and Navajo Indians. The few national troops who were quartered in Santa Fé were a burden rather than an aid, since taxes, already very heavy, had to be levied in order to pay them. Nor was much financial support forthcoming from Mexico City, as the various governments which existed there from time to time were always in need of money. Besides, the trade between Missouri and New Mexico over the Santa Fé trail had considerably lessened the latter's economic dependence upon the central government, and had brought New Mexico into close contact with the "great republic of the north." Many New Mexicans were actively engaged in this commerce, which had flourished for about twenty-five years. The continuance of the trade was a necessity for the very existence of the government of New Mexico, since its officials and employees were paid largely out of the funds derived from the duties and fees collected from the Santa Fé traders. The governor himself, Manuel Armijo, was financially interested in this traffic, had business relations with many merchants from the United States, and learned to respect the power and ability of the American people.[144] During the fall of 1845, just before he became governor for the last time, he invited a number of American traders to the Palace of the Gov-

[144] Lansing B. Bloom and Thomas C. Donnelly, *New Mexico History and Civics* (Albuquerque, 1933), 177-178, 185-187, 201, 209-210; *"Barreiro's Ojeada Sobre Nuevo Mexico"* (Lansing B. Bloom, ed.), *New Mexico Historical Review,* III, 150-151; Smith, *The War with Mexico,* I, 284-285; *Southwest Historical Series,* I, 57, 83-84, 91, 101-103; Gregg, *op. cit.,* XIX, 329-333, XX, 73, 77, 223.

ernors, where, "in his toast to the Americans, he manifested in the strongest terms his wish for the peace and welfare of the two countries: he said, that if war were declared, there would be no fighting by the people of New Mexico." [145]

Although the governor and most of the people of New Mexico were probably not unfriendly to the United States immediately before the outbreak of hostilities, they realized, when war actually commenced, that Mexico, after all, was their mother country, and that it was their patriotic duty to resist the invasion of the American forces. To be sure, there was little real enthusiasm to fight, but a vigorous minority demanded action. As early as March, 1846, the federal government informed Armijo that war might be expected, and authorized him to make preparations for defense.[146] On June 6, before news of the declaration of war had reached Santa Fé, the governor issued a proclamation to the troops under his command, pointing out that Mexico was threatened with the loss of Texas, which "the Giant our Neighbor has usurped from us," and that the United States wanted the left bank of the Río Grande to be the boundary of this "usurpation." He called upon his men to be prepared for action, and declared that it was not only courage and discipline that he desired of them, but also constancy and endurance, so that they might prepare themselves "for trials yet harder than those in the past from the wretchedness of our Treasury." He hoped that they would be "filled with enthusiasm and courage upon seeing for a Second Time

145 *Daily Missouri Republican*, Jan. 1, 1846.

146 Smith, *The War with Mexico*, I, 289, 293; Read, *Illustrated History of New Mexico*, 417-418; Ralph Emerson Twitchell, *The History of the Military Occupation of the Territory of New Mexico from 1846 to 1851* (Denver, 1909), 75.

the enemy that in 1841 surrendered his pride at Your presence." He concluded: "[You] shall find at the Head of Your lines in every exigency your Comrade and best Friend, Manuel Armijo." [147]

About eleven days after the above proclamation was issued the first news of the proposed invasion of New Mexico by the United States reached Santa Fé. Manuel Álvarez, the American consul, on his own initiative, had an immediate interview with Armijo and tried to convince him that it would be "better for himself and the people under his government to capitulate." It would be far better, argued Álvarez, "to become an inconsiderable portion of a powerful republic, than a considerable one of [a] nation continually engaged in revolutions" and unable to defend its citizens from the murder, rapine, and plunder of hostile Indians. Apparently he had little success in convincing Armijo, whom he characterized as "a great man in small matters" but "a small one in great affairs." However, he seems to have fared better with the governor's confidential advisors, who, according to Álvarez, were "rather easily won over," because they could look forward to political advancement in a free, elective state.[148]

During the latter part of June, shortly after the news of the proposed invasion reached New Mexico, a rumor circulated that the outposts of the American army were about two hundred miles from Santa Fé, and that in a few days an officer with a flag of truce would arrive in the capital to arrange for the surrender of the province.[149] This report produced great excitement. The

147 Lansing B. Bloom, "New Mexico under Mexican Administration, 1821-1846," *Old Santa Fé*, II, 352-353.

148 Álvarez to Buchanan, Sept. 4, 1846, Consular Reports, Santa Fé, MSS., State Department. See also Smith, *The War with Mexico*, I, 289.

149 *Täglicher Anzeiger des Westens*, Aug. 25, 1846; *Southwest Historical Series*, I, 185-186.

padres, who had considerable influence over the people, at once began to spread anti-American propaganda, attempting to kindle a fire of patriotism among the ignorant masses. They declared that the American troops were a reckless band of destructive adventurers who would pillage towns, rob the people of their property, desecrate churches, and destroy the Catholic faith. They also asserted that the invaders would debauch the women, and would brand them upon the cheek as the Mexicans did their mules upon the hip.[150] Many of the wealthier classes made hurried preparations to leave Santa Fé, and a number of farmers in the vicinity drove their cattle into the mountains. Alcaldes in Santa Fé and Taos went from house to house to collect arms and military equipment, and attempted to induce the men to come to the defense of their country.[151]

Governor Armijo was very excited when he heard how close the American troops were to Santa Fé, and at once sent out spies to confirm or refute the rumor which had been circulated.[152] Meanwhile, he decided to dispose of his merchandise to Albert Speyer, fearing that it might fall into the hands of Kearny's troops. On July 1, while making arrangements for the sale of his goods, Armijo became irritated with Speyer, and apparently with every one in general. "Damn the Americans! Damn the Mexicans!" he cried, and immediately ordered his guns loaded and called a guard to put Speyer in the calaboose. As the trader kept his composure, the governor finally vented his wrath upon the officer who had not immediately answered his summons, thus end-

150 *House Ex. Docs.*, 30 cong., 1 sess., no. 41, p. 27; *Daily Missouri Republican*, Sept. 4, 7, 24, 1846; Connelley, *Doniphan's Expedition*, 65; Smith, *The War with Mexico*, I, 293.

151 *Daily Missouri Republican*, Aug. 20, Sept. 7, 1846.

152 *Weekly Reveille*, Aug. 10, 1846; *Daily Missouri Republican*, Aug. 20, 1846; *Täglicher Anzeiger des Westens*, Aug. 27, 1846.

ing the incident.[153] On the same day Armijo presided at an extraordinary session of the departmental assembly, informed it of the "urgent circumstances" in which New Mexico found itself as a result of the advance of the American army, and recommended that the remaining members of the assembly be summoned, so that that body might meet and "decree measures in accord with their prerogatives." This recommendation was agreed to without discussion.[154] On the following day Armijo issued a proclamation calling into the service all men who were physically fit, and ordering the people to drive their herds of cattle into the mountains.[155] Later that day a rumor reached the capital that five thousand American troops were marching on Santa Fé and that an additional thousand would arrive at Taos on July 4.[156] But some of Armijo's spies soon returned and reported that they could find no trace of the American army anywhere. Thereupon, the governor asserted that all the rumors were "humbug" and had been spread by speculators. He regretted having sold his merchandise, and inveighed against the ingratitude of certain foreigners – among others, Josiah Gregg. He no longer appeared to believe in an army of invasion, and the departmental assembly which had been called to meet on July 3 and 4 did not convene.[157]

But Armijo was soon disillusioned, for about July 10 an express from the United States arrived in Santa Fé bringing a report that four thousand American

153 *Täglicher Anzeiger des Westens,* Aug. 25, 1846.

154 Bloom, "New Mexico under Mexican Administration," *Old Santa Fé,* II, 356.

155 *Täglicher Anzeiger des Westens,* Aug. 27, 1846.

156 *Ibid.*

157 *Ibid.;* Bloom, "New Mexico under Mexican Administration," *Old Santa Fé,* II, 356.

troops were advancing upon New Mexico.[158] This news, together with other more or less authentic information on the same subject, was transmitted by the governor to the departmental assembly on July 13. Ortiz, one of the deputies, presented a motion that in view of the urgent circumstances in which New Mexico found herself, the governor be authorized to "take all those measures which may seem proper for the conservation of the National Territory" and to exercise such dictatorial powers until the end of the war. The deputy explained that his object was to free the governor from "any sudden need to consult the Assembly." But the motion failed to pass at this time.[159] Meanwhile Santa Fé was in a state of great excitement, since the people were expecting the early arrival of the invading army. All business was suspended. A number of troops had responded to the governor's call and were quartered in the city; but they were poorly clad, fed, and armed, and, like Armijo, had little military experience. Two weeks passed without any further news of the American army, and by that time the excitement had subsided, a number of people again beginning to doubt the existence of an invading force.[160]

But shortly after midnight on August 6 a courier galloped into Santa Fé and brought the governor "certain and all too positive news" that more than five thousand United States troops were six days' journey south of Bent's Fort, and that they were "boasting in a loud voice" that they were coming to take possession of New

158 *Weekly Reveille,* Aug. 31, 1846.

159 Bloom, "New Mexico under Mexican Administration," *Old Santa Fé,* II, 357-358.

160 *Daily Missouri Republican,* Aug. 24, 1846; *Missouri Statesman,* Sept. 4, 1846.

Mexico at all costs.[161] About August 7 [162] the principal citizens of New Mexico held a conference in the capital in order to discuss what steps, if any, should be taken to resist the invading army. The majority, including Governor Armijo, wanted to surrender without fighting, but a vigorous minority contended that the enemy should be resisted. The latter opinion prevailed. A plan of action was then formulated "in which Messrs. Pino and Baca were entrusted to take charge, with General Armijo, of the forces which should repel the enemy." [163]

On August 7, Armijo acquainted the president of the departmental assembly with the news which had been brought by the courier on the previous day, and asked him to induce that body to declare itself in permanent session, in order that "by using its legislative powers it may aid the Government with its knowledge and foresight, which may furnish it with means to save the Department." [164] The assembly convened in special session on the following day and received a communication from the governor similar to the one sent to its president. After some discussion by several deputies about the "dismal news" which had been received, Antonio Sena declared that in his opinion a decree should be promulgated which, "in view of the pressing circumstances," should invest Armijo "with extraordinary authority," so that he "might take discretionary measures for the sustenance of the forces operating under his command." The assembly finally agreed that such a

161 Armijo to Sr. Presidente de la Excma. Asamblea Departamental, Aug. 7, 1846, in *Santa Fé Republican* (Santa Fé, N.M.), May 3, 1848.

162 Turner, Diary, Aug. 10, 1846, MS., M.H.S.; Read, *Illustrated History of New Mexico*, 417-418.

163 Read, *Illustrated History of New Mexico*, 418. See also Turner, Diary, Aug. 10, 1846, MS., M.H.S.

164 Armijo to Sr. Presidente de la Excma. Asamblea Departamental, Aug. 7, 1846, in *Santa Fé Republican*, May 3, 1848.

decree should be prepared and that it should be presented for adoption the next morning.[165] Accordingly on August 9 the departmental assembly adopted and issued a decree authorizing Armijo "to dictate all those measures which may be necessary for the conservation of the national honor which, for the moment, is threatened by the Republic of North America, our neighbor." The second article of the decree vested the governor with "extraordinary powers to maintain the military forces at his command; the enlargement of powers to last until the end of the war." The last article stipulated that the national and departmental incomes be held liable for the "preferential payment of the debt which may exist for the maintenance of the war, without there being granted any other inversion than that proposed for the purpose." [166] Meanwhile, on August 8, Armijo had issued a bombastic proclamation to the people of New Mexico in which he asked them to be ready for war, and assured them that he was prepared to sacrifice his life and interests in the defense of his country.[167]

Four days after the governor's proclamation Captain Cooke reached Santa Fé. Having left Bent's Fort at the same time as the Army of the West, he had traveled rapidly and on August 9 passed through Las Vegas. During a brief visit there he was entertained by the alcalde, who secretly dispatched an express across the mountains to inform Armijo of his arrival.[168] On August

165 Bloom, "New Mexico under Mexican Administration," *Old Santa Fé*, II, 361-362.

166 "Decreto de la Asamblea," [Aug. 9, 1846], in *Santa Fé Republican*, May 3, 1848. See also Bloom, "New Mexico under Mexican Administration," *Old Santa Fé*, II, 363-364.

167 Read, *Illustrated History of New Mexico*, 418-420.

168 Armijo to Excma. Asamblea Departamental, Aug. 10, 1846, in *Santa Fé Republican*, May 3, 1848; Cooke, *Conquest of New Mexico and California*, 21.

12, Cooke, at the head of his detachment of twelve dragoons, rode into Santa Fé. After traveling over a long crooked street, he suddenly found himself in front of the guardhouse, where, on seeing his dragoons, the Mexican soldiers "howled out their 'alarm' " in so hideous a manner that he mistook it for a threat. At this point he thought it might not be amiss to display his flag of truce. He made his way through the crowd of soldiers and people in and near the plaza, and finally reached the Palace of the Governors, in front of which his trumpeter sounded a parley. After some delay an officer conducted him into the building, where, in a long room with a carpeted earth floor, he was introduced to Armijo. The latter was seated at a table, and near-by stood six or eight military and civil officials. The governor, according to Cooke, wore "a blue frock coat, with a rolling collar and a general's shoulder straps, blue striped trousers with gold lace, and a red sash." [169] Armijo arose when the captain was presented to him. Cooke stated that he had a letter for him from the commander of the American army and inquired what time would be the most convenient to deliver it. The governor said that he had ordered quarters for him, and hoped that he would remain as long as he wished. Shortly after this interview Cooke, accompanied by an interpreter, returned to the Palace of the Governors on his official visit. Armijo thought that the approach of the American army was rather sudden and rapid, and inquired "very particularly" whether Kearny was a general or a colonel. Cooke was then permitted to walk about town, and the ever-alert captain of dragoons used this opportunity to note the amount and condition of the Mexican ordnance.[170]

[169] Cooke, *Conquest of New Mexico and California*, 28.

[170] *Ibid.*, 27-30.

During this time and afterward Magoffin was active in spreading propaganda among the New Mexicans. His wife appears to have been a relative of the governor, over whom he exercised considerable influence.[171] Entertaining liberally and dispensing ample supplies of claret and champagne, he interviewed Armijo, Archuleta, the militia officers, and many of the rich men of the province who were then in Santa Fé. He assured them that the only object of the United States was to take possession of New Mexico as a part of the territory acquired by the annexation of Texas, and to give "peace and quietude" to the people.[172] On the night of August 12, at ten o'clock, Magoffin brought Armijo to Cooke's quarters, where a secret conference was held. What happened at this meeting is not as yet entirely clear, but it is known that Cooke and Magoffin had a long conversation with the governor. Using Kearny's letter of August 1 and probably also his proclamation of July 31 as proofs, they tried to convince Armijo that the American troops were coming to New Mexico to give peace and protection to its inhabitants. They stated that Magoffin had been dispatched by President Polk in order to inform the governor and the people of New Mexico with whom Magoffin was acquainted that this was the only object of the United States. Probably Magoffin also argued at this time that American rule would increase the price of real estate and make New Mexico prosperous. Cooke asserts that it was finally settled that a commissioner should return with him, that they should start at sunrise, and that the governor "would march next day 'with six thousand men.' " The commissioner chosen was Henry Connelly,

171 Magoffin, *Down the Santa Fé Trail and into Mexico* (Drumm, ed.), 84; Connelley, *A Standard History of Kansas and Kansans,* I, 131, 134.

172 Turner to Magoffin, Jan. 14, 1849, Magoffin MSS., General Accounting Office, Washington, D. C.; Connelley, *A Standard History of Kansas and Kansans,* I, 124-127, 134; Benton, *Thirty Years' View,* II, 683.

an American merchant who had long been a resident of Mexico.[173] Whether Armijo would resist the American troops, probably neither Cooke nor Magoffin knew.

At Armijo's invitation Cooke made his final visit to the Palace of the Governors shortly after sunrise on August 13. It was a visit of courtesy, and chocolate, bread, and cake were served on silver plate. The captain thought the refreshments excellent and was convinced that the Spaniards or Mexicans alone knew how to make good chocolate. "But meanwhile," recorded Cooke, "the Governor is bowing me out, with a suspiciously good-humored smile, and deafening trumpets and drums seem beating to arms. I mount and ride forth, with my escort in compact order; and I pass that same guard-house, and hear the same sullen howl of the sentinel, which I still misunderstand; and rising in my stirrups I turn and with a defiant gesture, call out, in good English, 'I'll call again in a week.' "[174]

Even before Cooke left Santa Fé, plans had been drawn up by the governor and his associates to resist the advance of the American army at Apache canyon, about fifteen miles from the city; and after the captain's departure hurried preparations were made to put them into effect. Armijo had called upon the federal government, as well as upon the governments of Durango and Chihuahua, for military support to help New Mexico repel the invader, but with no result. It is true that as early as July 1, Colonel Mauricio Ugarte, comandante general of Chihuahua, had promised to send five hundred cavalry and the same number of infantry as soon

[173] Magoffin, *Down the Santa Fé Trail and into Mexico* (Drumm, ed.), 84, 169; Connelley, *A Standard History of Kansas and Kansans,* I, 124, 132, 134; Cooke, *Conquest of New Mexico and California,* 31, 33; Smith, *The War with Mexico,* I, 294.

[174] Cooke, *Conquest of New Mexico and California,* 31-32.

as New Mexico needed them; yet these troops never arrived in time for service.[175] Forced to rely upon his own resources, the governor finally assembled a body of militia, rancheros, Indians, and regulars, most of whom were inadequately trained, armed, and equipped. They left Santa Fé between August 13 and 16, cursing the gringo heretics, who, they said, would be defeated and driven back in disgrace.[176] But Armijo, who was less sanguine of success, privately executed a will and power of attorney on August 14 – evidence that he expected to be engaged in battle or to be forced to flee the country.[177] Early on the morning of August 16, the governor, with the regular dragoons, left Santa Fé for the canyon, where about three thousand men were assembled under Colonel Pino. The ravine constituted a strong natural defense which could easily be held against a superior force. The position chosen by the Mexicans was at the lower end of the canyon, where the passage was about forty feet wide. They felled trees, blocked the road with timber, and placed their cannon on an elevated point about three hundred yards to the rear. Besides, they began to throw up entrenchments.[178]

While Armijo's troops were taking their position at Apache canyon, Cooke was riding eastward to report to Colonel Kearny. But on August 14, the day before he

---

[175] Turner, Diary, Aug. 13, 1846, MS., M.H.S.; *Daily Union,* Oct. 22, 1846; Smith, *The War with Mexico,* I, 289-290, 293-294. See also Ugarte to Armijo, July 1, 1846, in the appendix of the present volume.

[176] Álvarez to Buchanan, Sept. 4, 1846, Consular Reports, Santa Fé, MSS., State Department; *Boonville Commercial Bulletin,* Sept. 24, 1846; Smith, *The War with Mexico,* I, 293.

[177] Ralph E. Twitchell, *Old Santa Fé* (Santa Fé, 1925), 257-258.

[178] Álvarez to Buchanan, Sept. 4, 1846, Consular Reports, Santa Fé, MSS., State Department; *Daily Missouri Republican,* Sept. 24, 1846; *Daily Union,* Oct. 23, 1846; *Täglicher Anzeiger des Westens,* Sept. 24, 1846; Connelley, *A Standard History of Kansas and Kansans,* I, 124; Smith, *The War with Mexico,* I, 293-294, 516.

could do so, four Mexican dragoons met the Army of the West near Las Vegas and gave the colonel Armijo's reply to the letter which had been delivered by Cooke. In it the governor stated that he could not acknowledge the Río Grande as the boundary line between the United States and Mexico, that the New Mexicans had risen *en masse* to defend their country, and that it was his duty and inclination to put himself at their head. "If you get the country," stated Armijo, "it will be because you prove the strongest in battle. I suggest to you to stop at the Sapello, and I will march to the Vegas. We will meet, and negotiate on the plains between them." [179] Despite this suggestion Kearny continued toward Santa Fé, and that evening camped a mile from Las Vegas. There he made a speech to the Mexican dragoons in which he said: "The road to Santa Fé is now as free to you as it is to myself; say to my friend, General Armijo, I shall soon meet him, and I hope it will be as friends. I come here as the friend of the whole Mexican people, and not as their enemy. My government considers New Mexico a part of the United States, and I intend to extend her laws over it. All who obey me, and do not resist, I will respect, and make secure in their property, their persons, and their religion. All who take up arms against me, I will treat as enemies." [180] He stated further that not "an onion or a pepper would be taken from them without a full equivalent in cash." [181] Upon departing, the lieutenant of the dragoons embraced Kearny, Turner, and Emory in true Mexican fashion.[182]

---

179 *Daily Union,* Oct. 22, 1846. See also Johnston, Journal, Aug. 14, 1846, Letters Received, MSS., O.F.S., A.G.O.; *House Ex. Docs.,* 30 cong., 1 sess., no. 41, pp. 25-26; *Daily Missouri Republican,* Sept. 24, 1846.

180 *Daily Union,* Oct. 22, 1846.

181 *Daily Missouri Republican,* Sept. 24, 1846.

182 *House Ex. Docs.,* 30 cong., 1 sess., no. 41, p. 26.

On the same evening – August 14 – Kearny had an interview with the alcalde and the two captains of militia of Las Vegas, and informed them that he had come to take possession of their country and hoped that this could be accomplished without bloodshed. He stated that he had no doubt that the occupation would be peaceable if he could talk to the people and explain the advantages which they would derive from American rule; he therefore asked the alcalde to assemble the inhabitants of Las Vegas in the plaza next morning by eight o'clock, when he would address them.[183] About seven o'clock on the morning of August 15 the Army of the West marched through Las Vegas and encamped a short distance beyond, while Kearny, his staff, and the commanders of the various divisions remained in the town. Accompanied by the alcalde and the two captains of militia, they ascended to the top of one of the flat-roofed houses, from which Kearny addressed one hundred and fifty or two hundred people who had gathered in the plaza.[184] He said: "Mr. Alcalde and people of New Mexico: I have come amongst you by the orders of my government, to take possession of your country, and extend over it the laws of the United States. We consider it, and have done so for some time, a part of the territory of the United States. We come amongst you as friends, not as enemies; we come to you as protectors, not as conquerors; we come amongst you for your benefit, not for your injury. Henceforth I absolve you from all allegiance to the Mexican government, and from all obedience to General Armijo. He is no longer your governor [great sensation]; I am your governor. I shall not

183 *Daily Union,* Oct. 22, 1846.

184 Johnston, Journal, Aug. 15, 1846, Letters Received, MSS., O.F.S., A.G.O.; *Daily Missouri Republican,* Sept. 24, 1846; *Daily Union,* Oct. 23, 1846.

expect you to take up arms, and follow me, to fight your own people, who may be in arms against me; but I now tell you that those who remain peaceably at home, attending to their crops and herds, shall be protected by me in their property, their persons, and their religion; and not a pepper or an onion shall be disturbed or taken by my troops, without pay, or without the consent of the owner. But listen! He who is found in arms against me, I will hang. From the Mexican government you have never received any protection. The Apaches and the Navajos come down from the mountains and carry off your sheep and your women whenever they please. My government will correct all this. They will keep off the Indians, protect you in your persons and property, and I repeat again, will protect you in your religion. I know you are all good Catholics, and that some of your priests have told you all sorts of stories; that we would pollute your women, and brand them upon the cheek as you do your mules upon the hip. It is false. My government respects your religion as much as the Protestant religion, and allows each man to worship his Creator as his heart tells him is best. Her laws protect the Catholic as well as the Protestant, the weak as well as the strong, the poor as well as the rich. I am not a Catholic myself; I was not brought up in that faith; but at least one-third of my army are Catholics. And I respect a good Catholic as much as a good Protestant. There goes my army! You see but a small part of it. There are many more behind. Resistance is useless. Mr. Alcalde, and you two captains of militia, the laws of my country require that all men who hold office under it, shall take the oath of allegiance. I do not wish for the present, until things get settled, to disturb your mode of government. If you are prepared to take the oath of allegiance, I shall continue you in office and support your authority." [185]

After a brief delay, due to the reluctance of one of the captains to change his citizenship, Kearny concluded the ceremony by administering the oath of allegiance to the alcalde and the two captains of militia. The spectators uncovered their heads; each of the three officials held up his right hand and made the sign of the cross by crossing his thumb and index finger; and then the general,[186] in a solemn manner, administered the following oath: "You do swear to hold faithful allegiance to the United States, and to defend its government and laws against all its enemies, in the name of the Father, Son and Holy Ghost." [187] Kearny then shook hands with the three men and commanded all citizens to obey them. Upon grasping the hand of the alcalde, he turned to the people and declared that he shook hands with all of them through their alcalde, and greeted them as good citizens of the United States. At the conclusion of the ceremony, the people raised a "faint shout." [188] What their real feelings were, can only be surmised.

On the evening of August 14, Kearny had been informed that a strong force of Mexican troops was sta-

[185] Lieutenant Emory's record of Kearny's speech. *Daily Union*, Oct. 23, 1846. See also *House Ex. Docs.*, 30 cong., 1 sess., no. 41, pp. 27-28.

[186] On June 30, 1846, Kearny was commissioned brigadier-general. Adjutant-general Jones sent him the commission on July 3, but it did not reach him until early on the morning of August 15, just before the ceremony above described. Jones to Kearny, July 3, 1846, Letters Sent, XXII, MSS., O.F.S., A.G.O.; Johnston, Journal, Aug. 15, 1846, Letters Received, MSS., *ibid.;* Francis B. Heitman, *Historical Register and Dictionary of the United States Army* (Washington, 1903), I, 586.

[187] *Daily Missouri Republican,* Sept. 24, 1846. See also Johnston, Journal, Aug. 15, 1846, Letters Received, MSS., O.F.S., A.G.O.

[188] Johnston, Journal, Aug. 15, 1846, Letters Received, MSS., O.F.S., A.G.O.; *Daily Missouri Republican,* Sept. 24, 1846; *Daily Union,* Oct. 23, 1846.

tioned at a defile just beyond Las Vegas in order to stop the advance of the American army. This news spread rapidly among the soldiers. Standards were unfurled, speeches were made to the volunteers, and a plan of attack was carefully devised and communicated to the troops.[189] Immediately after the general had administered the oath of allegiance to the officials of Las Vegas on the morning of August 15, he rejoined the army, which then advanced rapidly toward the defile. The infantry were ordered to scale the mountain to the right, while the dragoons, mounted volunteers, and artillery were commanded to proceed through the canyon. The artillerymen lighted their matches, and the mounted troops with drawn sabres rode forward at a trot. But when they came to the pass they could not find the enemy. Nor did the infantry have any better success. Apparently the report had been false or the Mexicans had fled.[190] The army continued its march and on the same day – August 15 – passed through Tecolote, and on the following day, through San Miguel. In each place Kearny made a speech similar to the one he had delivered at Las Vegas, and also administered the oath of allegiance to the local officials. Meanwhile, reports had come in that the Mexicans were fortifying themselves at Apache canyon, fifteen miles from Santa Fé. Rumor placed the number of the enemy at anywhere from one to twelve thousand. Some of the troops, though anxious to fight, doubted whether the Army of the West could engage such numbers successfully.[191]

---

189 Turner, Diary, Aug. 14, 1846, MS., M.H.S.; *Täglicher Anzeiger des Westens,* Sept. 24, 1846; *Daily Union,* Oct. 23, 1846.

190 Johnston, Journal, Aug. 15, 1846, Letters Received, MSS., O.F.S., A.G.O.; *Täglicher Anzeiger des Westens,* Sept. 24, 1846; *Jefferson Inquirer,* Sept. 29, 1846; Hughes, *Doniphan's Expedition,* 71-72.

191 Turner, Diary, Aug. 15, 16, 1846, MS., M.H.S.; Turner, Journal, Aug. 13, 1846, MS., *ibid.;* Johnston, Journal, Aug. 15, 16, 1846, Letters Received, MSS.,

While Kearny was occupying Las Vegas, Tecolote, and San Miguel, the Mexican troops at Apache canyon were in a sad plight. They appeared anxious to resist the American advance, but Armijo argued that Kearny's army was too strong for them. "Pino offered to attack if he could have a part of the regulars, but the governor was determined to keep them all for his own protection. Then he was called a traitor, and retaliated by calling the people disloyal and cowardly. They threatened him; and he, more afraid of his own army than of Kearny's, urged the militia to go home and let the regulars do the fighting. Threatened again, he forbade the people to come near his camp; and finally he turned his cannon in their direction." [192] The result was that on August 16 and 17 the officers dismissed the troops, who departed immediately for their homes; and thus New Mexico's army ceased to exist.[193] Armijo himself, accompanied by sixty dragoons, fled rapidly southward by way of Galisteo, and by August 20 reached the town of El Manzano, over eighty miles from Apache canyon. From that point he wrote a letter to the comandante general of Chihuahua asserting that most of the people of New Mexico were in favor of the American government, and promising to explain verbally why he had retreated from Santa Fé.[194] On the other hand, the people of New Mexico accused Armijo of cowardice.[195] As a matter of fact, neither the governor nor most of his troops, even though they had publicly proclaimed their zeal for battle, had much real enthusiasm to fight the Army of

O.F.S., A.G.O.; *Täglicher Anzeiger des Westens,* Sept. 24, 1846; *Daily Missouri Republican,* Sept. 24, 1846.

192 Smith, *The War with Mexico,* I, 294-295.

193 *Ibid.,* 295; Read, *Illustrated History of New Mexico,* 431-433; *Boonville Commercial Bulletin,* Sept. 24, 1846.

194 *Diario Oficial* (México, D. F.), Sept. 10, 1846; *Daily Union,* Oct. 31, 1846.

195 *Diario Oficial,* Sept. 10, 1846.

the West.[196] "Thus ended," wrote an old Santa Fé trader, "a two or three weeks preparation for a fight and is withal not a bad specimen of Mexican warfare." [197]

Not long after Armijo joined the army at Apache canyon, a report reached Santa Fé that great confusion prevailed there, and that a fight would probably break out among the Mexican troops. Soon afterward another rumor spread through the city that the governor had been assassinated by his own soldiers, and that the Mexican dragoons, who were known to be a rough lot, were returning to the capital to rob and murder the Americans.[198] When the news arrived that Armijo had fled and that the troops had dispersed to their homes, great excitement prevailed throughout the city. Fearing the approach of the American soldiers, many families left their homes "to hide themselves in the deserts," for they were apparently of the opinion that Kearny's army was composed of "cruel and sanguinary savages." In order to quiet their fears, Juan Bautista Vigil y Alarid, who had become acting governor upon Armijo's flight, issued a proclamation to the people of Santa Fé on August 17. In it he described the unfounded apprehensions of the inhabitants, and tried to allay them by reproducing Kearny's proclamation to the people of New Mexico on July 31, which had reached Santa Fé sometime before. The acting governor also ordered Kearny's proclamation to be posted "in the public places." [199] Vigil's actions may have stopped the exodus from the capital, but many of its inhabitants still believed what the padres

196 Connelley, *A Standard History of Kansas and Kansans,* I, 124.

197 *Boonville Commercial Bulletin,* Sept. 24, 1846.

198 *Ibid.*

199 Álvarez to Buchanan, Sept. 4, 1846, Consular Reports, Santa Fé, MSS., State Department; Read, *Illustrated History of New Mexico,* 430-431; Bloom, "New Mexico under Mexican Administration," *Old Santa Fé,* II, 373-374.

had told them and looked forward to the entrance of the American troops with misgivings.[200]

The first report of Armijo's flight reached Kearny during the night of August 16, when the army was encamped on the Pecos river, forty-five miles from Santa Fé.[201] Next day the report was verified from several different sources. The troops were disappointed that after a long and arduous march they had been deprived of an opportunity to fight the Mexicans.[202] Early on August 18 the Army of the West broke camp twenty-nine miles from the capital, and following a fatiguing journey over a slippery and rocky trail entered Santa Fé about five o'clock that afternoon. The dragoons rode in front, the infantry came next, and Colonel Doniphan's regiment brought up the rear, while the artillery remained on a hill immediately southeast of the city. With drawn sabres the troops proceeded through the streets of the capital and displayed their flags "in the gayest and most gorgeous manner." Along the line of march were many children who gazed at the wonderful spectacle with curious eyes; men "with surly countenances and downcast looks" who regarded the soldiers "with watchfulness, if not terror"; and black-eyed women who peered "through latticed windows," a few beaming with pleasure but many sobbing aloud. At last Kearny reached the Palace of the Governors, where he and his staff dismounted, entered the building, and in a large room met the acting governor and twenty or thirty prominent men of the city. The general talked to the

200 Edwards, Journal, Aug. 18, 1846, MS., M.H.S.; *Weekly Reveille,* Sept. 28, 1846.

201 Turner, Diary, Aug. 17, 1846, MS., M.H.S.; Edwards, Journal, Aug. 17, 1846, MS., *ibid.; Daily Missouri Republican,* Sept. 24, 1846.

202 Johnston, Journal, Aug. 17, 1846, Letters Received, MSS., O.F.S., A.G.O.; Turner, Journal, Aug. 16, 17, 1846, MS., M.H.S.; *Daily Union,* Oct. 23, 1846.

Mexicans in a conversational manner, and his remarks were similar in content to the addresses he had previously delivered at Las Vegas and at other places. When Kearny had finished, Vigil treated his guests to wine and brandy. At this time, and as the sun was setting, the Stars and Stripes were hoisted over the Palace, and immediately a salute of thirteen guns was fired by the artillery. Soon afterward the general and his staff were entertained at supper by Señor Ortiz, while the hungry and thirsty troops crowded into the taverns and saloons. That night Kearny slept on the carpeted earth floor of the Palace of the Governors, and his weary troops lay down to rest in their tents on the outskirts of Santa Fé.[203]

On the morning of August 19, Kearny made a formal address to the people. Many of the inhabitants of Santa Fé, together with all the officers in dress uniform, assembled on the plaza in front of the Palace of the Governors. At about ten o'clock General Kearny, accompanied by his interpreter, ascended a small platform. To his left were Acting Governor Vigil and the three alcaldes of the city; to his right were Colonel Doniphan, and Majors Sumner and Clark.[204] With the same punctilio that characterized his every action, Kearny then addressed the people as follows: "Mexicans! I have been sent by the government of the United States in order to take possession of this country, the province of New Mexico, as a territory of that republic. By the annexa-

[203] Edwards, Journal, Aug. 18, 1846, MS., M.H.S.; Johnston, Journal, Aug. 18, 1846, Letters Received, MSS., O.F.S., A.G.O.; *Daily Missouri Republican*, Sept. 24, 1846; *Weekly Reveille*, Sept. 28, 1846; *Jefferson Inquirer*, Sept. 29, 1846; *Daily Union*, Oct. 23, 1846; Hughes, *Doniphan's Expedition*, 78-79; Cooke, *Conquest of New Mexico and California*, 38-39; Connelley, *A Standard History of Kansas and Kansans*, I, 124; Smith, *The War with Mexico*, I, 295-296.

[204] Turner, Diary, Aug. 19, 1846, MS., M.H.S.; *Täglicher Anzeiger des Westens*, Sept. 28, 1846; Connelley, *Doniphan's Expedition*, 62; Hughes, *Doniphan's Expedition*, 79.

tion of Texas to the United States, the Río Grande was established as the boundary line between Mexico and the United States, and our republic consequently demands its rights by reason of that annexation. I come, therefore, not to bring war but to maintain peace, and the soldiers whom you saw marching into your city yesterday, have my orders to contribute to this in every way. You see in me the governor of New Mexico, and I herewith declare that all acts of the former government relating to this territory are null and void, that its laws are no longer valid, and that its offices are abolished. I herewith offer you the protection and security of the American constitution and the American laws, and consider all of you who choose to remain here as citizens of the United States and subject to its laws. And I herewith declare that any hostile act by such a person against the government of the United States will be regarded by me as treason and punished as such. To those among you who are not inclined to become citizens of the United States, I offer opportunity and time to leave this territory. I will not force one of you to become a citizen of a new state. However, I advise you to remain here and follow your occupations in peace; for that which the Mexican government has promised you a hundred times and has never been able to carry out, I offer you on the part of the mightiest republic in the world: freedom of person and conscience, security to your property, and protection to your occupations. The spirit of our constitution will not permit any interference of politics in religion, and religion forms no part of our laws. We allow every one to worship God according to the dictates of his own conscience. You may therefore be assured, Mexicans, that I shall protect religious freedom. But while I cannot force anyone of you to become a Protestant, I also cannot force anyone of my own people to become a Catholic. We shall protect the freedom of the individual without question as to what faith he is, for religion forms no part of our laws (loud hurrah!). General Armijo will soon return here, and when he comes back I demand of all of you that you injure him in no way, whatever injustice you may accuse him of. For this, laws exist, and we allow no one among us to seek his rights by means of personal force. Armijo is equal to all of you as a citizen, and for that very reason alone he deserves from us the protection which our government permits its citizens to enjoy. In a very short time I shall move to the South and send many of my troops to all parts of this country, in part to drive the wild hordes of Indians from your neighborhood, and in part to take possession of this land with all its towns. I do not expect that anyone will resist me, but believe rather that they will peacefully submit to me. If the latter should not occur, we shall try the strength of our arms against such individuals, and the stronger will then be right. For this purpose I do not need you, however. Follow your business and occupations and let me with my soldiers make peace. And let me tell you that diligence and industry are the noblest qualities that adorn the American citizen. Therefore follow your occupations peacefully, and if one of my men injure you, be assured that punishment will follow his offense. Live in peace with one another and obey the laws of your new state." [205]

[205] Lieutenant Kribben's record of Kearny's speech. *Täglicher Anzeiger des Westens,* Sept. 28, 1846. After recording Kearny's address, Kribben wrote: "Mr. Kearny may have said a little more, and may have expressed himself more in detail as to the religious conditions; however, I believe the above represents his speech quite literally." *Ibid.* For Hughes's versions of Kearny's address, see Connelley, *Doniphan's Expedition,* 62-63, 201-202.

No sooner had Kearny concluded his address than shouts of *"Viva el General!"* and *"Viva el Nuevo Gobernador!"* were heard on all sides. The general then administered the oath of allegiance to Vigil and the alcaldes.[206] Following this ceremony, Vigil read his answer to Kearny's speech. He said: "General: The address which you have just delivered, in which you announce that you have taken possession of this great country in the name of the United States of America, gives us some idea of the wonderful future that awaits us. It is not for us to determine the boundaries of nations. The cabinets of Mexico and Washington will arrange these differences. It is for us to obey and respect the established authorities, no matter what may be our private opinions. The inhabitants of this department humbly and honorably present their loyalty and allegiance to the government of North America. No one in this world can successfully resist the power of him who is stronger. Do not find it strange if there has been no manifestation of joy and enthusiasm in seeing this city occupied by your military forces. To us the power of the Mexican republic is dead. No matter what her condition, she was our mother. What child will not shed abundant tears at the tomb of his parents? I might indicate some of the causes for her misfortunes, but domestic troubles should not be made public. It is sufficient to say that civil war is the cursed source of that deadly poison which has spread over one of the grandest and greatest countries that has ever been created. To-day we belong to a great and powerful nation. Its flag, with its stars and stripes, covers the horizon of New Mexico, and its brilliant light shall grow like good seed well

206 *Täglicher Anzeiger des Westens,* Sept. 28, 1846; *Daily Missouri Republican,* Sept. 24, 1846; Hughes, *Doniphan's Expedition,* 81.

cultivated. We are cognizant of your kindness, of your courtesy and that of your accommodating officers and of the strict discipline of your troops; we know that we belong to the republic that owes its origin to the immortal Washington, whom all civilized nations admire and respect. How different would be our situation had we been invaded by European nations! We are aware of the unfortunate condition of the Poles. In the name then, of the entire Department, I swear obedience to the Northern Republic and I render my respect to its laws and authority." [207]

After Vigil's address the people began to disperse. At this time a white-haired old man on crutches approached Kearny and grasped his hand. Overcome by emotion, he fell on the general's breast and wept quietly for some time. At length Vigil and the alcaldes urged the old man to move on, but Kearny protested: "Let him remain; he will soon have wept enough. Heaven knows the oppressions this old man had to bear!" [208]

Three days later, on August 22, Kearny issued a proclamation to the people of New Mexico in which he announced his intention of holding "the Department with its original Boundaries (on both sides of the Del Norte) as a part of the United States & under the name of 'the Territory of New Mexico.'" He absolved all persons from allegiance to the Republic of Mexico and proclaimed them citizens of the United States. He concluded: "The Undersigned has taken possession of it [New Mexico], without firing a Gun, or spilling a single drop of blood, in which he most truly rejoices,

[207] Ralph Emerson Twitchell, *The Leading Facts of New Mexican History* (Cedar Rapids, 1912), II, 210-211. See also *Täglicher Anzeiger des Westens,* Sept. 28, 1846.

[208] *Täglicher Anzeiger des Westens,* Sept. 28, 1846. See also Hughes, *Doniphan's Expedition,* 81.

& for the present will be considered as Governor of the Territory." [209]

When Kearny occupied Santa Fé without resistance, he fulfilled the fond wish of the president of the United States. On learning of the general's accomplishment, Polk recorded in his diary: "Gen'l Kearny has thus far performed his duty well." [210] Winfield Scott wrote Kearny: "Your march upon and conquest of New Mexico . . . have won for you, I am authorised to say, the emphatic approbation of the Executive." [211] The occupation of Santa Fé without bloodshed, which was hailed by the American press as a great feat and denounced by the Mexican press as a disgrace to the Mexican nation, was due primarily to Kearny's peace propaganda, favorable conditions in New Mexico, Magoffin's influence over Armijo, Archuleta, and other Mexicans,[212] the arguments of Manuel Álvarez, rumors in

209 Kearny, Proclamation, Aug. 22, 1846, Letters Received, MSS., O.F.S., A.G.O. See also *House Ex. Docs.*, 30 cong., 1 sess., no. 60, pp. 170-171.

210 *The Diary of James K. Polk* (Quaife, ed.), II, 170.

211 *House Ex. Docs.*, 30 cong., 1 sess., no. 60, p. 164.

212 That Magoffin helped Kearny to occupy New Mexico peaceably seems clear; but the contention that he was solely responsible for New Mexico's non-resistance can no longer be maintained. Magoffin's claim to distinction rests upon his own statement in 1849, about five months after Kearny's death, and upon Benton's *Thirty Years' View,* published in 1858. Benton, however, was a biased witness, because he was a friend of Magoffin's. Besides, Benton, the father-in-law of Frémont, did not like Kearny, largely on account of the Kearny-Frémont feud during the Mexican war, and is therefore not a reliable source when he belittles the general's accomplishments by exalting those of Magoffin. We now have available all the papers which the latter filed with the War Department in support of his claim for compensation in 1849, and which Benton intimated would substantiate Magoffin's contention. But none of them prove that Magoffin was solely, or even mainly, responsible for Kearny's peaceable conquest. The most favorable statement in support of Magoffin's contention was made by Henry S. Turner, who wrote Magoffin on January 14, 1849: "Having been Chief of Genl. Kearny's Staff when he entered New Mexico in 1846, at the head of the Army of the West, I distinctly remember the services rendered by you to the Government, and to the

New Mexico exaggerating the size of the American army, and Kearny's considerate treatment of the Mexican spies and of the inhabitants of Las Vegas, Tecolote, and San Miguel.

Gibson remained in Santa Fé from August 18 until December 4, 1846. During that time a number of events occurred in New Mexico in which he did not participate. Early in September, General Kearny made a tour of the country south of Santa Fé and returned to the capital firmly convinced that the natives were favorably disposed toward the United States. He established a civil government in New Mexico on September 22, when he promulgated a code of laws, issued a declaration of rights, and appointed officers for the Territorial government. Three days later he departed for California with some of his troops, after leaving orders for Colonel Doniphan to command the military forces in

---

General, in enabling the latter to accomplish successfully the object of that expedition: *viz.*, the conquest of New Mexico without bloodshed, or resistance on the part of the inhabitants. This was much desired by our Government at the time; and I have no hesitation in saying that the Genl. was greatly aided in bringing it about, by your acquaintance with, and the influence you exercised over, the leading men of the country. The activity and zeal displayed by you, on that occasion, in behalf of American interests, were frequently and highly commended by Genl. Kearny." On August 26, 1846, when Magoffin reported to Marcy from Santa Fé, he made no claim that he was solely responsible for the peaceable occupation of New Mexico. Indeed, he then contended that Kearny's proclamation of July 31 played a great part in causing Armijo's officers to decide not to fight. Magoffin wrote: "Armijo left this place [Santa Fé] early on the 16th with 150 Dragoons and joined his army, called his officers together and wished to know if they were prepared to defend the territory. They answered they were not, that they were convinced by the proclamation they had seen from Genl. K. that the U.S. had no intention to wage war with New Mexico, on the contrary promised them all protection in their property, person and religion. Armijo, *apparently*, appeared very much exasperated, gave orders for the troops to be dispersed." Magoffin MSS., General Accounting Office, Washington, D.C.; Connelley, *A Standard History of Kansas and Kansans*, I, 123-135.

Albert Speyer
From a photograph taken in 1861

James Wiley Magoffin
From an oil painting made in 1852

New Mexico until the arrival of Colonel Price with reinforcements from the United States. The Second regiment of Missouri mounted volunteers, under the leadership of Price, reached Santa Fé during the latter part of September and the early part of October. Meanwhile, Kearny had ordered Doniphan's regiment to make a campaign into the Navajo country, and then to proceed to Chihuahua and report to Major-general Wool. Gibson eventually joined Colonel Doniphan's forces in the latter expedition, which was destined to be as eventful as Kearny's march to Santa Fé.

On September 23, in accordance with instructions from the War Department, General Kearny issued an order that as soon as all of Colonel Price's troops reached Santa Fé, Colonel Doniphan should proceed with his regiment to Chihuahua and report for duty to Brigadier-general Wool.[213] But on his way to California, Kearny learned of the depredations of the Navajo; and therefore on October 2, when encamped on the Río Grande near La Joya, he ordered Doniphan to send a military expedition into the country inhabited by these Indians. The colonel was authorized to force the Navajo to surrender all their white prisoners, as well as all property stolen from the New Mexicans, and to exact security from the Indians for their future good conduct. After he had fully complied with these instructions, he was to proceed to Chihuahua, as directed by the order of September 23.[214] Doniphan left Santa Fé on October 26 to execute the instructions of General Kearny, and on the following November 22 made a treaty with the Navajo. Returning to the Río Grande near Socorro on

213 Kearny, Order No. 30, Sept. 23, 1846, Letters Received, MSS., O.F.S., A.G.O.
214 Kearny, Order No. 32, Oct. 2, 1846, *ibid.*

December 12, he marched down the river to Valverde, where he found an encampment of Santa Fé traders who were awaiting his arrival.[215]

While Doniphan was penetrating the Navajo country, Colonel Price decided to organize a detachment to join Wool's forces in Chihuahua. On November 17, 1846, Price ordered Lieutenant-colonel Mitchell, of the Second regiment of Missouri mounted volunteers, to select one hundred men to open communication between the army in New Mexico and the troops commanded by Brigadier-general Wool, and to reconnoiter the route between Santa Fé and the city of Chihuahua. Since the object of the expedition was important, he directed Mitchell to be careful to select both officers and men with reference to their intellectual and physical efficiency, and to see that their horses were in a condition to perform the duty required.[216] Mitchell finally chose the quota from the many volunteers who offered their services, selecting Gibson as assistant quartermaster. Early in December the detachment, which was called the "Chihuahua Rangers," left Santa Fé and on the sixteenth of that month overtook Colonel Doniphan near Valverde.[217] As the colonel was on his way to Chihuahua, the Rangers became a part of his command.[218]

In the meantime the department of Chihuahua made an effort to defend itself against American invasion. As early as July, 1846, Colonel Mauricio Ugarte, comandante general, marched from the capital with about

[215] *Senate Ex. Docs.,* 30 cong., 1 sess., no. 1, p. 496; Connelley, *Doniphan's Expedition,* 307. A more detailed account of Doniphan's expedition against the Navajo will be given in the next volume of this series.

[216] See the appendix of the present volume.

[217] *Weekly Reveille,* Feb. 22, 1847; *Täglicher Anzeiger des Westens,* Feb. 20, 22, 23, 1847; *Journal of William H. Richardson* (Baltimore, 1848), 37-43.

[218] A more detailed account of Doniphan's march to Chihuahua and of the Battle of Sacramento will be given in the next volume of this series.

three hundred and eighty men to go to the aid of Armijo. Passing through El Paso del Norte about August 13, he advanced to a point about eight miles south of Socorro, when he decided to retreat because he learned of Kearny's occupation of Santa Fé by superior forces.[219] Not long afterward the city of El Paso del Norte, whose inhabitants were not very eager to fight, organized an expedition and on October 12 dispatched it to the north to forestall invasion. But on arriving at Doña Ana, the men, as well as the officers, became panic-stricken, and all returned to their homes in great haste.[220] When the news of this debacle reached the city of Chihuahua, Governor Trias hastened his military preparations and in a short time assembled a body of soldiers to march to the defense of El Paso.[221] In November he issued a proclamation exhorting these troops "to chastise the enemy if he should have the audacity to set foot upon the soil of this State." [222]

Shortly after this proclamation was issued, the soldiers marched from the city and in December arrived at El Paso. At that place their ranks were augmented, bringing their total number to about twelve hundred officers and men, with four pieces of artillery. The inhabitants of El Paso provided them with money, horses, and supplies. Soon a courier brought the news that Colonel Doniphan's forces were approaching Doña Ana. At this juncture Colonel Gavino Cuilty, in command of the Mexican troops, announced that he had been stricken

219 *Diario Oficial,* Sept. 10, 1846; *Daily Union,* Oct. 31, 1846; Wislizenus, *Memoir of a Tour to Northern Mexico,* 42.

220 Smith, *The War with Mexico,* I, 300-301; *Daily Missouri Republican,* Jan. 19, 1847.

221 Ramón Alcáraz, *The Other Side: Or Notes for the History of the War between Mexico and the United States* (Albert C. Ramsey, ed., New York, 1850), 168.

222 *Daily Missouri Republican,* Jan. 19, 1847.

with a disease which the army surgeon had diagnosed as brain fever, and that he would therefore be forced to retire to Chihuahua immediately. Accompanied by his adjutant and the accommodating surgeon, Cuilty departed from El Paso in considerable haste, leaving the command to Lieutenant-colonel Luis Vidal. After proclaiming martial law in El Paso, Vidal, on December 21, advanced three miles from the city, and then decided to halt and build a fortification. He told his soldiers that the American forces consisted of three hundred straggling men in tatters and with no artillery. This body, he asserted, could easily be surrounded and lanced like so many rabbits. Apparently he was not eager to do the lancing in person, for he delegated this pleasure to Lieutenant-colonel Ponce de León, second in command. On December 24, Ponce, at the head of at least five hundred cavalry, seventy infantry, and fifteen artillerymen with a two-pounder howitzer, marched to the north in search of Doniphan's troops, while the adroit Vidal, with the remainder of the expedition, remained securely encamped three miles above El Paso.[223]

Doniphan's army, which consisted of 856 effective men armed with rifles but without artillery, crossed the Jornada del Muerto in several sections, and by December 23 all companies had reached Doña Ana.[224] The appearance and actions of the troops in some respects justified Vidal's description of them, because the majority were dirty, unshaven, and without uniforms, and lacked the strict discipline of the regular army. However, they could not be justly described as "rabbits" easy to be lanced; for, despite a certain outward laxity, they

223 Smith, *The War with Mexico*, I, 301; Alcáraz, *The Other Side* (Ramsey, ed.), 168-169.

224 *Senate Ex. Docs.*, 30 cong., 1 sess., no. 1, p. 497.

were "as full of fight as game cocks." [225] On Christmas day, at about three o'clock in the afternoon, the advanced detachment of Doniphan's army, numbering nearly five hundred men, arrived at Bracito, or Temascalitos, where they decided to encamp. The soldiers scattered over the prairie in search of wood and water, while a small group of officers started to play a game of cards. Shortly afterward a guard rushed into camp with the news that the Mexican troops were close at hand and were rapidly advancing upon them. Doniphan hurriedly gathered his scattered forces and formed them "in open order on foot as skirmishers." The enemy halted half a mile away and drew up in line of battle. Their dragoons were dressed in uniforms of blue pantaloons, white belts, green coats trimmed with scarlet, and "tall caps plated in front with brass, on the tops of which fantastically waved plumes of horse-hair, or buffalo's tail." They were armed with carbines, polished sabres, and long lances with small colored flags at the ends. Before Doniphan had completed the formation of his troops, a Mexican officer waving a black flag rode within a hundred yards of the American lines and demanded that their commander go to the Mexican army and confer with its commander. He stated that unless this request was complied with, the Mexicans would charge and take him, and then would neither ask nor give quarter. Doniphan's reply, according to his own account, "was more abrupt than decorous – to charge and be damned." [226] Thereupon the officer rode away to carry the message to his commander.

---

225 George F. Ruxton, *Adventures in Mexico and the Rocky Mountains* (London, 1847), 175-176.

226 *Senate Ex. Docs.*, 30 cong., 1 sess., no. 1, p. 497; Hughes, *Doniphan's Expedition*, 260-261; Edwards, *A Campaign in New Mexico with Colonel Doniphan*, 84.

No sooner had the officer reached the Mexican lines than Ponce ordered his men to charge the gringos. They advanced in perfect formation and with great rapidity, opening fire at a distance of four hundred yards from the American forces. The latter had been directed not to discharge their arms until the enemy came within rifle shot. When the Mexicans were about one hundred yards from his lines, Doniphan gave the command, and his troops poured forth such a devastating fire that the enemy ranks were thrown into great disorder. Ponce then directed his dragoons to charge the American supply wagons, but there too he was repulsed. In the midst of the fighting Captain Reid, at the head of twenty mounted men, sallied forth and attacked several times that number of Mexican dragoons, completely routing them. The Howard company captured the two-pounder howitzer – the only cannon used by either side in the conflict. Captain Thompson, of the First dragoons, acted as Doniphan's aid and adviser, and, according to the colonel's report, was of "the most essential service in forming the line and during the engagement." After approximately forty minutes of fighting, the enemy retreated from the battlefield. Their casualties were sixty-three killed or mortally wounded, about one hundred and fifty slightly wounded, and a few prisoners. The American losses were none killed and seven slightly wounded. That night Doniphan's troops feasted upon the provisions and wine captured from the enemy, and two days later entered El Paso in triumph.[227] Then, wrote a Mexican patriot, "the detested American stand-

[227] *Senate Ex. Docs.*, 30 cong., 1 sess., no. 1, pp. 497-498; *House Ex. Docs.*, 30 cong., 1 sess., no. 56, p. 318; *Missouri Statesman*, Apr. 16, 1847; *Weekly Reveille*, Mar. 1, 1847; Hughes, *Doniphan's Expedition*, 262-269; Smith, *The War with Mexico*, I, 302.

ard was raised in the plaza of the city. This sad event was the last important occurrence of the mournful year 1846." [228]

Although Colonel Doniphan learned in El Paso that General Wool had not advanced upon Chihuahua, he decided to continue his march to the capital of that state.[229] As soon as the War Department was informed that Wool did not intend to invade Chihuahua, it requested General Taylor to notify Doniphan, hoping to stop the colonel's proposed expedition.[230] But Taylor was unable to transmit the message in time; so Doniphan, unaware of the desires of the War Department, made preparations for his march. After waiting some time for the arrival of his artillery, he left El Paso with 924 effective men on February 8, 1847. He was accompanied by a large number of American traders with about 315 wagons, whom he soon organized into a battalion of infantry. Following a toilsome journey over a desert country, the expedition approached the city of Chihuahua during the latter part of February.[231]

Ever since August, 1846, the department of Chihuahua had been making preparations to meet an American invasion. Governor José María de Yrigoyen, an elderly man of moderate views, took the first steps in this direction,[232] but during the latter part of August he was forced to resign because the populace demanded more action. Señor Angel Trias, whose bitter hatred of the gringos made him a favorite at this time, succeeded Yrigoyen

228 Alcáraz, *The Other Side* (Ramsey, ed.), 171.

229 *Senate Ex. Docs.*, 30 cong., 1 sess., no. 1, p. 498.

230 Marcy to Edwards, Mar. 25, 1847, Military Book, XXVII, MSS., O.R.D., A.G.O.

231 *Senate Ex. Docs.*, 30 cong., 1 sess., no. 1, pp. 498-499; Hughes, *Doniphan's Expedition*, 286-301.

232 Expediente 1148, Año de 1846, MSS., Secretaría de Relaciones Exteriores, Archivo General, México.

and began a vigorous campaign to put the department in a state of preparedness.[233] He undertook a tremendous task, for many obstacles had to be surmounted. Writing from the city of Chihuahua on August 30, 1846, a Mexican stated: "It has been three days since the excellent Señor Trias entered upon his duties as Governor. He has displayed the energy and activity which might be expected from his genius and patriotism. He takes not a moment's repose. He has reanimated public spirit. All is action and movement among the citizens, who hurry to enrol themselves on the registers. But we want everything, everything. There is no powder – there are not arms enough, and the few that we have are much out of order; there is no lead; there is no copper, nor pieces of artillery; there is no money, and, finally, no time to create resources, and prepare for a regular resistance, for men cannot perform miracles. Notwithstanding this, I do not believe that the same thing will happen here, which has happened in New Mexico. But it is necessary that those who direct public opinion should enlarge upon, and cause the nation and the new government to see the difficulties which surround us, owing to the criminal neglect of the iniquitous cabinet of Paredes and his crew, whom God curse! The other adjacent departments are frigid spectators of what is passing here. From Durango we have not a man – not a look of protection. Zacatecas the same thing. . . We have already lost New Mexico; we shall lose Chihuahua by the same neglect; and, in succession, Durango and other departments will be lost. Raise your voices, and cry out, in order that the New Government may send us prompt

[233] *El Republicano,* in *Daily Missouri Republican,* Nov. 4, 1846; *Täglicher Anzeiger des Westens,* June 7, 1847; Smith, *The War with Mexico,* I, 304-305.

assistance, for here we shall finish by becoming victims."[234]

When the preceding letter was written, the people of Chihuahua anticipated that the department would soon be invaded by American forces coming by way of El Paso del Norte and Presidio del Norte. Since the latter expedition did not materialize and the former was delayed until 1847, the Mexicans were given more time to perfect their defense. In the fall of 1846, José A. Heredia was named comandante general of the department; and although Trias and many others disapproved of this appointment, they coöperated with the general in making preparations to repel the invader. "Volunteers" were forcibly enlisted, cannon were cast and mounted, ammunition and clothing were manufactured, arms were assembled and repaired, and a forced loan was levied upon the inhabitants of the department.[235] The priests and public officials told the people that Doniphan, in order to stimulate his soldiers to greater energy and courage, had promised that if they won the battle they would be allowed two hours to ravish the women, two hours to sack the city, and two hours to burn it.[236] Heredia finally assembled about two thousand troops and decided to defend Chihuahua at the Sacramento river, about fifteen miles north of the city. There a favorable position was chosen, and for two or three weeks the soldiers were busy throwing up fortifications and redoubts. On the night of February 27,

[234] *El Republicano,* in *Daily Missouri Republican,* Nov. 4, 1846.

[235] *Ibid.; Täglicher Anzeiger des Westens,* Nov. 27, 1846, June 5, 7, 10, 1847; Alcáraz, *The Other Side* (Ramsey, ed.), 168; Smith, *The War with Mexico,* I, 305-306.

[236] *Daily Missouri Republican,* May 18, 1847. See also *Southwest Historical Series,* I, 265-266.

Heredia with all his troops encamped behind the defenses which his men had labored so hard to erect.[237] "The enemy were to appear on the following day," wrote a Mexican chronicler, "according to the news received of their approach, and that night was a festival in the camp. In every tent, in every friendly group, cheerful toasts were drunk to the liberty of the country, the young men abandoning themselves to the illusive delirium of expected triumph, and thinking more of their expedition to New Mexico, to assist their brethren, and to cast off the American yoke, than of the approaching encounter, which they looked upon as less important than it was." [238]

At sunrise on Sunday, February 28, Doniphan broke camp at the hacienda of Sauz, about fifteen miles north of the Sacramento river. Having been informed that the Mexicans had entrenched themselves at a favorable position near that river, he prepared to engage them in battle. The commissary, company, and merchant wagons were formed into four parallel lines, with intervals of fifty yards between the lines. The artillery marched in the center interval, the first battalion in the right, and the second battalion in the left. Ahead rode about two hundred mounted troops, among whom were the Chihuahua Rangers. This arrangement gave compactness to the American army, effectually concealed its numbers, enabled it to deploy to the front, rear, or either flank, and made it possible for the wagons to form a corral sufficiently large to protect the whole force if necessary. The troops continued to march in this order until they reached the field of battle. When they arrived

[237] *El Republicano,* Mar. 22, 1847, in *Daily Picayune* (New Orleans), Apr. 10, 1847; Alcáraz, *The Other Side* (Ramsey, ed.), 173.

[238] Alcáraz, *The Other Side* (Ramsey, ed.), 174.

within a mile and a half of the Mexican position, Doniphan directed them to turn sharply to the right in order to ascend a plateau from which the enemy could be successfully attacked. The fighting began about three o'clock in the afternoon and lasted approximately three hours.[239] During that time the Americans made spirited charges upon the enemy defenses and completely routed Heredia's enthusiastic but inexperienced forces, many of whom had never before "heard the whispering of a cannon ball." Captain Thompson, of the First dragoons, and Lieutenant Wooster, of the Fourth artillery, acted as Doniphan's aids and advisers, and were largely responsible for the arrangement and movement of the troops before and during the engagement. The American casualties were one killed, one mortally wounded, and seven less seriously wounded.[240] Heredia reported to the Mexican government that because of the "complete dispersion" he could not give the exact number of his killed and wounded, but stated that they could not be less than "80 to 100."[241] Doniphan, however, estimated that the Mexican losses were three hundred killed, about the same number wounded, and forty prisoners.[242] Heredia admitted that he lost everything in his camp except a small amount of ammunition.[243] That night Doniphan's men went to sleep on the battlefield, which was made hideous by the cries of the

239 *Senate Ex. Docs.*, 30 cong., 1 sess., no. 1, pp. 498-513; Rives, *The United States and Mexico, 1821-1848,* II, 371-372.

240 Wooster to Jones, Mar. 7, 1847, Letters Received, MSS., O.F.S., A.G.O.; *El Republicano,* Mar. 22, 1847, in *Daily Picayune,* Apr. 10, 1847; *Senate Ex. Docs.*, 30 cong., 1 sess., no. 1, pp. 500-501.

241 *El Republicano,* Mar. 22, 1847, in *Daily Picayune,* Apr. 10, 1847.

242 *Senate Ex. Docs.*, 30 cong., 1 sess., no. 1, p. 501.

243 *El Republicano,* Mar. 22, 1847, in *Daily Picayune,* Apr. 10, 1847. See also Expediente 1143, Año de 1847, MSS., Secretaría de Relaciones Exteriores, Archivo General, México.

wounded and the dying Mexicans. Next morning Lieutenant-colonel Mitchell entered the city of Chihuahua with about two hundred troops, and the day afterward Colonel Doniphan followed with the remainder.

The news of the American victory in the Battle of Sacramento, as this engagement was called, was received in the United States with wild acclaim. In Missouri and elsewhere Doniphan immediately became a hero. On reporting the small American losses and the heavy Mexican casualties to the War Department, General Zachary Taylor wrote: "This disparity of loss seems incredible; but I have it from the official report of Colonel Doniphan." [244] The adjutant-general informed Doniphan that the courage and skill displayed by the troops in the Battle of Sacramento reflected "the highest credit upon the officers & men." [245] No one was more pleased with the victory than President Polk, who recorded in his diary: "The battle of Sacramento I consider to be one of the most decisive and brilliant achievements of the War." [246]

Doniphan remained in Chihuahua until the latter part of April, when, following the receipt of instructions from General Zachary Taylor, he broke camp and started for Saltillo. Gibson, however, did not accompany the Missouri volunteers on their last march. After the occupation of Chihuahua, he had been ordered to report to the commanding officer at Santa Fé; but as no troops were returning to New Mexico at that time, he was forced to delay his departure until April 4, when he joined a small caravan of traders bound for New Mexico. He arrived in Santa Fé a month later and on June 27 was mustered out of service. He remained there

---

[244] *House Ex. Docs.*, 30 cong., 1 sess., no. 56, p. 360.

[245] Jones to Doniphan, May 6, 1847, Letters Sent, XXIII, MSS., O.F.S., A.G.O.

[246] *The Diary of James K. Polk* (Quaife, ed.), III, 10.

until April 28, 1848, when he began his return journey to Missouri. While residing in Santa Fé, Gibson kept no journal, for in his opinion the important occurrences during most of this period were adequately recorded in a newspaper which he edited.[247]

Several newspapers had been started in Santa Fé prior to the American occupation, but all were short-lived. As early as 1834, Antonio Barreiro, deputy to the Mexican congress, established the first, *El Crepúsculo de la Libertad,* which appeared weekly for about a month.[248] Ten years later Donaciano Vigil began the second, *La Verdad,* which was published weekly from February 8, 1844, until early in May, 1845.[249] The third, *El Payo de Nuevo-Mejico,* also a weekly, made its appearance on June 28, 1845, but was soon discontinued.[250] All of these journals were published in Spanish and were printed by a press which appears to have been brought across the plains from the United States in 1834.[251] It was "a very small affair of royal size – Ramage patent, with iron bed and iron platten [platen]." [252] Soon after Kearny entered Santa Fé he used this press to print proclamations, laws, broadsides, orders, notices, and regulations; and his successors continued to operate it for the same purposes until the summer of 1847.[253]

247 George Rutledge Gibson to Charles Gibson, Oct. 22, 1873, MS., M.H.S.

248 Gregg, *op. cit.*, XIX, 331-332; Douglas C. McMurtrie, "The History of Early Printing in New Mexico," *New Mexico Historical Review,* IV, 373-375; Bloom and Donnelly, *New Mexico History and Civics,* 185.

249 Douglas C. McMurtrie, *"El Payo de Nuevo-Mejico," New Mexico Historical Review,* VIII, 133-134; Bloom and Donnelly, *New Mexico History and Civics,* 185.

250 McMurtrie, *"El Payo de Nuevo-Mejico," New Mexico Historical Review,* VIII, 130-138; Bloom and Donnelly, *New Mexico History and Civics,* 185.

251 *Missouri Republican,* Aug. 26, 1834; Gregg, *op. cit.*, XIX, 332.

252 *Jefferson Inquirer,* Oct. 13, 1846. See also *Weekly Reveille,* Oct. 19, 1846; *Jefferson Inquirer,* Nov. 17, 1846.

253 *Jefferson Inquirer,* Oct. 13, Nov. 17, 1846; *Weekly Reveille,* Mar. 1, 1847; Hughes, *Doniphan's Expedition,* 120-121; McMurtrie, "The History of

But Kearny had found the press inadequate for the work required; so before leaving for California he ordered a new one from St. Louis.[254] Early in November, 1846, Augustus P. Ladew, a type founder of that city, filled the general's order, and the quartermaster at St. Louis immediately sent the press, type, paper, ink, and other printing materials to Fort Leavenworth, whence they were shipped to New Mexico in the spring of 1847.[255] On reaching Santa Fé, the press was placed in charge of the quartermaster, who had operated the first printing establishment for the army.[256] In the late summer of that year Oliver P. Hovey, formerly a member of the Howard county mounted volunteers under Doniphan, and Edward T. Davies, a volunteer serving under Price, both of whom were young Missouri printers, engaged the use of the new press for six months in order to publish a newspaper, which they decided to call the *Santa Fé Republican*.[257] It was this paper which Gibson edited.

The *Santa Fé Republican* was the first American newspaper published in New Mexico. Printed half in English and half in Spanish, it hoped to interest the native Mexicans as well as the newcomers from the United States. Its initial issue appeared on September 10, 1847, when it announced that it would be published once a week and that the subscription price would be

---

Early Printing in New Mexico," *New Mexico Historical Review*, IV, 373, 380, 383, 389, 390-391.

254 Philip G. Ferguson, Diary, Sept. 2, 1847, MS., M.H.S.; *Jefferson Inquirer*, Nov. 17, 1846; *Saint Louis Daily Union*, Nov. 6, 1846; *Daily Missouri Republican*, Nov. 7, 1846.

255 Ferguson, Diary, Sept. 2, 1847, MS., M.H.S.; *Saint Louis Daily Union*, Nov. 6, 1846; *Daily Missouri Republican*, Nov. 7, 1846; *Weekly Reveille*, Nov. 9, 1846; *St. Louis Daily New Era*, Nov. 7, 1846.

256 Ferguson, Diary, Sept. 2, 1847, MS., M.H.S.

257 *Ibid.;* George Rutledge Gibson to Charles Gibson, Oct. 22, 1873, MS., M.H.S.; Connelley, *Doniphan's Expedition*, 558; *Santa Fé Republican*, Sept. 10, 1847.

two dollars "for the term of Six Months; payments invariably in advance – no subscription for less than three months." Its motto was: "We Die But Never Surrender." [258] In the very first number Gibson stated the reasons for starting the newspaper and outlined a rather ambitious program. The paper, he wrote, would provide the inhabitants of New Mexico with the latest and most authentic news from "the States," and would supply them with information concerning the movements of the army, the "stirring events" of the war, and the subjugation of the hostile Indian tribes. It would pay particular attention to the proceedings of the first Territorial legislature, and to the introduction of American laws and institutions into New Mexico. Considerable space would be devoted to the development of the territory's agricultural and mineral resources, to the improvement of the moral, social, and intellectual welfare of the people, and to "the general amelioration of the condition of the Population." News of a partisan, slanderous, or purely personal nature would be excluded.[259]

Although the *Santa Fé Republican* continued to be published until about 1849, Gibson ceased to be its editor during the latter part of December, 1847. After his resignation the owners expressed the hope that the paper might be conducted in the future with the same tact and ability as it had been in the past.[260] Gibson remained in Santa Fé until April 28, 1848, when he began his return trip to "the States." Traveling rapidly eastward over the Santa Fé trail, he reached Fort Leavenworth exactly a month later. He left that post as soon as possible

258 *Santa Fé Republican,* Sept. 10, 1847.

259 *Ibid.* Gibson presented a file of the *Santa Fé Republican* to the Missouri Historical Society in 1874. The first number is dated September 10, 1847, and the last, April 22, 1848.

260 *Ibid.,* Dec. 25, 1847.

and shortly afterward arrived in Weston, where he was greeted by his wife and five-year-old son, James. But his stay at home was brief, for in 1849 he was smitten by the California gold fever and traveled one of the overland trails to the mines. In a letter to his wife during the latter part of that year he stated that he was "doing as well as the miners generally." [261] He returned to his home in Weston about 1851, having had enough of mining life. Gibson and his family soon moved to Auburn, Illinois, a small town a few miles south of Springfield. There, on January 20, 1853, his second son, George Rutledge Gibson, Jr., was born.[262] His third child, a girl named Eugenia, was born on March 18, 1860.[263] How long Gibson resided in Auburn has not been ascertained, but about 1864 he removed to Mattoon, Illinois, where he appears to have engaged in agriculture and the practice of law.[264] In 1875 he traveled west to California, leaving his family in Mattoon. After spending some time in that state and in the Territory of Arizona, he returned home on November 26, 1878.[265]

But his "nomadic temperament" soon reasserted itself, and on June 30, 1880, at the age of seventy, he bade his family and friends good-bye and again left Mattoon, destined never to return.[266] Once more he journeyed to California, where he became associated in business with his brother, James. His brother died early in 1885; so

[261] Joseph M. Gibson to Eliza Jane Gibson, Feb. 17, 1850, Gibson MSS., William McCord Harris, New York City. See also *Santa Fé Republican*, July 18, 1848.

[262] *National Cyclopedia of American Biography* (New York, 1893), III, 248.

[263] Tombstone Inscription, Eugenia Gibson, Dodge Grove Cemetery, Mattoon, Ill.

[264] *Mattoon Gazette*, July 3, 1885; *Daily Journal-Gazette* (Mattoon), May 12, 1906; *Mattoon Commercial*, May 17, 1906.

[265] *Mattoon Gazette*, Nov. 29, 1878; *Mattoon Commercial*, Dec. 5, 1878.

[266] *Mattoon Gazette*, July 2, 1880, July 3, 1885.

Gibson decided to return to Mattoon after settling James's estate. Before his plans could be carried out he was stricken with cholera morbus, from which he died on June 28, 1885, at Woodland, Yolo county, California. "The unexpected messenger," declared the *Mattoon Gazette,* "who does not wait for perfected plans called him away from those he loved, with little warning." [267] Funeral services were held in Woodland, and, like many a soldier in the Army of the West, he was laid to rest thousands of miles from his family and friends.

[267] *Ibid.,* July 3, 1885. See also *Mattoon Commercial,* July 2, 1885.

AUTHOR'S FOREWORD

AUTHOR'S FOREWORD

The following pages [268] were prepared for the private inspection of my family only, and consequently contain many things which, if intended for the public eye, would not have been inserted. The diary was most carefully kept, and made up each day notwithstanding the fatigues and hardships of the march, and is accurate in all respects. In the infantry we could not enjoy the excitement of the chase or see the face of the country bordering the route that the mounted troops did, who were continually scouring the country for amusement as well as provisions. We, of course, saw nothing except what was immediately on our route, and had not the benefit and pleasure of examining at our leisure anything which curiosity might prompt us to inspect. Being in advance of the whole army from Bent's Fort until we struck the settlements, that portion of the narrative possesses the most interest. And being in front with the regulars from that time until we reached Santa Fé, we had means of observation which was denied to other volunteers; and in taking possession of the town [we] saw as much as could be seen or known by any except the general and his staff.

The march was effected in the most unfavorable season of the year and under circumstances the most disadvan-

268 Gibson divided his journal into six sections. His foreword relates only to the first section and a part of the second. To the first section, which covers the period from June 27 to August 18, 1846, he gave the following title: "Geo. R. Gibson's Diary of the March from Fort Leavenworth under Genl. Stephen W. Kearny in the months of July and August, 1846, to Santa Fé for the occupation of New Mexico."

tageous, many having left Fort Leavenworth with insufficient supplies of clothing and those little comforts and necessaries so highly valued on the plains. Besides, the season was an unusually dry one, and our suffering for water was often tormenting and painful. Men who march from twenty to thirty-five miles a day require more and better water than horsemen, the exercise creating a thirst which only those who have experienced it know. Besides, the infantry force was too small to permit it to delay the army, and we either had to fall back and come up after the country was taken or undergo all the long and hard marches which the dragoons and mounted volunteers made. As an alternative we chose the last and accomplished it. General Kearny, who keeps his counsels to himself, no doubt had information which caused him to push forward with all possible expedition from Bent's Fort and thus obtain peaceably the occupation of a country which otherwise might have cost some valuable lives and perhaps much blood. The delay of a few hours to [Las] Vegas might have given the Spaniards time to organize or at least to muster a force which would have given them confidence and brought on an engagement. That it is better as it is no one can deny, an effective resistance being out of the question.

I have no apologies to make for the diction, though very faulty in many parts. That it lacks coloring to give it interest and in some instances to make it a faithful picture, I know; but as it is written, so let it be. The time allowed me and the difficulty of improving what is once written by altering, has determined me to give the plain, unvarnished narrative of what transpired as noted at the time – perhaps after all the best plan. Sometime it may be of interest to my family, the only persons for whose benefit it has been compiled. The journal is made up of such things as came to my knowledge while at Santa Fé, and such things as I noticed peculiar to the country that deserved mention. As far as it purports to be within my own knowledge, it is true; and so far as statements are made upon the information of others, I had the best of reasons to believe them true.

With these remarks I hand it over with a hope that it will not be found entirely devoid of interest, as the contents relate to the occupation of a country once a part of the dominions of Montezuma, more latterly of Mexico, and now of the United States.

GEORGE R. GIBSON

Santa Fé
October 16, 1846

ACROSS THE PLAINS TO BENT'S FORT

ACROSS THE PLAINS TO BENT'S FORT

It is unnecessary to mention the various causes which led to the declaration of war by the United States against Mexico. The tendency of things had been this way for a long time, and in the spring of 1846 hostilities broke out on the Texas frontier, which resulted in a formal declaration.[269] General Taylor [270] was at the head of the

[269] The United States made no formal declaration of war on Mexico, but the act of May 13, 1846, served the same purpose. The law was entitled: "An Act providing for the Prosecution of the existing War between the United States and the Republic of Mexico." It asserted that a state of war existed "by the act of the Republic of Mexico." On the same day President Polk issued a proclamation announcing the existence of a state of war. United States, *Statutes at Large,* IX, 9-10; Richardson, *Messages and Papers of the Presidents, 1789-1897,* IV, 470.

[270] Zachary Taylor was born at Hare Forest, Orange county, Virginia, November 24, 1784. Shortly afterward his family moved to Kentucky, where he spent much of his youth. As early as May 3, 1808, he was commissioned first lieutenant in the Seventh infantry, and thereafter was promoted rapidly in the service. Leading an expedition into the Everglades of Florida, he defeated the Seminole Indians in the famous Battle of Okechobee, December 25, 1837. For this victory he was breveted brigadier-general. In 1841 he was placed in charge of the Second military department with headquarters at Fort Smith, Arkansas, and three years later was transferred to the command of the First military department with headquarters at Fort Jesup, Louisiana. Acting under various instructions from the War Department, he advanced from Fort Jesup into Texas during the early summer of 1845, and assumed command of the Army of Occupation. On April 25, 1846, a small detachment of his troops was destroyed by the Mexicans a short distance east of the Río Grande – an occurrence which prompted Polk to assert that Mexico had "shed American blood upon the American soil." Taylor won victories over the military forces of General Arista at Palo Alto and Resaca de la Palma, Texas, on May 8 and 9, 1846. He occupied Matamoras, May 18, 1846, and defeated the Mexicans at Monterrey, September 21-23, 1846, and at Buena Vista, February 22-23, 1847. He was commissioned major-general on June 29, 1846, and resigned from the army on January 31, 1849. Meanwhile, in

main army on the lower Río Grande, and had met the enemy in two or three successful battles before anything was done towards the invasion of the upper provinces of this unfortunate and distracted country. But our government took active measures for this purpose as soon as possible and ordered two expeditions to be fitted out, each a separate and distinct *corps d'armée*: the one from San Antonio de Béxar against Chihuahua, [and] the other from Fort Leavenworth against Santa Fé. General Wool [271] was placed in command of the former, and

1848, he was elected president of the United States on the Whig platform. He died in office, July 9, 1850. His body was first interred in the cemetery at Capitol Hill in Washington, but was later removed to Louisville, Kentucky. *House Ex. Docs.*, 30 cong., 1 sess., no. 60, pp. 79-141, 295-298, 345-346; *Letters of Zachary Taylor from the Battle-fields of the Mexican War* (William H. Samson, ed., Rochester, 1908); Heitman, *Historical Register*, I, 949, II, 396-397; Grant Foreman, *Pioneer Days in the Early Southwest* (Cleveland, 1926), 281-282, 304; Smith, *The War with Mexico*, I, 140-261, 384-400.

[271] John Ellis Wool was born in Newburgh, New York, February 20, 1784. On April 14, 1812, while engaged in the study of law at Troy, New York, he was commissioned captain in the Thirteenth infantry, and on the following October 13 fought at the Battle of Queenston Heights, Canada, where he was wounded. After a number of promotions he was made inspector-general, April 29, 1816. During a portion of the thirties he was in command of troops in the Cherokee country in Alabama, Georgia, North Carolina, and Tennessee. On June 25, 1841, he was commissioned brigadier-general, which was his rank at the outbreak of the Mexican war. On June 11, 1846, the adjutant-general directed him to proceed immediately to San Antonio, Texas, where he was to organize an expedition to capture the city of Chihuahua. After receiving some general instructions from Taylor, Wool left San Antonio during the latter part of September, 1846, and marching by way of Presidio del Norte, arrived at Monclova on October 29. On November 24 he left Monclova for Parras, which he reached on December 5. Nearly two weeks later he received orders to abandon the Chihuahua expedition and unite his forces with the Army of Occupation. He participated in the Battle of Buena Vista, February 22-23, 1847, and was breveted major-general for gallant and meritorious service in this conflict. He retired from the army, August 1, 1863. On November 10, 1869, he died at Troy, New York, where he was buried. *Letters of Zachary Taylor* (Samson, ed.), 15; *House Ex. Docs.*, 30 cong., 1 sess., no. 60, pp. 328, 410-411; Heitman, *Historical Register*, I, 1059-1060, II, 42; Smith, *The War with Mexico*, I, 266-276; Grant Foreman, *Indian Removal* (Norman, 1932), 188, 269, 271, 279.

General Stephen W. Kearny of the latter; which [*i.e.*, Kearny's] was of an unusual character, being through a country uninhabited for nearly a thousand miles by civilized men and over arid plains destitute of water or provisions or inhabitants, except the savage. The route had only in part ever been visited by troops, all that part south of the Arkansas being known only to traders and their employees, mountain men, and a few adventurers, all of whom gave glowing accounts of the climate, and such descriptions of the inhabitants [and] their manners and customs as were calculated to excite the deepest interest. Besides, public attention had been directed in a very great degree to this department a short time previous by the publication of Gregg's *Commerce of the Prairies* and Kendall's *Santa Fé Expedition,* both books generally circulated and read.

As soon, therefore, as an expedition was ordered, mounted companies were organized throughout Missouri, supposing that would be the only kind of force employed, and Platte and the adjoining counties were not less prompt to volunteer in this service than the balance. The governor, however, failed to make a requisition on them for this species of troops, and they were defeated in their expectations by the intermeddling and ignorance of a few men of influence at home and at Jefferson City.

General Kearny, destitute of infantry and well knowing its importance, expressed great desire to have some,[272]

[272] Writing to Governor Edwards, of Missouri, on June 16, 1846, Kearny declared: "We always look upon Infantry with their Bayonets, as the main Pillar & Strength of an Army." Kearny to Edwards, June 16, 1846, Letters Received, MSS., O.F.S., A.G.O. On July 2, 1846, when Kearny reached Fish's ferry on the Kansas river, he again wrote the governor of Missouri: "I have with me 2 Cos. of Infy., one from Cole, the other from Platte county. I wish I had more." Kearny to Edwards, July 2, 1846, Kearny Letter Book, MS., M.H.S.

and a company from Cole county, which was disappointed in going south to join General Taylor, came to the fort and was mustered into the service.[273] This acted as a stimulus to the citizens of Platte who had organized as mounted men and been rejected; and some of them determined to enter the service in the one capacity if they could not in the other, although they well knew the hardships, the difficulties, and [the] trials that awaited an army over the Great Plains. Captain William S. Murphy finally succeeded in converting his mounted company into infantry, who met in Weston [274] on Saturday, June 28,[275] 1846; and at noon of that day [they] left for the fort, which they reached in the evening, and were mustered in [276] (George R. Gibson, at the request of Captain McKissack, reading the rules and articles of war) in spite of the contemptible efforts made by a few knaves and demagogues to detain them at home as competent only for the defense of the frontier. The

[273] Early on the morning of June 11 the Cole county volunteer infantry left Jefferson City on the steamer "Balloon" and four days later arrived at Fort Leavenworth. On June 17 they were mustered into service as infantry company A, Missouri volunteers. *Jefferson Inquirer,* June 17, 1846; *Weekly Reveille,* June 22, 1846; Connelley, *Doniphan's Expedition,* 566.

[274] Weston was first settled in 1838, although several streets were laid out and some lots sold during the previous year. Growing at a rapid pace, it had a population of about one thousand by January, 1845. At the same time it could boast of sixteen dry-goods stores, ten groceries, eight commission houses, two drug stores, two tinsmith shops, and one brewery. It soon became one of the principal starting and outfitting points for prairie travel. *Weston Journal,* Jan. 11, 1845; W. M. Paxton, *Annals of Platte County, Missouri* (Kansas City, 1897), 23.

[275] June 27. *Weekly Reveille,* July 6, 1846.

[276] On a copy of the company's muster roll, which was dated June 27, appears the following certificate: "I certify that the above is a true copy from the Muster Roll of my Company as mustered into the service of the United States by Capt. W. M. D. McKissack, U.S. Army, June 27, 1846. [Signed] W. S. Murphy, Captain." The company was mustered into service as infantry company B, Missouri volunteers. Connelley, *Doniphan's Expedition,* 568.

infantry force consisted of: company A, William Z. Angney, captain, Alexander Irvine, first lieutenant, Lucian Eastin, second lieutenant, and 65 privates; [and] company B, William S. Murphy, captain, V. R. Van Valkenburgh, first lieutenant, George R. Gibson, second lieutenant, and 74 privates – all hardy, honest, intelligent, and public-spirited young men of Platte, and either farmers or the sons of farmers or mechanics.

When mustered in, it was confidently expected that the two companies would elect a major to command the battalion; and General Kearny had even gone so far as to order one [*i.e.*, an election] to be held the next day by Colonel Doniphan. But a few men who aspired to the command and who regarded more their own interest than that of the company, when they found they could not succeed, so poisoned the mind of the general that he revoked the order, to the great mortification of our company, who expected to have a field officer of their own choosing and also, it was said, of company A. Had we not been occupied, this might possibly have been prevented. But we were all too busy procuring arms, ammunition, and supplies, and mustering in men to listen to what was said or done, and the consequence was the command devolved upon the senior captain. Nor was it until after we left the fort and were *en route* that the particulars and cause of its failure [*i.e.*, the failure to hold an election] came to our knowledge, when the previous impression that the election was merely postponed was confirmed.

Major Walker,[277] the paymaster, advanced to all the

[277] Benjamin Walker, a native of Vermont, was graduated from the United States Military academy on July 1, 1819, when he was promoted in the army to third lieutenant in the ordnance corps. On October 3, 1821, he was transferred to the Third infantry, and during the next fifteen years served at a number of frontier posts, including Jefferson Barracks, Fort Leavenworth,

men who would receive it, ours amongst others, forty-two dollars in lieu of clothing for twelve months, the better to enable them to procure a suitable outfit and settle their business. However, after the payment we mustered in some men who in consequence failed at that time to receive this allowance of three dollars and fifty cents a month, it being supposed the bill before congress increasing it to this amount would pass. While making the payment, lots were drawn by the officers of the two companies for seniority, when Captain Angney obtained the age of Captain Murphy [278] and thereby became the commander of the battalion, the election of a major having failed.[279]

Sunday morning we received orders to be ready to march Monday positively. And instead of remaining some days at the fort [280] as we expected, we found our-

---

and Fort Jesup. On December 17, 1839, he was made paymaster with the rank of major, and acted in this capacity until his death. At the outbreak of the Mexican war he was stationed at Jefferson Barracks; but in June, 1846, he left St. Louis for Fort Leavenworth and became the chief paymaster of the Army of the West. After the war he returned to Jefferson Barracks and made St. Louis his permanent residence. He died at his home in St. Louis, May 28, 1858, and was buried in the cemetery at Jefferson Barracks. *Weekly Reveille,* June 22, 1846; *Daily Missouri Republican,* May 29, 30, 31, 1858; George W. Cullum, *Biographical Register of the Officers and Graduates of the U.S. Military Academy, at West Point, N.Y.* (New York, 1868), I, 189-190; Heitman, *Historical Register,* I, 995.

278 William S. Murphy, born on July 14, 1814, was a merchant in Weston at least as early as 1840. "He was handsome, intelligent, and full of energy and courage," recorded a personal acquaintance. He died in Weston, December 18, 1856. Paxton, *Annals of Platte County, Missouri,* 34, 223.

279 On June 29, 1846, Colonel Kearny issued the following order: "Capt. Angney being the Senior Officer of the Infantry Battalion (2 Companies) Missouri Volunteers, will assume the command thereof, and prepare it to march from this Post today." Kearny, Order No. 5, June 29, 1846, Letters Received, MSS., O.F.S., A.G.O.

280 Fort Leavenworth was established in 1827. A traveler gave the following description of the post as it appeared early in July, 1846: "The nearest buildings and block-houses of the Fort are situated about four hundred yards from the steamboat landing, on the summit of the first swell of land which

selves hurried away with hardly time enough to make the necessary requisitions for provisions, stores, arms, equipments, etc., and as a consequence had no time to prepare for our personal comforts or even to get such things as we had collected at Weston for the campaign. Many were without blankets, shoes, or shirts except what was on their backs, and had to depend entirely upon the sutlers for procuring these indispensable articles. And many had only such as were not well suited to the march, being old; and particularly the shoes and boots too tight or worn, so as to be of but little service. When it is remembered that we were mustered in with

gradually rises from the river. The ground then declines towards the west for the distance of 100 yards, and again rises very slightly for about the same length of space, on the summit of which swell are located the western buildings of the Fort. The area of ground occupied by the buildings, lawns and streets, is but little short of 20 acres, in the form of a square. At each corner is planted a block-house, to be used by artillery-men or rifle-men. On the east side the buildings are of brick, two stories high, with double porticoes running their whole length, used by the troops as quarters. On the north side, the buildings are principally of brick, two stories, and occupied by the principal officers of the Fort as offices and family residences. These buildings are also fronted by porticoes and piazzas. The west side is not so closely built up. The arsenal and two or three buildings near the south-west corner of the Fort, are of brick, and the balance are large frame houses, occupied as quarters for officers and privates. The south side is altogether occupied by a long line of stables, and yard for artillery. South of the arsenal about one hundred yards, on a beautiful piece of ground, stands the hospital, a building of considerable size and very comfortably constructed. The building is completely surrounded by porticoes, which afford pleasant retreats for the convalescent. Besides the public buildings of the Fort, several small log and frame houses are to be seen on the northern and western suburbs occupied by the families of regular soldiers, and of persons laboring for the Government. The powder magazine is located near the centre of a beautiful lawn finely shaded by forest trees, and in the heart of the Fort. It is completely fire and bomb proof. West of the Fort, is the parade ground. It is a beautiful space, and admirably calculated for the purpose. South-west, at the distance of half a mile, is the Government farm, about eleven hundred acres of which is now under cultivation. Provender for the horses in the Fort, is the principal production." *St. Louis Daily New Era,* July 10, 1846. See also *Southwest Historical Series,* II, 101.

44 privates (men) and left with 66, and only had 36 hours to get ready for a march of 1,000 miles and to be absent 12 months or probably longer, it will be seen at once that neither the officers nor men had time to devote to anything else. Nor could we possibly have done it had not all the men used the greatest activity and most untiring efforts, as wild mules had to be caught and broken, and oxen to be yoked up that never had worked together. Many of our friends were at the fort Sunday, and particularly Monday, anxious for our welfare and contributing their aid where they could to relieve our labors; and the few things we obtained from Weston were through their instrumentality.

In obedience to orders the two companies left between three and four o'clock and barely made out to go about three miles to camp, which the captain, myself, one wagon, and several men did not reach until some time after night, being detained to complete our requisitions and to load a team we had kept back. Only those who have experienced it know the feelings of men leaving their homes and firesides for perhaps the last time and maybe to find a grave upon some bloody field of battle: the tears trickling down some father's cheek as he takes his son by the hand and tells him to do his duty and above all things to have a Spartan's courage and never to come back dishonored or disgraced, as I saw one; the cordial parting of bosom friends and their requests to be remembered, as I saw many others; the anxious looks of those to be left; and the resolute mind and lofty determination of those who had engaged in the service of their country.

Our company was provided with one mule team, two ox teams, one loose horse belonging to the captain, two extra mules, and provisions for fifteen days commencing

July 1, besides such things as in the hurry and confusion could be gathered besides the government stores, etc. The first night was a sample of what we might expect, as we had raw pork and sea bread for supper and the green grass for a bed, our teams not getting up in time [for us] to raise tents, gather wood, or cook supper. Yet we bore it all without a murmur, though it looked very uncomfortable to lie down on the grass in the open air without camp fires and many without blankets. Sentinels had been posted, and all was soon quiet in camp, and we were now fairly on the road. The only troops left by us at the fort were the artillery and General Kearny,[281] his staff, etc., all of whom were to leave the next morning.

The army now consists of the portion of the First regiment of dragoons who accompanied us, 420 strong, under the command of Major Sumner;[282] the regiment of mounted volunteers commanded by Colonel Doniphan numbering 806 strong; the battalion of artillery, Major Clark, 220 strong; the battalion of infantry; besides, a large train of quartermaster and commissary teams, baggage wagons, servants, etc.; and Captain Hudson's company attached to Major Sumner's command.[283] Sumner's command [consists of] 420 men [and] 16 officers; Doniphan's command, 806 men [and] 30 officers; Clark's command, 220 men [and] 12 officers; Angney's command, 148 men [and] 7 officers; general staff, 10; making a grand total of 1,659, exclusive of

281 For a biographical sketch of Colonel Stephen W. Kearny, see *Southwest Historical Series,* I, 185.

282 Captain Edwin V. Sumner, with two companies of the First dragoons, left Fort Leavenworth on July 6, 1846, but was not placed in command of all the dragoon companies until his arrival at Bent's Fort on July 31. Kearny, Order No. 11, July 31, 1846, Letters Received, MSS., O.F.S., A.G.O.

283 Captain Hudson's company of Laclede Rangers was not attached to Sumner's command until July 31, 1846. *Ibid.*

traders, teamsters, etc., August 17. The total of present and absent, June 29, 1,612; aggregate, June 29, 1,701.

JUNE 30. We left camp early in the morning, the weather being pleasant, and had a good road all day through the magnificent scenery of the Stranger,[284] a tributary of the Kansas. General Kearny and the troops we left at the fort yesterday, came up and passed, but we all camped together on a small stream [285] where the grass was abundant and timber and water plentiful. We found that our guides had taken the wrong road and that we were several miles out of our way, but the road was equally [as] good as the other. Corporal McFarland had a severe attack of cramp colic today, and a detail was made to attend to him and have him brought to camp in the wagon. Of course there was a great deal of speculation today as to the fate of the army. Some thought we would be recalled and the war ended in a few weeks, others that we should have a fight first and not get back before spring, and some that our force was sufficient to overawe the authorities and take Santa Fé as we did. "The States," Mexico, our friends, the route we were to take from the Arkansas, and all such subjects were the constant themes of conversation. We marched today about twenty-two miles.

JULY 1. A mule escaped from us this morning as we were about to leave camp, and two men were sent to try and get him; but they returned without any tidings of his whereabouts, and we came on without it. It [*i.e.*, the weather] was very warm, and we stopped about noon at a small stream skirted with timber and a thick undergrowth to wait for the cool of the evening and to

[284] Stranger creek, now called Stranger river, flows into the Kansas river at the present town of Linwood, Leavenworth county, Kansas.

[285] A tributary of Stranger creek. Turner, Diary, June 30, 1846, MS., M.H.S. Their encampment was not far from the present Tonganoxie, Kansas.

rest our teams. There Mr. Nye's son and others from Weston overtook us with some things which were forwarded that were very acceptable. All day our road was through the country watered by the Stranger and its tributaries, with hills and valleys, woodland and prairie, all in view from the high grounds, and presenting scenery as varied and magnificent as can be found. In this delightful country nature has done more than art has or can accomplish to furnish large rural parks more elegant than royalty ever luxuriated in.[286] And to add to its beauty we oftentimes through the day had General Kearny and staff and the artillery in view, winding their way over the hills and valleys; and the sound of a bugle to remind us that we were no longer citizens, but soldiers under military law beyond the precincts of civilization and on their way to fight the battles of their country. The day being warm, we suffered much from the heat by attempting to keep up with the general, who is reputed one of the most expeditious travelers who ever crossed the plains. But good and healthy water was plentiful, and had we then known what we were to suffer afterwards on the march for the want of it, we should have thought ourselves well off in this respect at least. We passed Major Rich's [287] team up to the axles in mud; he succeeded, however, in getting it out and camped with us.

As we approached the Kansas, the hills became higher, and the whole country more broken and difficult

286 On June 30, Lieutenant Lucian J. Eastin, of the Cole county infantry, wrote: "We marched about 18 miles, and passed through the most beautiful country I ever beheld. . . Sometimes we would ascend upon an elevated plain, and far in the distance could be seen rising mound after mound and elevated ridges, dotted here and there with timber, – and the tall grass would be ruffled by the gentle breeze until you imagine it was the rising waves of the ocean." *Jefferson Inquirer,* July 15, 1846.

287 William H. Rich was a sutler. *Daily Missouri Republican,* June 22, 1846.

of ascent or descent for teams; and in consequence the road was more winding and serpentine. Yet we all got along well except at a small stream seven or eight miles from the river, where the artillery met with some delay and hard pulling. But by doubling teams, we crossed over tolerably well. We had orders from Captain Angney to cross the Kansas, and although it was late in the evening and a good camping place at this creek, we marched on. We soon came to the Kansas bluffs and passed the artillery, who were camping about three miles from the river; and at dark we struck the bottom, which is a sand bank half a mile wide, and which we found exceedingly bad to pass through. The oxen fell down in the road, the heat, long march, and hard pulling in the hills and sand completely using them up. But by putting all the cattle that could be used to one wagon, with the assistance of the men at the wheels they [*i.e.,* the wagons] were finally brought to camp one at a time about eleven o'clock. Company A, with a good deal of trouble and considerable delay by oxen falling out of the boat while at the landing, crossed over and camped on the other side. They refused to cross our company after waiting awhile, and we camped on the bank of the river in the deep sand.

The men were very much fatigued by the long march, and many had sore feet; and all of our teams were completely used up without anything to eat, as there was no grass in the bottom. Captain Murphy ordered double rations to be issued, and at two o'clock all were prepared to do justice to salt pork and bread and coffee and then lie down and sleep soundly on the sand without blanket or covering of any kind. They had had nothing to eat since morning, and some of the guard, as we learned afterwards, not since the preceding evening, on account of being on post when we ate breakfast. They were men belonging to company A, and as the rear guard was with us, remained all night and appeared to have no desire to join their own company. The men were not sparing of imprecations upon Captain Angney, who required us to make such a forced march to the great injury of men and teams, merely to have the reputation of keeping up with mounted troops. Several of our men were on the sick report but none dangerously ill, as they had all been sent to the wagons when taken [sick]. Both companies were regretting that we were prevented from electing a major and were thus deprived of the services of a man who could use more judgment. We marched about twenty miles and found ourselves at Fish's ferry, belonging to some Delaware Indians.[288]

JULY 2. Early in the morning we crossed the Kansas without any difficulty, and General Kearny, at the request of Captain Murphy, permitted us to camp (Captain Angney wishing us to go on); which we did (with the general) about a mile from the river, to refresh our teams (which had nothing to eat since yesterday morning), to wash, to repack our wagons, and to make some better preparations for the long march before us. The artillery came up as we landed the last boatload and immediately crossed and camped with us. Company A, instead of stopping, went on, by which they gained one day of us. Our camp was on the slope of a hill of very gradual ascent, with a ravine skirted with hazel and a few trees close to our tents, the remainder of the country being prairie, except along the river.

Through the day it [*i.e.,* the camp] presented a lively

---

288 Fish's ferry, owned by Pascal Fish, a Shawnee Indian, was located at or near the present town of Eudora, Douglas county, Kansas. It was one of the early ferries on the Kansas river. George A. Root, "Ferries in Kansas," *Kansas Historical Quarterly,* II, 276-277.

and animated appearance, all being busy at something. Fresh oxen, or rather unbroken fat cattle, were given us to take the place of those that were lame or given out by the hard service marching from the fort; and in the evening the men were quite lively and active putting the yoke on their necks for the first time, which was done to save time and start early in the morning. Some [oxen] cut freaks that produced a good deal of merriment; and one that was very restive jumped down the bank of the ravine with his mate, which caused a piece of his tail to be pulled off, [the soldiers] having tied them [*i.e.,* the tails] to keep them [*i.e.,* the oxen] in a proper position in their new sphere. We got an extra yoke of oxen, and some of the men were up all night making a yoke for them, which was completed; and another [was] also [completed] to take along to be used in case any accident happened to one, having been detained at camp yesterday morning to make a rude one to use in place of one that split. General Kearny had a beef slaughtered, and we had plenty of fresh meat. Here I wrote letters to Bird and Mrs. Gibson, and several others did the same [*i.e.,* wrote letters]. In the evening the camp presented a pretty appearance, the weather was fine, the men all merry and exchanging visits to know how the military life pleased them; and the sound of the bugles at retreat gave a military air to the surrounding country. The teams of the artillery containing their provisions and camp utensils failed to get up, and at the request of Captain Turner [289] we loaned them our camp kettles and

[289] Henry Smith Turner was born in King George county, Virginia, April 1, 1811. Graduating from the United States Military academy on July 1, 1834, he was promoted in the army to brevet second lieutenant in the First dragoons. During the next twelve years he served at various frontier posts, such as Fort Des Moines, Jefferson Barracks, Fort Leavenworth, and Fort Gibson. From August 9, 1839, to April 5, 1841, he was on professional duty

pans and a tin cup of coffee from each mess and some other things; for which Captain Fischer,[290] who commanded the company for whom they were obtained, seemed very thankful. Mr. Robidou,[291] who goes out as

at the cavalry school of Saumur, France, and later assisted in the preparation of cavalry tactics for the United States service. On March 3, 1837, he was commissioned first lieutenant in the First dragoons, and April 21, 1846, captain, although the latter commission did not reach him until the following August 15. From 1844 to 1846 he was acting assistant adjutant-general of the Third military department with headquarters at St. Louis. On June 19, 1846, Colonel Kearny appointed him acting assistant adjutant-general of the Army of the West. Continuing with Kearny to California, he participated in the Battle of San Pascual, December 6, 1846, in which he was wounded by a lance. He was breveted major for "gallant and meritorious conduct" in this action, as well as for similar service at San Gabriel and the Plains of Mesa, California, January 8-9, 1847. He resigned from the army on July 21, 1848. Except for a brief residence in California during the middle fifties, he spent the rest of his life in or near St. Louis, where he died, December 16, 1881. Turner, Diary, Aug. 15, 1846, MS., M.H.S.; Kearny, Order No. 1, June 19, 1846, Letters Received, MSS., O.F.S., A.G.O.; *Missouri Republican,* Dec. 17, 1881; Cullum, *Biographical Register,* I, 454; J. Thomas Scharf, *History of Saint Louis City and County* (Philadelphia, 1883), II, 1407.

290 Woldemar Fischer, a native of Prussia, was captain of company B, light artillery, Missouri volunteers, which was composed entirely of Germans from St. Louis and vicinity. Richard H. Weightman was captain of company A, also from St. Louis. Both companies constituted a battalion, which, on June 27, 1846, was temporarily placed in command of Fischer, the senior officer. He continued to command the battalion until July 10, when Major Meriwether Lewis Clark, who had just arrived from Fort Leavenworth, was ordered to take charge. Kearny, Order No. 4, June 27, 1846, Order No. 8, July 10, 1846, Letters Received, MSS., O.F.S., A.G.O.; *Täglicher Anzeiger des Westens,* June 9, 1846; Connelley, *Doniphan's Expedition,* 573-580.

291 Antoine Robidou was born in St. Louis, September 22, 1794. Migrating to New Mexico in the early twenties, he established his residence there, and for many years hunted and trapped in various parts of the Rocky mountains. His brother, Joseph, founded St. Joseph, Missouri, to which town Antoine removed before the Mexican war. On June 4, 1846, he was engaged as interpreter for the Army of the West, and subsequently translated into Spanish all of Kearny's speeches to the Mexicans. He was severely wounded in the Battle of San Pascual, California, December 6, 1846. He was tall, slender, and athletic, had polished manners, and possessed a striking personality. He died at St. Joseph, August 29, 1860. Kearny to Robidou, June 4, 1846, Kearny Letter Book, MS., M.H.S.; *Liberty Tribune,* Sept. 7, 1860; Scharf, *History of Saint Louis City and County,* I, 558-559; Magoffin, *Down the Santa Fé Trail and into Mexico* (Drumm, ed.), 136-137.

interpreter, guide, etc., for the general, paid us a visit, and we spent the evening very pleasantly.

JULY 3. After a good night's rest we broke up camp early in the morning and passed over a country of rich and varied scenery, our road [for] the first ten miles being up the valley of the Kansas [and] along the Oregon road, which we struck about a mile from camp. We passed an Indian hut or two with some good corn enclosed with a fence, and had no difficulty, as the country was prairie, except crossing a few small streams which were very muddy, particularly one or two. We left General Kearny and [the] artillery, who were resting and waiting for their teams, and marched alone. We met some mounted volunteers returning on the hunt of stray horses, who informed us that company A had kept the Oregon trail until they crossed the Wakarusa and were a long day's march out of their way. Instead of being before us, they are now behind us.[292] We are now fairly on the prairies, which extend to Mexico and the mountains, and timber is scarce; in fact [there is] none, except where water is usually found. The big hill is between the Oregon and Santa Fé roads, and is a high, steep, and rocky ridge requiring hard pulling to get up. It is about three miles from the Santa Fé road, and the prospect from its summit is magnificent and extensive, embracing the valley of the Kansas and its tributaries. When we reached the summit, we found ourselves apparently on a table-land extending some distance, it being the divide

[292] On July 3, 1846, Lieutenant Eastin, of company A, wrote: "After we had gone about ten miles, an Indian overtook us, and said we were on the Oregon road. We despatched a messenger back to ascertain the fact. In place of going on to Santa Fé, we found we were on our road to Oregon. As we had enlisted for the wars, we retraced our steps, and encamped at the same place we started from in the morning." *Jefferson Inquirer,* July 15, 1846.

which separates the Kansas valley from that of [the] Blue, which empties into the Missouri.

We followed the Santa Fé road a mile and a half and after a march of twenty miles camped at Shuck Grove, or, as we called it, the Willow springs.[293] A private from the Cole mounted company overtook us tonight and stayed with us. We learned from him that company A had broken two axles at the Wakarusa, where they were detained, and that they had sent back to the general's camp. They are in a bad fix and considerably in our rear. We have nothing but small willows to cook with, which we made answer our purpose very well by making a fireplace of rock, which retained the heat. The water is good, our company all in fine spirits, and for the first time our supper ready by dark. Sore feet is now a common complaint in camp. Every night we have a property guard to guard stock and the camp, but no countersign, as we only have to guard against rogues.

JULY 4. All were anxious to pay some respect to the day, and it seemed peculiarly proper at this time for us to do so, but as we had no spirits and could not observe it in the usual manner, we pulled up stakes and took the road. In ten miles we came to Rock Branch,[294] where we found plenty of indifferent water in pools, which we soon left with the expectation (from what we were told) of finding better in two or three miles. The day was excessively hot, and all the company suffered extremely from thirst, to relieve which they pushed forward at a rapid gait, expecting every moment to find water. In

[293] The Army of the West reached the Santa Fé trail one and a half or two miles east of Willow springs, which is about ten miles southwest of the present city of Lawrence, Kansas. *Ibid.*, Aug. 11, 1846.

[294] Rock creek, a tributary of the Wakarusa river. They reached Rock creek not far from the present Globe, Douglas county, Kansas.

this, however, they were disappointed and had to march twenty miles under a burning sun before they came to any. Many were sick, lame, and exhausted – completely overcome by the heat, thirst, and long march we were by necessity forced to make. Amongst others I suffered very much myself and could not attend to the company, the other officers being in advance; and as a consequence the men dispersed over the prairie in search of something to relieve them, being totally unable to control themselves, and thereby added greatly to their fatigues and suffering.

Some at last reached 110,[295] where they found Captain Murphy and water, and he returned on horseback with several canteens full, which enabled us to reach camp. As the evening advanced, straggling parties came in, and about dark we were all enabled to reach camp in a crippled condition, some having to be sent for and brought in on the extra mules. We marched today about thirty miles, the whole distance through prairie, and camped at 110, a small stream where we found both wood and water in abundance. Captain Hudson and company,[296] who were also suffering from thirst, overtook us in the evening and went off the road two or three miles, where he camped, six miles in our rear. He had lost his way and crossed the Kansas too low down and came by Westport, which threw him sixty miles out of his way and behind us. Mr. Robidou estimated our day's march at thirty-two miles, which most probably is not over the mark. Coffee and water made us feel better, and the men were soon wrapped in their blankets and the camp quiet, all needing repose after one of the longest

[295] 110 Mile creek. They crossed this creek near the present town of Scranton, Osage county, Kansas.

[296] The Laclede Rangers, of St. Louis.

and hardest day's marches we were destined to make.

JULY 5. As the men and teams were not sufficiently recovered from the fatigues of yesterday, the captain determined to make a short march, and we only went eight miles to Bridge creek and camped. The country in the vicinity of 110 is good, and timber can be seen on several small streams tributary to it. We have no further news yet of company A and those in our rear. Lieutenant Elliott,[297] of Captain Hudson's company, and five men, their front guard, passed us after we had camped, examining the road for water. He furnished us with the names of several creeks and some distances, which we found useful. We camped early in the day and spent the evening fishing in a pool of the creek, having brought along some hooks, and caught plenty of bass, perch, catfish, and chubs of respectable size. Our captain, who prides himself on his angling, beat me both in number and weight, but when it came to the table operations I was his full match. The weather was dry and pleasant,

[297] Richard Smith Elliott, son of William P. and Emily Elliott, was born in Lewistown, Pennsylvania, July 10, 1817. At the age of sixteen he started to work in the printing office of the local newspaper owned and edited by his father. In 1843, after a varied career as printer, editor, publisher, and lawyer, he was appointed Indian sub-agent at Council Bluffs. While serving there he became an occasional correspondent of the St. Louis *Reveille,* contributing both prose and poetry under the pseudonym "John Brown." Early in 1846 he moved to St. Louis, where he practiced law. At the outbreak of the Mexican war he enlisted in the Laclede Rangers, and on May 28 was elected first lieutenant of the company. Elliott became a regular correspondent of the *Reveille* during his service with the Army of the West. Returning to St. Louis in 1847, he soon entered the real estate business with Hiram W. Leffingwell, the firm being known as Leffingwell & Elliott. In 1853 he named and helped to found the town of Kirkwood, Missouri, a suburb of St. Louis. Thirty years later he published his reminiscences: *Notes Taken in Sixty Years.* He died at his home in Kirkwood, December 12, 1890, and was buried in Oak Hill Cemetery. Oak Hill Cemetery (Kirkwood), Records, MSS.; Reginald Heber Elliott, Scrapbook; *Weekly Reveille,* Aug. 19, 1844, July 28, Aug. 4, 1845, June 1, 1846; *St. Louis Republic,* Dec. 13, 15, 1890; Elliott, *Notes Taken in Sixty Years.*

but the mosquitoes troubled us very much, literally swarming in our tents.

JULY 6. We left Bridge creek early in the morning and passed Lieutenant Elliott and crossed several little streams, the names of which were unknown to us. The country would admit of considerable settlements, as timber is on all of them, though the strips are narrow. Wild turkeys and deer signs were seen, but we killed nothing and had to be satisfied with salt meat. Today we marched easily twenty-five miles and camped within sixteen of Council Grove, according to the table of distances furnished by Lieutenant Elliott. We have no news from the general and troops in our rear. Mr. Swan was taken quite sick, but generally they [*i.e.,* we] got along very well.

JULY 7. We left camp early and marched through a country similar to that we passed over yesterday, crossing several small streams with timber, their branches visible all around. The scenery is pretty, but prairie greatly [*i.e.,* generally] prevails. We found good spring water at Rock creek, and also at another east of it, the name of which is unknown to us. The day was fine with some appearance of rain, but the sun set in a gorgeous panoply, lighting up the west with its richest tints and most golden colors. Swan was better, and all the men [were] in fine spirits. After we had camped, Sergeant McClure and a detachment passed us, going to Council Grove to get timbers suitable for axletrees, tongues, yokes, etc., it being the last timber on the route which will answer that purpose. They will get it out, ready to put in the wagons and take along when the troops come up. The general sent us word by him that he would camp tomorrow night at Diamond spring, and instead of laying by as we intended, we shall have to travel tomorrow.

General Kearny and the other troops, as we learned from the same source, camped six miles in our rear. We marched today eighteen miles and camped at the famous spring known as the "Big John." [298]

JULY 8. We left Big John early to keep before the others through the day and in two miles came to Council Grove,[299] a pretty place, the prairie grass looking like a Kentucky meadow. But there was a heavy fog which limited our view and prevented us from making such observations as we intended of this well-known spot.

---

298 George C. Sibley, one of the three government commissioners who surveyed the Santa Fé trail between 1825 and 1827, gave the following account of the discovery and naming of this spring: "'Big John' Walker first discovered the remarkably fine spring that bears his name. He was one of a small party that accompanied me in the summer of 1827 for the purpose of correcting the previous survey of the road, and to mark it where necessary by heavy mounds of sod, etc. Walker found the spring on the 13th of June, 1827, brought me some of the water (our camp was near by) and asked me what name it should have. I directed to cut in large letters 'Big John's Spring' on a Big Oak that grows near it. He laughed, and with his knife and hatchet soon performed the work in excellent style. This Spring is on Gravel Creek, short of two miles easterly from Council Grove. It was discovered on my return from my correcting tour, after we had been *sixteen miles* beyond the Grove." *Western Journal,* v, 180.

299 "It was here," wrote Sibley, "that the Mexican Road Commissioners, with their train of forty men, Surveyors, Secretary, Interpreters, Hunters, Guard, etc., met the chiefs and head men of the Osages in Council (agreeably to previous arrangement) and concluded and signed a treaty securing the right of way and permanent use of the road through the territory claimed by those tribes. After the completion of this formality, and the Indians had departed perfectly content (August 12, 1825) it was suggested by G.C.S. to have the name of the place, as inserted in the treaty, carved in large and legible characters on the trunk of a venerable White Oak tree that stood and flourished near the entrance of our council tent, and also to add the date and distance from Fort Osage. Colonels Reeves and Mather readily assented, and Capt. S. Cooper was directed to have it promptly executed. Capt. C. employed a young man of the party known to be remarkably expert in *lettering* with his pen knife and tomahawk, by name John Walker, commonly called in camp *'Big John,'* in reference to his gigantic size, who executed the order very neatly and substantially – thus 'Council Grove' came to be the name and designation of the place." *Ibid.,* 178-179. See also *Southwest Historical Series,* I, 46.

Our road was through prairie, except Council Grove bottom about one mile wide, but we could see timber in all directions along the tributaries of Council Grove creek. In the evening, after a march of seventeen miles, we reached Diamond spring,[300] a large and fine one, and generally considered the best on our route. The general, [the] artillery, Captain Hudson's company, and company A all came up as we reached camp, company A considerably worsted and in low spirits. We were all assigned quarters in and around the spring by Adjutant Johnston,[301] and presented a more military and warlike appearance than we have before. The general seemed to be satisfied with our progress. Besides the soldiers, there is a heavy train of commissary and quartermaster teams and baggage wagons, which swells the number of men, and with the loose mules adds to the magnitude and display of the rear.

Council Grove is the last place from which a single

300 The discovery and naming of Diamond spring were also described by Sibley: "The Diamond of the Plain. This treasure was, in fact, discovered first by 'Old Ben Jones,' a hunter of our first party, on the 11th August, 1825. It is thus noted in my 'Pencil Sketches,' at the time: 'This Spring gushes out from the head of a hollow in the prairie, and runs off boldly among clean stones into Otter Creek, a short distance – it is very large, perfectly accessible, and furnishes the greatest abundance of most excellent, clear, *cold* water – enough to supply an army. There is a fountain, inferior to this, in the Arabian Desert, known as "The Diamond of the Desert." This magnificent Spring may, with at least equal propriety, be called *The Diamond of the Plain.* We found it a most excellent camping place. A fine Elm tree grows near to and overhangs the Spring.' On the 10th and 11th June, 1827, I encamped here with my party (as noted above) – during our stay I made requisition of 'Big John' and his carving implements once more, to inscribe on the stooping Elm 'Diamond of the Plain'– which was promptly done – the tree has since been cut away I believe. The fountain is now generally known as 'The Diamond Spring.'" *Western Journal,* V, 180-181. See also *Southwest Historical Series,* I, 47.

301 Kearny appointed Abraham Robinson Johnston regimental adjutant on June 16, 1846. Kearny to Jones, June 16, 1846, Letters Received, MSS., O.F.S., A.G.O.

individual can return in safety to "the States," and hereafter it will be necessary to be cautious how we leave the company, as we might fall in with some of the wild and savage Indians of the plains. It is an important point, as after this no timber can be found on the route to repair anything broken. The bottom is about a mile wide, covered with a heavy growth consisting of almost every variety found in "the States." The soil is alluvial and very rich, and a considerable population could be supported on it and its tributaries, four or five of which can be seen from the high ground on the south side, with timber on all. A settlement at this point, where supplies could be obtained or fresh animals [purchased] for any given out, would very much diminish the drawbacks of a march across the plains. Mr. Gregg sets it down at a hundred and sixty miles from Independence,[302] but I estimate it at only a hundred and fifty. I think, though, I am rather under than over the mark. A blacksmith and wagon shop with a few soldiers, established here by the government, would be of great benefit, as the little streams crossed to reach it do more damage to teams than twice the distance up the Arkansas.

Up to this place we found the sameness of the prairie very fatiguing, as there is nothing to break the monotony. Game of all kinds is scarce, hardly even a bird to be seen. Rattlesnakes and prairie snakes, both a large and small species, are common, but appear not to be dangerous or disposed to bite except when provoked. The grass so far has been abundant and good, and the climate very similar to western Missouri. Council Grove creek is now a small stream, but gives unequivocal evidence of sending down great floods at some seasons of the year.

302 This is an error. Gregg estimated the distance from Independence to Council Grove at one hundred and forty-five miles. Gregg, *op. cit.*, XX, 93.

JULY 9. After we got up this morning, we found a small rattlesnake in our blankets. It had slept between the first lieutenant and myself and near the captain's face. It was soon dispatched for its intrusion, and we thought but little more about it. We received orders to start early and march to Cottonwood Fork, estimated at twenty-seven miles, and all was bustle in camp to get off. Here we procured several things from Major Rich which we wanted badly, and particularly a *wee drap*. Last night all we wanted to complete our happiness was one of Joe's best juleps, a long straw, and well feet. In the morning the men were tolerably well. But it commenced raining soon after we left camp and continued so throughout the day, and we were wet to the skin and did not reach camp until after night, in a severe thunderstorm. The company was very much crippled up by the long march in such bad weather, and all had to lie down and sleep in their wet clothes without a mouthful to eat, as it was not possible to start a fire with green cottonwood in such weather or to cook with the rain pouring down in torrents. My feet were so swollen I had to cut my boots off, and the night was very stormy, but we were all soon sound asleep. There would have been no temperance men in camp tonight if they had had spirits, but we had to content ourselves with the hope of getting some in the morning. Today we met Somers returning to Westport with one of Mr. Perry's teams, which had broken down. A Negro driver was the only person with him.

JULY 10. The morning was damp and disagreeable, the men very much out of humor and in a good tune to fight the Mexicans if they could meet them. They obtained some whiskey from Major Rich at four dollars and twenty-five cents per gallon, which gave more life.

And as wood was scarce, wet, and hard to kindle, we dug pits and cooked with twigs, after helping Mr. Billingsby's team up the hill. Soon after leaving camp a severe thunderstorm blew up, and we were not only drenched and pelted but had to wade many places knee-deep and to plunge along through the mud the best we could. After marching eight miles, we camped in the open prairie with Mr. Billingsby and had plenty of brandy at a dollar and fifty cents per quart, which helped us all very much, as we were chilled and wet. We also obtained many other articles, particularly clothes, tobacco, and some sardines which we found very good and palatable. We had no wood except what we hauled in our teams, but made out to cook supper. Some quartermaster teams were camped near us. Today the other troops remained with the general, encamped on Cottonwood on account of the weather; but we had orders to march, which gave a good deal of dissatisfaction.

JULY 11. Another severe thunderstorm came up last night, worse than any we yet had, and completely soaked everything in camp. Some of the tents blew down, a hard blow such as is common on the prairies accompanying it, and this morning we found ourselves wet, chilled, and without even wood to cook breakfast.[303] Our tents being single and without flies and not very good, everything was wet except the articles in our trunks, the water running under our tents in a perfect stream, though situated on the top of an elevated piece of ground. Notwithstanding the prospect of rain, the camp was active

[303] Lieutenant Eastin, of company A, wrote: "About 12 o'clock at night it seemed as if the windows of Heaven were opened for the rain poured down in torrents. In a few moments I found myself surrounded with water. It was running thro' the tent like a perfect sluice. We had to get up on boxes and stand upon them: some men got in the wagons. Next morning we had to travel through mud and water." *Jefferson Inquirer,* Aug. 11, 1846.

preparing to start and reach Turkey creek, as we cannot remain where we are without wood. Our breakfast was made off the remnants of what we cooked last night with the wood we brought with us, and a little coffee in some of the messes which they made out to warm. Yet the men started off apparently in good spirits, laughing at their troubles, company A and the quartermaster teams with us. And all the low places [were] full of water, which we marched through up to our knees. We have all been wet for the last twenty-four hours and will have to remain so until we reach timber eighteen miles ahead.

After marching about ten miles, we began to pass out of the section visited by the storm and soon had dry grass and dry ground to march upon; and in eight miles more camped at one of the Turkey creeks, where we obtained indifferent water by digging, and where not a stick of timber was to be seen nearer than six or seven miles. By scouring all the country around, we made out to collect twigs and weeds enough to cook, and as it had cleared off and was a pretty evening, slaughtered a beef we picked up on the road, and had plenty of beef soup for supper. We also took advantage of the sun, having camped early to dry our clothes and blankets, which we effected in a great measure, at least sufficiently to keep them from spoiling. Buffalo gnats were exceedingly troublesome to us, literally filling the atmosphere, swarming all over us, and getting in our eyes, ears, nose, mouth, etc. We witnessed the false appearance of water on the plains, so often noticed by travelers, and which has deceived so many into a belief that they were near to and approaching a lake or pond. We appear to have marched all day over a great level plain dividing the waters of Cottonwood from those of the Little Arkansas. Some antelopes were seen for the first time, and everywhere their tracks could be seen mixed with those of deer. Several [men] are on the sick report, and many complaining of sore feet and unable to march in the ranks. The general and troops with him camped about five miles in our rear. We marched eighteen miles today.

JULY 12. This morning the weather was settled, pleasant, and the men all in fine spirits. We struck our tents at an early hour and continued our march up the Little Arkansas bottoms, which we followed all day, the river distant six or eight miles, and the country very level. All the troops we left behind passed us on our march and camped on the Little Arkansas, where wood is scarce but water plentiful. At this season it is usually a small stream, a mere branch, and we found it so now, but swollen and muddy by the late rains. Its channel, or bed, indicates, though, like all western streams, that at some season of the year it sends down a considerable flood.

We reached camp about three o'clock after a march of twenty-five miles and had to wait several hours for our teams to come up. We found the general and troops with him here, and all camped together on both sides of the stream. Today buffaloes were seen for the first time, but none killed. They were not far from the river. We found the grass here very fine, better than we have had for some time and more abundant. The day was warm and oppressive,[304] and the men generally took a bath in the river; and I took a shave and wash, which had the usual

304 "The day was excessively hot," recorded Hughes on July 12. "The thermometer, though exposed to the breeze, stood at ninety-five degrees Fahrenheit. The earth was literally parched to a crust, and the grass in many places crisped by the heat of the sun. In the distant horizon, upon the green plains, might be seen ephemeral rivers and lakes, inviting you to drink of their seemingly delicious waters. It is all, however, a tantalizing illusion; for as you approach the enchanting spot, the waters recede." Hughes, *Doniphan's Expedition*, 46.

good effect. Our company shave, wash, and put on clean clothes oftener than any other, and consequently present a much neater and more healthy appearance. The bluffs of the Arkansas, which we have seen at a distance yesterday and today, present a singular and very fine appearance, resembling a city in all respects. We supposed them to be clay or sand.

JULY 13. We broke up camp early, and after marching a few miles I got in the wagon and rode within five miles of camp, not being well. The country is very flat and water scarce, though we crossed several streams now dry and camped on Cow creek, having made twenty-five miles. It is warm, and the wagons full of lame and sick. Amongst those complaining was the first lieutenant, but he marched at the head of the company all day. The appearance of the country generally has changed, and we have evidently passed into a climate and region different from any behind us. A few elms and underbrush are scattered along the water courses, but wood is scarce and dwarfish, and fern, sage, and thistles plentiful. The grass is thin, short, and dry, affording but scanty pasturage. The only timber is boxwood, white elm, cottonwood, willows, and ash. We saw a little game today, but as usual none was killed. On the prairie about five miles from camp we left a little bull that was in our ox team; he gave out and could not be got along. And the mule team was the last to come up, being considerably worsted. This evening our camp is hungry and wolfish, but presents a handsome appearance on both sides of the river. We have in company the same as last night. Quite an incident occurred here: our coffee mill, which is the only one in [the] company, met with an accident and was considerably damaged but not rendered altogether useless.

JULY 14. We left camp early and in a few miles came to a prairie-dog village, the first of any size we had seen. But we saw no dogs, probably because they had been alarmed and driven in by the companies ahead of us. The country is generally level and similar to that we have been passing over for the last day or two. Ten miles from the Arkansas we passed a high ground which affords a good view of the bottom of the river as well as [of] the country around. The bottom extends from its base to the river, and contains ponds and muddy water, which the company very gladly drank. Here we found plenty [of] indications that we were in the buffalo range, and all were on the lookout, but none was killed or seen.

We marched eighteen miles today and camped on the Arkansas at an early hour. We found the Arkansas a broad and pretty stream with low banks, sand bars, and islands, one of which is opposite our camp. At this time the river was high, and there being no wood on our side, the men had to wade and swim the channel between us and the island to get some. Its water is muddy like the Missouri, and its bottoms very broad. Sunset was magnificent, the air balmy, and all the company enjoyed it, bathing, smoking, writing, cooking, laughing, and talking. The general and troops with him camped half a mile above in the bend, except Mr. Billingsby, who joined us again tonight, and from whom I purchased some articles, amongst others a blanket. Our spirits were considerably elevated by reaching this place, as it was set down by all as a point of considerable importance. We now regarded ourselves as amongst the untamed savages of the plains, the country being visited frequently by all the warlike tribes from Texas to the Nebraska and Rocky mountains.

JULY 15. Sunrise was pretty this morning and the

camp in motion early. Soon after taking up our line of march, we passed a Delaware Indian with fresh buffalo meat to sell, the first Indian we have seen on the plains. After a march of seven miles we reached Walnut creek, a clear, cool, and pretty stream, which we had to wade. Here we filled our canteens and marched on, and found no other water until we reached the Pawnee Fork, about thirty miles, making our day's march thirty-seven miles. It was the longest and hardest day's march we have had, and the men suffered a great deal, not more than thirty being in the ranks in marching order. We found Ash creek perfectly dry, and Captain Murphy with canteens went ahead on horseback to get some [water] and meet us; which he did after night, a mile or two from camp, having had to go five or six miles to the river.

It appears to be a great level plain over which we marched, dividing the Arkansas from Walnut creek, and we were on the road from six o'clock until after night. The day was warm and the soil sandy and dried up, the grass resembling the sod of an old common, and the infantry annoyed very much by the dust raised by the mounted troops who were passing us all day. All the low places were dry, except a few buffalo wallows and ruts in the road, [where the water was] muddy, filthy, and covered with green scum, which the horses of the mounted men refused to drink. Yet the men drank it with avidity; they suffered so much from thirst. They used all kinds of expedients which were said to allay thirst, such as keeping silver in the mouth, bullets, etc., but it was all to no purpose and seemed to have no effect. Sore mouths are common, the lips being swollen and parched by the hot sun and constant prairie winds. The mouth becomes slimy, the tongue swollen, and articulation difficult. We passed several dog towns, one of considerable size, and we saw and heard barking many of these little animals, made so famous by travelers. They appear to be a species of squirrel rather than dog. Buffaloes and antelopes were seen several times today, and a very pretty chase took place by some horsemen after an antelope, which escaped them all, though [they were] well mounted. The horsemen have been riding in all directions over the plains in search of grass, water, and game, and greatly have the advantage of us in all respects. Near Ash creek there is a pretty point of rocks called the "Pawnee Rock," [305] on which they say a volunteer [306] of the Howard company was buried yesterday. Timber on the Arkansas and Walnut creek on each hand could be seen all day, ten or fifteen miles distant.

We reached the Pawnee Fork an hour after dark, many so much worn out by the long march and hardships of today that they tumbled into their blankets without supper, too tired to cook or to hunt fuel. Tonight we had to cook supper with buffalo manure for the first time, which we found a good substitute in dry weather like the present. The smell of the smoke is not agreeable, and some rather than use it went without cooking. But to men hungry and fatigued, as most of us were, there was nothing repulsive, and we soon became used to it, except

[305] Robinson, of company D, Missouri mounted volunteers, wrote: "The rock is singular in its appearance, rising abruptly in the midst of the prairie, and on it are carved innumerable names. In this vicinity we saw the first great herd of buffaloes we had met with. I climbed up the rock, from the top of which I witnessed one of the grandest sights ever beheld. Far over the plain to the west and north was one vast herd of buffaloes; some in column, marching in their trails, others carelessly grazing. Every acre was covered, until in the dim distance the prairie became one black mass, from which there was no opening, and extending to the horizon." Robinson, *A Journal of the Santa Fé Expedition* (Cannon, ed.), 12.

[306] Nehemiah Carson, of Glasgow, Missouri, died on July 13, and on the following day was buried in a vault hollowed out of the top of Pawnee Rock. Ruff, Notes, July 13, 14, 1846, MS., M.H.S.; *Täglicher Anzeiger des Westens*, Sept. 5, 1846; Connelley, *Doniphan's Expedition*, 164-166, 559.

our cook, who always preferred a little wood. A box of sardines obtained sometime since from Mr. Billingsby and carefully preserved for hard times like this, a little bacon, and fried cakes composed our supper, except a cup of coffee before we went to bed; after which I felt myself pretty well, laid down, and slept soundly. We found the river too high to cross from late rains, and all the troops, except those with Captain Moore,[307] were detained here. And the army is now all together except the regulars and one or two companies. We found plenty of buffalo meat in camp and for the first time enjoyed the luxury of feasting on a choice piece of this celebrated animal, cooked by one of the company.

JULY 16. This morning all is life in camp, the weather delightful, and the whole bend of the river strung with tents, horses, oxen, men, wagons, mules, etc., besides many traders and their caravans whom we have overtaken. Having had but little fresh meat, we enjoyed a breakfast of buffalo meat, coffee, and some first-rate bread by Walter, who is the best cook in the army. Mr. Billingsby stayed with us last night, and joined us in our morning meal. Many were engaged writing letters all morning, as there will be an opportunity to send them

[307] Benjamin Davis Moore was born in Paris, Bourbon county, Kentucky, September 10, 1810. Later he removed to Illinois, from which state he was appointed midshipman in the United States navy, February 2, 1829. Resigning after a few years of training at sea, he was commissioned first lieutenant in the Mounted rangers, November 6, 1832, first lieutenant in the First dragoons, September 19, 1833, and captain in the First dragoons, June 15, 1837. On June 5, 1846, he was ordered to proceed from Fort Leavenworth with two companies of the First dragoons in order to detain the trading caravans of Armijo and Speyer, who were reported to be taking arms and ammunition to New Mexico. Although he made rapid marches over the Santa Fé trail, he was unable to overtake the caravans. He was killed in the Battle of San Pascual, December 6, 1846. Heitman, *Historical Register,* I, 721; Paxton, *Annals of Platte County, Missouri,* 80; Magoffin, *Down the Santa Fé Trail and into Mexico* (Drumm, ed.), 63.

back. Though very anxious to do likewise, I could not find time, and had to neglect my correspondence and attend to my duties as a soldier. We made a requisition for provisions, the time for which we had drawn having expired, and in addition to flour, meat, coffee, sugar, and salt, drew some rice, an article we had not obtained heretofore. We also procured a large tent for our own use, not having room enough. Mr. Seafert, a private in our company, was discharged here this morning for inability to discharge a soldier's duty. He was laboring under delirium tremens. Many of our friends and acquaintances of other companies called to see us this morning, and a thousand inquiries were made how each got along, and their hardships, trials, troubles, and difficulties related. Today some of our men procured corn bread and milk from some traders camped near us; they had brought a cow with them. A private in one of the mounted companies was drowned yesterday or day before in attempting to swim the river.[308] The bluffs of the Arkansas are in sight, distant ten miles. Company A camped higher up than we did, and we saw but little of them here. I called at Major Rich's, in hopes I should find some letters or papers, but there was nothing for any of our company. The bluffs back of our camp are

308 Arthur E. Hughes, of the Laclede Rangers, was drowned while attempting to swim across Pawnee Fork on July 14. A few days before, he and several others had been sent ahead as an express to stop some provision wagons. On July 15, according to John T. Hughes, he was "decently buried with the honors of war on the East bank of Pawnee Fork, at the foot of a bluff, about 200 yards above the point where the Santa Fé road crosses the said stream. His name is engraven in large capitals on his tomb-stone." Frank S. Edwards wrote: "He received a prairie burial; wrapped in his blanket and clothes, he was placed in his grave, and, without any form, it was filled up and covered over with stones, to prevent the wolves from meddling with the body." Turner, Diary, July 15, 1846, MS., M.H.S.; *Weekly Reveille,* Aug. 10, 1846; *Weekly Tribune,* Sept. 5, 1846; Edwards, *A Campaign in New Mexico with Colonel Doniphan,* 30.

pretty, and buffaloes are said to be plentiful the other side of them. The river is falling fast, and we have orders to cross it today, and all are busy preparing to be ready to break up camp by noon. Before leaving we exchanged an ox team for a horse one [*i.e.,* team] and large wagon, to our great joy, as the oxen were nearly given out; and [we] added another yoke to the other ox team, leaving the remaining oxen.

About noon we broke up camp and in one mile reached the ferry, where everything was crossed in a wagon bed made for that purpose, which answered very well; and [we] pulled the wagons across with ropes. After reloading our teams and getting all together, it was late, and we only marched two miles to camp, company A having first crossed and gone to camp. Some of the other companies were crossed and camped, but their teams were still on the north side, as they crossed on a log, and all were busy trying to get over either themselves or their baggage. We found plums and wild cherries abundant along the river and of a good quality, and the day was cool and beautiful, and all enjoyed it very much. Here also, for the first time, I noticed a large thistle, the leaves a light blue, and the flower a rich white one, similar in size and appearance to a hollyhock but more delicate when close to it, now called "Mexican poppy." Spanish gourds [and] wild Silenes, or, as some call them, "soap-root," are common on the bottom.

This evening we are before all the troops, except Captain Moore's command consisting of the regulars [and] the Jackson and Saline companies. Tonight both companies are cheerful and determined to get a good start of the general and other troops in the morning. Wolves and game of all kinds are plentiful; the former we hear all around camp. This evening a private in company A killed a deer, but we got none of it. It appears to be a prairie-dog town all the way from the river to our camp, and we saw numbers of this little animal, some of which the men shot at as they sat at their holes but hurt none. Our camp is a beautiful spot on the Pawnee Fork, the river winding its way down by the camp of the other troops, which we can see, with elm, wild cherry, willow, etc., scattered along its banks. The climate is evidently cooler and drier than [in] Missouri. This evening two or three blankets are not uncomfortable, and the atmosphere is clear and bracing. But it all may have originated from the late rains which raised the river so much.

JULY 17. We broke up camp early and continued passing through cities of prairie dogs, some of which the men tried to shoot and some young ones to catch, in both of which they failed. We were soon followed by the other troops, and as we marched along could perceive one of the mounted companies winding its way to the Arkansas a mile or two on our left. Just at this time something was seen on the high ground on our right, supposed to be buffaloes. Our captain, Doctor Moore our surgeon, and some others on horseback went in pursuit, when one proved to be a buffalo and three others wild horses, which scampered off leaving all behind. We were too far off, though, to see whether the famous black, or as some say white, horse was with them. The different mounted companies have been coming up all day with stragglers, wagons, oxen, beef cattle, etc., and as far as can be seen, both in front and rear, we had a column like the picture in the journey of the Israelites.

For several days past we have met with great numbers of grasshoppers of an unusual size and apparently too full and fat to perform the feats of this generally active little animal. They are almost as thick as long, sluggish and clumsy. The whole army have suffered from the effects of saline water, many of the mounted companies very much; amongst others our first lieutenant, who came to camp with the wagons. The general and artillery are behind, and we marched today about twenty-six miles. We have had no timber on our route, nor is there any at camp except the drift on the river bank. The soil is sandy, very dry, and the grass, except on the bottom, apparently dead. The weather is pleasant, of an agreeable temperature, and many [are] in the wagons from weakness – sore feet or sickness. The country wears a different aspect from any we have heretofore passed through, being generally very level and almost without a stick of timber as far as the eye can reach, except a tree here and there (on the islands), which does not impede the view. We have plenty of buffaloes and witnessed several chases, some of which [*i.e.,* buffaloes] were killed. We also saw a prairie hare [with]in a few miles of camp. They are double the size of the rabbit but made very much like it, in color a shade lighter, and in action its equal.

JULY 18. We broke up camp early and soon found ourselves on the road with the mounted companies, [which were] strung out for several miles before us. The Arkansas, like all western streams, is crooked and is here serpentine and regular in its bends, presenting a scallop-like appearance as you ascend it, the bend this side being short and on the opposite very sweeping. Our road was from point to point, leaving the big bend and bottom on our left, and by the time our line was stretched across the base of one of these bends, a distance of three or four miles, a buffalo and antelope were jumped up in the bend near the river by some mounted men who were on the lookout for game. And they soon had an animating and exciting race in presence of nearly the whole army, all of which could be distinctly seen, as the chase was on a bottom of great extent. After a long run of several miles at full speed, and [after] half a dozen guns [*i.e.*, shots] or more, the buffalo was brought down. But the little antelope, too fleet for its pursuers and too small a target for hunters at a long shot, made its escape, though several tried to take it both ways. Our servant, Walter, killed a bull today, but he said the meat was no good and brought in none. Walter thought himself quite a victor and was much elated at his success. The whole country from the Little Arkansas is like a slaughter pen, covered with bones, skulls, and carcasses of animals in every state of decay.

Captain Murphy is quite sick today and confined to the wagon, unable to keep on horseback. I am not well myself and was forced to ride a short distance to camp. The first lieutenant is also indisposed but kept on his feet all day.

We reached camp in good season, and I performed ablution in the river. At this place [the river is] broad, shallow, and filled with sand bars, the water so divided into small channels that it can almost be crossed without wetting the feet, and can be waded anywhere. Its banks on this side are low, and [on] the opposite [side are] bluffs [that are] nothing but sand, which gives to them a desertlike and singular appearance. Our camp is close to the river bank, above the other troops, and on the opposite shore large herds of buffaloes come down to the river for water. We saw numbers of them on both sides last evening and this morning. A good many of both companies went over to kill some; they shot eight or ten times, wounded a few, but got none. As they were returning to camp, they found half a dozen Pawnee on an island opposite us, from whom they purchased (for a trifle) dried buffalo meat. After dark the Indians came over to camp and wished to be friendly, but we knew their thievish propensity and want of faith, and told them to leave, which they did. We marched today about twenty-six miles, and Mr. Billingsby came into camp quite sick. We administered to him such things as we had, and gave him such accommodations as our situation would permit.

JULY 19. All the mounted companies were soon before us this morning, and in consequence we saw but little game or anything to give us interest. This morning we found that Mr. Morgan was not so badly hurt as we feared at the time, or had reason to expect, by his wagon accidently running over his breast and shoulders when about to leave camp. He is better and likely to do well. We sent out some hunters this morning, but they returned through the day, without anything. Captain Murphy is quite unwell yet, but generally our sick are better today. Mr. Billingsby came to our camp quite sick. I myself was troubled with something like the splint, but made out to reach camp with the company.

Altogether we got along very well and camped a short distance below the dragoons, on the bank of the river as usual, after a march of twenty-five miles. We sent out some hunters again to try and kill some fresh meat, but they failed to bring in any. General Kearny and the artillery are encamped about eight miles in our rear. The country over which we passed today is similar to that we have been passing over for the past day or two. In our march we keep up the river, having it in sight nearly all the time.

Tonight we had considerable difficulty about our stock, which had been turned on an island, or rather [a] chain of islands, opposite us, as the grass was more abundant than on the mainland; and [they were] left there until after dark, instead of being brought over and placed under the guard. The teamsters and guard were sent over to hunt them up, but they could only find a portion, which they brought, the remainder having wandered to some of the islands, which were separated only by a shallow and narrow stream. Besides, the grass and undergrowth was very high and thick, and they could not be seen in a dark night like the present. As we were amongst Indian tribes who make a rule to steal all they can, and who pay no respect to our notions of *meum* and *tuum,* we considered it hazardous, if they were not already in possession of the missing head. But in the morning all were found, and our anxieties on this score relieved. It was late at night before all was quiet in camp.

JULY 20. After getting the missing horses and mules, we left camp early, Captain Murphy and Mr. Billingsby going on before on horseback. We passed several dog towns, and saw two large rattlesnakes in the road, killed by some person who preceded us. Several shots were fired at the dogs by our men, who are in this way permitted to practice with the musket; but they escaped better than their scaly companions, as none were hurt. After walking about twelve miles, my leg failed on account of the splint, and not being otherwise very well, I took an uncomfortable seat in the horse team and rode within five miles of camp. I was wakened up in the wagons by some of our men, who were complaining very much of Captain Angney and who refused to march under him, the companies having halted to rest, and the first lieutenant having gone to the top of a high ground some distance ahead to examine the country and see if a good camp ground could be had. As soon as I crawled out and ordered a march, they assumed their places and went on without a murmur, except at him. We soon came up to the first lieutenant, who resumed his place and command, and but little more was said about it. They complained that Captain Angney did not treat them well, and that he marched faster than necessary, as in a day we could go only as far as our teams. The men on foot all came into camp pretty well, but the wagons were loaded with lame and sick.

Mr. Billingsby came in at supper, but as yet we don't know where Captain Murphy is, and some uneasiness exists in camp lest he has fallen into the hands of some wandering Indian. But our mess think he is with some of the other troops tonight. Half a dozen commissary teams camp with us tonight, and the wagon master reported twenty-five or thirty Indians below camp, and that they shot at him as he was driving up his oxen about dark. Our first lieutenant, who is officer of the day, ordered all arms to be loaded and the guard to be increased, all of which was done. We marched twenty-four miles today, and I was quite unwell when we reached camp.

JULY 21. In the morning the whole company discharged their arms (having been loaded last night) and took up the line of march, and in three miles came to Captain Murphy, who had camped with a company of mounted volunteers. The day was warm, the road sandy and cut up with ravines more than it has been, and the men suffered much from heat [309] and the want of water, as we do not often strike the river, though it is seldom out of our view since we left the Pawnee Fork, a distance of

[309] On July 21, Lieutenant-colonel Ruff wrote: "Heat, great heat. Our march is under the Bluffs. No air. Desert, desolation, sand, & aridity. March 7 miles. Cross 2 dry sand creeks. . . Stop to graze. Resume march. Heat intense. Road continues under Bluff. Travel 7 miles. Prairie flattens. Heat, heat, heat." Ruff, Notes, July 21, 1846, MS., M.H.S.

about a hundred miles. About three o'clock we came to a few trees, the first we have had the pleasure of reposing under since we left the Pawnee Fork, though a few are to be seen on the Arkansas on the other shore and on the islands. The men enjoyed the shade very much, being quite exhausted when they reached them [*i.e.,* the trees], and we waited until our teams came up and were also refreshed. In about three miles we came to good camping ground and pitched our tents as usual on the bank of the river, where I had a pleasant bath on its sandy bottom. Nearly all the company did the same thing.

The evening being pleasant, I lay down upon the grass and watched the evening clouds as they pictured to the eye the various fleeting forms of things of life, and thought of home and those dear to me. They soon formed themselves into a black mass, and we were threatened for a while with a storm, which finally passed around, heaven's artillery making the valley ring. The wind gave freshness to the atmosphere and added to our comfort. Mr. Billingsby was very sick, and we gave him an emetic, which afforded some relief. We marched eighteen miles today. Several shots were fired at buffaloes, but none [were] killed.

JULY 22. This morning the air was fresh, temperate, and bracing, and the camp was in motion early. I was quite unwell – the effects of the saline water, heat, dust, and fatigue – and took a berth in the mule team, which I kept all day. Today our road was up an extensive bottom, almost on a level with the river and running back from two to four miles, without anything on either side which deserves the name of bluffs. We passed through beds of flowers all day, many very beautiful and abundant: one, the flower of which is exactly like the common morning-glory, but instead of a vine is a plant three or four feet high, the stems branching out close together and most generally giving a conical appearance or shape to it; one, in the bend of the river where the grass and rushes are high, of a purple color, many stems on a stalk and [a] soft velvetlike leaf, the stalk hard and easily broken and about waist-high; sage; and another plant, like thyme, also very common. Amongst the flowers was a pretty red one, the seed similar to a bachelor's-button, and the leaves like a geranium. Another flower, large beds of which we continue to pass every hour, is beautiful. The stalk is like a young green hemp stalk, and a flower on each branch at the end. The purple flower is Artemisia, I believe, and is frequently spoken of by Frémont, etc. Today we marched twenty-five miles, and had to leave the road and go two miles to find a suitable camping spot.

JULY 23. We broke up camp early and in two or three miles overtook the mounted companies. The Cole company had just committed one of their comrades, a Mr. Leslie,[310] a private, to his grave and were firing volleys

[310] Augustus Leslie appears to have been a sergeant. A member of the Cole company described his burial as follows: "His burial was the most solemn and peculiar of any scene I ever witnessed. I had his grave dug on a high point in the prairie with a neat vault cut in the bottom. At an hour by sun, on the next morning, we set out on foot, with the corpse, to pay the last respects to a friend and fellow-soldier. We marched in double file to the grave – wrapped the corpse in blankets (for we could not obtain any such thing as a coffin) and laid it in the tomb. Religious exercises were then had over the grave – singing and prayer conducted by Doct. Winston and assisted by many others of the company. After the religious ceremony, the usual military honors were paid the dead by firing three volleys over his grave; we then covered the vault with the staves of a flour barrel and placed heavy timbers on these to keep his body from the wolves and Indians. We then threw dirt over this, and then placed in a head board, with his name upon it. The whole company then wept over his grave as though he were a brother. The bugle sounded and the company wheeled off and resumed its position in the line of march." *Jefferson Inquirer*, Sept. 15, 1846. See also Connelley, *Doniphan's Expedition*, 173, 555-556.

over it. To be several hundred miles from home and to listen to such a requiem for the dead was calculated to arouse serious feelings. I said to myself [that] our friends look forward to the day when we shall exchange a hearty salutation, but our fate may be that of the poor private. He was entirely unknown in our company. We passed over what may be called "Arkansas bluffs," but they are more like the usual swells of the prairie. From the summit of one we had a magnificent view of the river and valley, both up and down, with the bluffs a mile or two back, the white sandstone projecting from near their summits. Today we passed all the mounted companies,[311] who are at least ten miles in our rear. I marched with the company eight or ten miles and was too unwell to proceed; so I fell in behind the big horse wagon, which afforded me a good shade the remainder of the day. Sergeant Aull and John Doyle are very sick and [so are] some others; and great complaints [312] are made by

311 Infantry company A passed the mounted volunteers as early as July 21. A member of the company wrote: "On the 21st, we passed the Regiment of mounted men without any difficulty. Our men were in high spirits. They would tantalize them as we passed by, telling them 'good bye,' – 'that they would have to pay a bounty of $20 to join the Infantry,' – 'that if they had any news or letters to send on to Bent's Fort, they would take it,' etc., etc." *Jefferson Inquirer,* Sept. 15, 1846.

312 The mounted volunteers also complained of the rapid marching. On July 27 a sergeant of company G, Missouri mounted volunteers, wrote: "We have been marched twenty-five miles a day for the past two weeks or more, and many of our horses are fast failing under this forced march. If it is continued throughout, the 1st Regiment of Missouri Mounted Volunteers, will compose a Regiment of Infantry, and march into Santa Fé on Foot. Curses are daily imprecated upon the heads of Col. Doniphan and Lt. Col. Ruff, who alone are charged with being the cause of our fast travelling, though they are not at all at fault, as they are only acting under orders from Colonel Kearney; at least so Col. Doniphan informed me last week. . . Another cause of complaint is that our coffee gave out a week since, and we have no chance to procure a supply until we reach Bent's Fort, two days' march from this place. We are told that pickled pork and bread baked in ashes, make a very healthy diet; and perhaps it does." *Missouri Democrat* (Fayette, Mo.), Sept. 9, 1846.

the men that Captain Angney should march so fast, and so far before our teams, over burning sands and a scorching sun. We reached camp early, after a march of twenty miles.

The road has been less even than usual, and we crossed the bed of a stream now dry, which has a few trees on its banks, the first we have seen on any tributary of the Arkansas since we left the Pawnee Fork, a distance of a hundred and fifty miles, though there are many small streams in that distance. The grass at our camp is abundant and high, and we have the usual floral specimens to ornament our camping ground. We had a high wind tonight after dark, and some fears were entertained that our tent would go down, but all went off well, and the storm otherwise was at a considerable distance. The lightning could be seen, but the thunder could not be heard. Yet the wind was plainly caused by the storm, which shows that in this atmosphere they are felt at a greater distance than one would suppose. We killed several rattlesnakes in our camp this evening, but none were found in our blankets in the morning as we anticipated.

JULY 24. An early start enabled us to enjoy the morning air, which was quite cool and refreshing, the wind in the evenings and mornings, since we struck the Arkansas, being from the north and from 11 A.M. to 5 P.M. from the south; which indicates something like a sea breeze or the regular trade winds of the ocean, which probably prevails in this region from a like cause in the summer months. In the morning I took passage in the horse team, the disease which all have suffered from having weakened me very much. Besides, my leg still was affected with a kind of splint, which was not very painful but prevented the free use of it, as it was swollen from half way up the shin to the foot.

The road we passed over today was an extensive bottom with nothing like bluffs on this side and only sand hills on the other, which are said to extend south a considerable distance. At a distance they look like bluffs with precipitous sides, which is the case with some, the winds having made them into all kinds of shapes. On our march we crossed several little streams with a few trees scattered along their borders, but all dry and their beds filled up even with the country around with a pretty, clean white sand. Our camp has one of these on our right and the river on our left, with some large but low cottonwoods scattered over the angle, which, in our estimation, add very much to the beauty of the camp as it has been such a rare occurrence for a long time. Sergeant Aull is quite unwell today, but I am better. The wagons are filled with sick in the same condition, except a few who have chills and several lame.

We made camp in good season after marching twenty-five miles, all becoming anxious to reach Bent's Fort, about four days' travel as is supposed, where both rest and washing can be done, and where we expect to put our feet upon Mexican soil, which is soon destined to add to our already extended Union. There we shall leave our native soil until new acquisitions are made and the Stars and Stripes float in Santa Fé. We are out of the buffalo range, and game of all kinds appears to be scarce, the country having but a little grass and that short and dried up. Lieutenant Reed and F. fell in company with us today, accompanying some wagons, and it was a source of great pleasure to meet them. It was like exchanging congratulations at sea. Captain Murphy was able to go upon duty today, though he had not recovered his strength.

JULY 25. We left camp in good season, continuing our march up the river. I continued with the company twelve or thirteen miles while the morning was cool and pleasant, during which I took off the head of a large rattlesnake that came out of a dog hole to sun itself. About ten o'clock it [*i.e.,* the weather] began to turn intensely warm, the wind being from the south over the sand hills, and about noon it blew a perfect sirocco, blinding from its severity and blistering where it touched.[313] It is scarcely credible that such a wind prevails anywhere in North America. The company, though, made out to get through it, and I, being in the horse team, did not suffer its full force and effects. Our road was up the bottom known as the Chickasaw, over which, a distance of twenty miles, we suffered from heat and want of water. The men suffered very much on these accounts and also from the sand, which was hot and in clouds.

We reached camp after a march of twenty-eight miles, pitching our tents as usual on the bank of the river, two or three miles below the upper end of the bottom. There is a Comanche camp a short distance above us, a war party against the Cheyenne. Several of the companies went up, but they failed to induce any of them to visit us. An express to Bent's Fort camps with us. The timber on the islands begins to be more abundant and to present

[313] Frank S. Edwards described the hot winds encountered while marching along the Arkansas: "While on our march along the banks of the river [Arkansas] a singular phenomenon occurred. Towards the middle of the day, while no breeze was stirring, we were met by successive blasts of heated air, so hot as to scorch the skin and make it exceedingly painful to breathe; and these continued upwards of two hours. The sky, at the time, was entirely cloudless; but these gusts bore no resemblance to an ordinary current of wind, but rather to a blast from a furnace." Edwards, *A Campaign in New Mexico with Colonel Doniphan,* 30-31.

a more forestlike appearance. All of the teamsters raised a shout when they came in sight of camp, as they knew water at least could be had if they could not find wood.

JULY 26. This morning I was too unwell to march with the company and took to my big horse team. About ten o'clock I had a severe ague, but the fever was light, and I rode all day over a delightful country, the scenery being splendid. We had a view of it for a great distance, the bottoms on both sides being very extensive; and the islands, which are numerous, [were] covered with grass and undergrowth to the water's edge, with only a tree here and there, looking more like the artificial work of a garden than natural scenery. The day was rather pleasant, a few drops of rain coming down occasionally, and the evening [was] delightful. Our camp is where Bent's Old Fort stood, forty-five miles from the present one, and very few vestiges of it now remain, scarcely enough to indicate its former size, though it was deserted only about twelve years ago.[314] The express camps with us again tonight. Timber is abundant at camp and begins to obstruct the view of the other shore and bottom. It is entirely cottonwood and willow. We reached camp in good season, but the mule team was belated. We marched about twenty-five or twenty-seven miles, and all are in good spirits on account of our near approach to Bent's Fort.

JULY 27. I was quite unwell all night and morning, having taken a dose of calomel, and was not with the company; nor [was] the first lieutenant, who is also complaining. We passed over a country something similar to yesterday, with the exception of the greater quantity of rock and timber, indicating our approach to the

314 If Gibson's statement is true, it contributes new and important information on the early history of Bent's Fort.

mountains, which, it is thought, can be seen on a clear day from the high elevations in the prairie. There was one isolated pile back from the river, in the bottom, of considerable size and height, its sides steep and rugged, which presented a pretty appearance.

In the evening a storm blew up and finally passed around, cooling and refreshing the atmosphere, and we camped with some cottonwood timber around us. We marched seventeen miles, and three or four men passed us at camp, going express to the fort. The day was pleasant for men who were well, but, like all others, very disagreeable to sick ones. The country generally is dry and parched, with many large cracks or fissures. It is poor and gravelly and nearly destitute of grass. Captain Angney was greatly disappointed when, instead of being at our camp within a few miles' march of Bent's Fort, he found himself twenty-three or twenty-four. As he is getting short of provisions, he went on and camped several miles ahead of us. The captain's box of sardines was opened for supper, and once for several days I made what might be termed a meal.

JULY 28. I found myself much better this morning and with a pocket full of quinine pills took the ox team, all leaving camp early to reach a point which we have had the utmost anxiety to see, as we shall then have a great many things settled about which various opinions are entertained. Soon after starting, we had presented to our view in front the Rocky mountains, which we were told was Pike's Peak, at a distance of a hundred miles, at the sight of which the company gave a shout. The air in the morning is cool and bracing, like it has been all the way up the river, but warm and very oppressive through the middle of the day. The soil is poor, gravelly, dry, and completely parched, with scarcely any grass or any growth upon it except a few weeds and several kinds of cacti, the bayonet plant being the most common.

About noon, after marching fifteen miles, we reached Captain Moore's camp, two miles below the fort, which had a reviving effect upon the company as we expect to remain here several days.[315] Our camp, as usual, is on the river bank, and by digging a well we procured good water. Wood also is plentiful, but grass is scarce and mixed up very much with weeds, poison oak, vines, and sage. We were soon exchanging salutations with our acquaintances in Captain Moore's command, and for once experienced one of the pleasures of a soldier on a long campaign. The first lieutenant's box of sardines, the last in camp, furnished us with a supper, and I found myself much better in the evening, having escaped a chill. All the company appear to be improving in health.

JULY 29, 30, 31. Bent's Fort. Contrary to our expectations we could learn no news here from Santa Fé:[316]

[315] With the exception of Captain Moore's detachment, which left Fort Leavenworth early in June, the infantry companies were the first troops to reach Bent's Fort. "The Infantry companies," asserted a member of the Laclede Rangers, "have out-marched, and reached the Fort in advance of all the mounted companies." Lieutenant Eastin, of infantry company A, wrote from Bent's Fort: "We arrived here on the 28th July, early in the morning,—only 29 days out from Ft. Leavenworth. We lost three days during the time, which leaves 26 days travel. This clearly proves that the Infantry can travel through this country as well, if not better, than the cavalry." *Jefferson Inquirer,* Sept. 15, 1846; *Saint Louis Daily Union,* Sept. 7, 1846.

[316] Most Americans who left Santa Fé for "the States" between May and August, 1846, reported that there would be little if any opposition in New Mexico to Kearny's occupation of that department. Charles Bent, Ceran St. Vrain, and other traders departed from Santa Fé on May 27, arriving at Westport and Independence a month later. Bent and St. Vrain immediately went to Fort Leavenworth, where they told Kearny that Armijo had informed them that he was expecting General Urrea with reinforcements from Sonora, Zacatecas, and Durango. "Mr. Bent is of the opinion," wrote Kearny to the adjutant-general, "that there can be no good feeling between Urrea & Armijo, & that if I can get there in time, the services of the latter may be made

whether they were collecting an army to meet us or not,

---

available against the former." Bent and his party of traders continued their journey to St. Louis, where they asserted that most of the people of New Mexico were well disposed toward the United States, and that if Urrea did not arrive with his troops "Col. Kearney would be able to march in and take possession of the country without serious resistance." On July 17, when Kearny met George T. Howard returning from New Mexico, Turner recorded in his diary that Howard represented "everything favorable to our object." George Bent, Boggs, Hatcher, and other Americans reached Bent's Fort from Santa Fé and Taos on July 3, and two days later E. L. Hempstead wrote a letter from the fort summarizing their opinion of conditions in New Mexico: "It is, however, thought by the wise ones in Santa Fé, that on the arrival of the troops [American], if a flag is sent in giving assurance of respect for persons and property, the country to the Río de Nòrte would be given up without a struggle." Rallston, an American trader, left Santa Fé about July 8 and arrived at Independence on August 13, when he reported that "it was pretty certainly known" that there would "not be even a show of fight on the part of the Mexicans," and that "the common people and Indians say that nothing can induce them to fight against the Americans." McKnight, Aubry, and other American traders departed from Santa Fé on July 16, and when they reached St. Louis the *Daily Union* stated: "One of the gentlemen named had a conversation with Governor Armijo on the day of his departure, and learned that no opposition would be offered to the march of the American forces." An American by the name of Waugh left Santa Fé on August 2, and on arriving at Council Grove declared: "There can be but little apprehension of any resistance at Santa Fé. Armijo, the Governor, manifested the greatest friendship for the Americans, and the traders who had arrived there felt themselves in no danger." Turner recorded on July 28 that recent letters to traders Glasgow and Leitensdorfer from their partners in Santa Fé represented "that the reduction of the province will be accomplished without bloodshed." On July 30, Lieutenant Kribben, then at Bent's Fort, wrote that the captured Mexican spies had brought information which, together with the opinions of men whose judgment he respected, led him to conclude "that, apart from a few skirmishes in the mountain passes, we shall find little work to do this side of Santa Fé." Thomas Fitzpatrick, Kearny's guide, wrote from Bent's Fort on July 31: "Late news which we received from Santafee would indicate that we shall have no fighting and indeed it has always been my opinion that there would not be a blow struck at Santafee whatever may be the case elsewhere." Kearny to Jones, June 29, 1846, Kearny Letter Book, MS., M.H.S.; Fitzpatrick to Andrew Sublette, July 31, 1846, Sublette MSS., *ibid.*; Turner, Diary, July 17, 28, 1846, MS., *ibid.; Daily Missouri Republican,* July 3, Aug. 20, 24, Sept. 7, 1846; *Missouri Reporter,* July 3, 1846; *St. Louis Daily New Era,* July 3, 1846; *Saint Louis Daily Union,* Aug. 24, 1846; *Weekly Reveille,* July 6, Aug. 10, 1846; *Täglicher Anzeiger des Westens,* Sept. 5, 1846; *Missouri Statesman,* Sept. 4, 1846; *Jefferson Inquirer,* Sept. 15, 1846.

whether they would receive us as deliverers or not; and we all began to think we should have to fight, thinking the Mexicans had cut off all communication. The only person who has come in from New Mexico was brought as a prisoner, and General Kearny, after taking him to camp where he could see our forces, dismissed him as either not an enemy or for effect, [so] that he might return and relate to his own people what a large army he had seen. Everything has been put in order, and all of our men appear clean shaved and with clean clothes, different in this respect from all the troops. Great numbers of letters were written, I myself having written to Mrs. Gibson and Bird, as teamsters and an express return to "the States." A bath in the river, with the rest we have had, has nearly restored my health. The general and all the troops with him have camped about nine miles below us at the mouth of the Purgatoire, and on the twenty-ninth Captain Moore and his command moved down to them; so that the whole army is there with him, except our battalion. Some fine fish were caught in the river by some of the men, but we did not find the fishing good.

On Thursday I visited the fort [317] and found it situated

[317] Early in 1846 an American gave the following description of Bent's Fort: "This establishment is constructed of what is termed in New Mexico *adobes* – a sun-dried brick, which becomes hard and firm, and durable. They are 18 inches long, 9 inches wide, and 4 inches thick. They are not made with as much precision as our brick, but when put up, make a wall that is strong and passable. The fort is an oblong, the wall about twenty feet in height, and sufficiently thick to resist all attempts with small arms. At the angles are round towers, commanding the outside of the walls; so with some swivels, and a couple of six-pounder brass pieces which we have, the place can be defended against any force that can be brought against it in this country. The area enclosed within the walls would probably comprise over an acre, which is subdivided by high walls; so, in case of a siege, all the horses, mules, cattle, wagons, etc., can be secured and protected inside the walls. Round the inside of the wall of the fort *proper,* are the storehouses, shops for blacksmith, gunsmith and carpenters, men's quarters, private rooms for gentlemen, dining room, kitchen, etc. Over the dining room, and perched

a hundred yards from the river in a dry, sandy, and gravelly soil, on a small rise, or swell, in the prairie. It is of mud brick, or adobe, quite convenient and capacious, affording all kinds of accommodation to travelers, such as repairing teams (for which they have a blacksmith shop), provisions, repairing guns (for which they are provided), procuring ammunition, horses, or mules, or articles from the store, which is filled with articles for the Indian trade. The view from the top of the fort is very fine, the river and its valley being visible a great way up and down, and the mountains in the west. At present it is crowded with all kinds of persons: citizens, soldiers, traders to Santa Fé, Indians, Negroes, etc.[318] The Indians were Arapaho, a fine-looking set of men, with mules to trade. As I was unwell and could not bear its confined air, I saw but little of its interior arrangements. However, they have a large dairy, and I

on the very top, overlooking all the buildings, is my sanctum. The buildings have flat roofs, covered with *adobes,* and rendered perfectly tight, affording a pleasant promenade, with a view of a vast extent of surrounding prairie, meandered by the river, with a back view of the Rocky Mountains – the Spanish Peak and Pike's Peak, towering amid the clouds and glittering in the sunshine. . . Our style of living is superior to that of ordinary Indian traders, having abundance of substantials. Flour, corn, beans and whisky we get from the Spanish settlements. Milk, poultry, butter, eggs, etc., are kind of indigenous affairs. All we lack is *murphys,* which we will try to raise the coming season. There were twelve cows kept at the fort to furnish milk for the winter, and now there are thirty that could be put in requisition, if necessary. The company keep a large stock of cattle, employing Mexicans to herd them." *Weekly Reveille,* May 18, 1846. See also *Southwest Historical Series,* I, 59.

318 Writing from Bent's Fort on August 3, a volunteer stated: "Such a collection of tribes or nations, as I never expected to see, is here congregated. Yesterday before the army left, I think I heard at one time, as many as six different languages, French, Spanish, German, English, Camanche, Arapahoe – a perfect Babel of a place not only from heterogeneousness of tongues but from differences of character of persons assembled. We had all sorts from the polished gentleman down to the rough daring man of the mountains, as well as the untamed savage who seemed to be sneaking about as if in search of a good opportunity to scalp some body." *Glasgow News,* Sept. 3, 1846.

saw some very fine calves near it. At a distance it [*i.e.*, the fort] presents a handsome appearance, being castle-like with towers at its angles, or, as we call them, bastions, with portholes, and only one large porta, or entrance, protected by a massive gate now open. But when you approach close, you find the design good but the execution rough, like all Spanish buildings of the same material as we have since found, but answering all purposes of protection, defense, and as a residence. They have a well, the water of which is very good, and I heard of juleps, lemonades, etc., but saw none, nor the ice.

Here we left John Doyle, a private of our company, who was too unwell to travel. When sufficiently recovered, [he] is to follow and rejoin us. He is in charge of Captain Weightman,[319] of the artillery, who is also

[319] Richard Hanson Weightman was born in Washington, D.C. He was a cadet at the United States Military academy from July 1, 1835, to April 28, 1837, but was never graduated. Later he removed to St. Louis, where he was living at the outbreak of the Mexican war. On May 28, 1846, he was elected captain of company A, light artillery, Missouri volunteers. After remaining at Bent's Fort for a short time on account of sickness, he rejoined the Army of the West near Las Vegas and entered Santa Fé with the rest of the troops. He fought in the Battle of Sacramento, February 28, 1847, and was mustered out of service, June 24, 1847. On May 10, 1848, he was appointed additional paymaster of volunteers and was honorably discharged, August 1, 1849. He was elected senator from the "state" of New Mexico on June 20, 1850, but never entered upon the duties of his office because of the abortive nature of this government. On September 1, 1851, after New Mexico had been organized as a territory, he was chosen its first delegate to the congress of the United States. Returning to New Mexico upon the expiration of his term of office, he engaged in the practice of law, and for a short time edited a newspaper at Albuquerque. On August 18, 1854, following an argument in Santa Fé with François Xavier Aubry, a trader and explorer, Weightman, in self-defense, stabbed him to death with a bowie knife. Not long afterward he returned to "the States" and helped to found Atchison, Kansas. He joined the Confederate army at the beginning of the Civil war and was killed in the Battle of Wilson's Creek, Missouri, August 10, 1861. He was buried at Springfield, Missouri. Robinson to Snyder, Mar. 17, 1913, Weightman to Snyder, Apr. 19, 1913, Snyder MSS., M.H.S.; *Weekly Reveille,* June 1, 1846; *Daily Missouri Republican,* Aug. 19, 1850, Oct. 15, 1851; *Appleton's Cyclopedia of American Biography,* VI, 421; Heitman,

unwell. Company A left a sick man in the same way and had their wagon taken to the fort and repaired. We also left our two loose mules with the quartermaster. The ground which they cultivate is off from the fort, but they had at it a good many horses, mules, and cattle. The river is broad here, with its sandy bottom and sand bars, apparently containing as much water as where we first struck it; which probably is the case at this season of the year, as there are but few tributaries below, which are not now dried up, until you come to the Pawnee Fork. According to my estimates we have marched 607 miles from Fort Leavenworth.

Historical Register, I, 1014; Edwards, *A Campaign in New Mexico with Colonel Doniphan,* 42; *Southwest Historical Series,* I, 287.

THE OCCUPATION OF NEW MEXICO

THE OCCUPATION OF NEW MEXICO

AUGUST 1. After nearly four days' rest we all became anxious to reach the place of our destination; so we drew rations, the sugar and coffee being short (only half), broke up camp, and today turned our faces once more towards Santa Fé. We passed by the fort, where we were delayed some time on account of having to leave John Doyle, and immediately crossed the Arkansas, which was considerably over knee-deep in some places; and [we] continued our march six miles up the river on the south side, when we encamped where our road leaves this stream, having ascended it 319 miles from the time we first struck it. We are in advance of all the troops, who remain today at the mouth of the Purgatoire. A part of the day was very warm, but the remainder pleasant; and as our march was short and we were in camp most of the time, we were comfortable. The evening was delightful. The camp fires having caught in the dry grass, a prairie rabbit was run out and caught after some whooping and sport. They appear whiter than the rabbit of "the States" but very similar in make and general appearance, except that they are again as big. Every man in camp was on duty today, and one of our greatest anxieties now is to reach the pure air and water of the mountains, where we expect a perfect and complete restoration to health. Colonel Owens [320] with his teams

320 Samuel Combs Owens, a prominent Santa Fé trader. *Southwest Historical Series*, I, 42.

is a half mile below us, and [there are] other traders between here and the fort, [all of] whom we passed, waiting for permission to advance. They are all willing to go before, but the general will not permit them to trade with the enemy. Consequently they follow in our rear.

AUGUST 2. Our road today was across deep ravines, or gullies, for several miles, when we came upon the divide between the Purgatoire and another tributary of the Arkansas, apparently a table-land, but the heads of branches intersecting it and making many ups-and-downs. We could see mountains on our right, which we supposed were the Spanish Peaks forty or fifty miles distant. They were in view all day. The first lieutenant was sick and confined to the wagon, and after marching about fifteen miles Captain Murphy injured his foot with his sword and had to fall back to the teams. The day was tolerably pleasant, but as we have had no water since we left the river, the battalion suffered very much, some men in our company being quite sick and unable to march.[321] I myself gave out, partly from this cause and partly because I had not recovered my strength. Captain

[321] The troops were starting to cross one of the worst deserts on the route to Santa Fé. Robinson wrote: "Next day [August 3] travelled 15 miles up the Arkansas. The country becomes a desert, extremely hot; the wind blows from it as from a heated oven, causing soreness of the eyes and bleeding at the nose. On the 4th of August we left the Arkansas, and travelled 30 miles across a desert country. This has been a trying day: the heat intense, thermometer 120; clouds of dust almost suffocate the men, who are in confusion, and grumbling. Water-mirage appears, but no water; and last and worst the dreaded Sirocco or hot wind blows, which burns us even through our clothes. The only vegetation here is some bunches of dry grass, and now and then a bunch of prickly pear, which seem to tell how desert a country it is. At the place where we encamped found some brackish water. Five horses died. The discontented men say, Let us be any where than in this desert." Robinson, *A Journal of the Santa Fé Expedition* (Cannon, ed.), 19-20. See also Turner, Diary, Aug. 2, 3, 4, 1846, MS., M.H.S.; Edwards, Journal, Aug. 3, 4, 1846, MS., *ibid.;* Hughes, *Doniphan's Expedition,* 61-63.

Angney, having tendered his services for the purpose and the men expressing a wish that he should march them on to water, took the company to camp, all being desirous not to wait for the teams, which were a considerable distance behind. We appear to have left all kinds of insects behind us, such as grasshoppers, flies, etc., as we have not been troubled with anything of the kind today. At our camp this evening we found two specimens of the horned frog, or lizard, a curious and rough-looking animal, harmless but disgusting in its appearance. All over their bodies they have little short horns or what looks like them, for they seem not to be a bony substance but [a] kind of gristle, which has caused the name. They are probably of the chameleon species, as they have the color of the soil on which they are found, which, of course, varies.

We marched about twenty-two miles and encamped on a stream, which at this time has only pools and is quite brackish and disagreeable. We dug a well, an expedient which furnished us with good water at our camp below the fort; but it failed us here, as it was no better than the branch. However, we drank it freely, being very thirsty, and felt the effects all next day and suffered the consequences, some of the men being very much weakened. We have no timber in sight except on the mountains, a long way off, but we have a species of brush, the name of which is unknown to us. It is thick and bushy and low, and furnishes a fine retreat for rabbits, great numbers of which appear to be here. Captain Cooke and a detachment of twelve men camp with us, sent forward with a flag to Santa Fé.[322] The

[322] Captain Philip St. George Cooke, in command of a detachment of twelve men of the First dragoons, was marching to Santa Fé ahead of the army in order to deliver Colonel Kearny's letter of August 1 to Governor

general and remainder of the troops camp a mile or two in our rear. This evening the weather was windy but pleasant. And a fire broke out in the brush, the lurid flames rising high, and the crackling of the dried brush alarming the prairie rabbits, almost the only tenants that we saw of this poor and barren country.

AUGUST 3. We took a very early start this morning, the sun just beginning to show itself after we were a mile upon our road; and [we] soon came to a range of hills and ridges, which presented a very different appearance from anything we have heretofore seen on our route. They generally run parallel to each other, our road being usually up the valley, or rather down it, as we go a south course. But occasionally we cross one [*i.e.,* a ridge] into another valley and pursue it a while. At the first hills and at various other places on our road today I found fine specimens of iron ore, together with volcanic remains. [At] several places near their summits, the face of the high hills presented the appearance of being artificial cornice work, the tops covered with cedar and pine. After marching six miles, we were delayed a short time to know which of two roads was the one we should follow, when Mr. Magoffin,[323] a trader, came up, and from his information

Armijo. On August 2, Cooke wrote: "At last, as the sun was setting, I saw the troops leaving the road to camp; and although there was no indication of water beyond, I kept on; and after I had entirely passed, came in sight of some tents, and directed there my course; I found it the camp of the small battalion of infantry who had marched the previous day. We were hospitably welcomed; but there was scant grass for the few animals, and the water of the little stream, the Timpe, was a weak but decided solution of Epsom salts. Variety in diet is pleasing; but extremes not always. Capt. Angney, the commander, had procured at the fort, some molasses, – for the consideration of a dollar the pint – and that, with strong thirst, helped down the tepid Timpe. After all its effects were moderate." Cooke, *Conquest of New Mexico and California,* 10-11.

[323] James Wiley Magoffin and José Gonzáles, Chihuahua traders, were

we sent our teams on the right and ourselves took the left, which, he said, was shorter but impracticable for wagons.

After crossing several ridges over which our road led us, we came to the Cedar Grove bluffs, where we found good water in a deep canyon, its sides lined with massive sandstone, and [we] filled our canteens. The country around here is very poor: sandstone, with the yellow and red oxides of iron intermixed with it, and gypsum of various kinds [are] mixed with the soil. And nothing is to be seen but chains of ridges, their sides perfectly sterile and their tops set with cedar and pine, some of which are very pretty, the trees large, and like they had been trimmed by art. The cedar all appears to be of the white species, and from their appearance many [are] of great antiquity. From the last named place we started for the Hole in the Rock, leaving behind Mr. Magoffin and Captain Cooke with his detachment, our road leading us over a country still more broken, one ridge having an elevation which would almost entitle it to the appellation of mountain, its top covered with low but large-bodied pines and cedars. The country over which we have marched today was quite rocky, sandstone greatly prevailing but mixed with almost all other kinds, iron giving its most striking colors. We saw more antelopes today than we have found anywhere on our route. There is scarcely anything like brush, and no timber except pine and cedar, and they only on the summits, except a few at the Cedar Grove bluff.

Today we marched twenty-eight miles and reached camp at dark, several of the men completely exhausted

accompanying Cooke to Santa Fé. Magoffin's mission was to help Kearny to occupy New Mexico peaceably.

by fatigue and want of water, which they had only at the Cedar Grove bluff. The road we came was dim and dusty, and we are in advance of all others except Captain Cooke, who camps on the east side of the Hole in the Rock, we on the west.[324] Where we struck this place it is a deep canyon, its bed and sides covered with large rock, as if it had been separated by some convulsion of nature. As our teams come around another road, we crossed over to its west bank and camped on the brow, with plenty [of] pine and cedar for fuel. The water was good, better than we have usually had, and though our teams were [until] after night getting up, we were all in our blankets in good season. The horse and mule teams were considerably worsted, and some had fears that we should have to abandon a portion of our stock as unable to be got to camp. But they were all finally brought up with a good deal of exertions, patience, and whipping.

AUGUST 4. We left camp early, our road being over a high, dry, and rather level country, probably a divide between two streams, with scarcely such a thing as grass to be seen or anything else except the low, brushy bush common [on] this side of the Arkansas. Captain Cooke

[324] Cooke recorded his experiences on August 3: "Next morning we were off betimes with the infantry; the scenery all day was wild, and strange to us; bare of trees or grass, – save on the ridges where cedars and pines were to be seen; our information indicated no water short of a very long march. But by taking a horse trail, and passing along a ridge, near noon, a good spring was found, and there we passed several hours under the shade of *piñón* trees, indulging in lunch, with claret wine and *piñón* nuts for dessert. In the afternoon, the road being very difficult, I got far ahead of the carriages; near sundown I overtook numerous infantry stragglers, suffering from extreme thirst. Just at dark, I saw the battalion camp fires, but beyond a rocky and deep ravine which we could not cross. We managed, however, to get water, and bivouacked above under the little cedar trees. I heard my sergeant discussing with his party, that extraordinary infantry, which, with our fine horses, we could not pass; but he said, 'if regulars were to straggle so, they would be considered mutinizing.'" *Ibid.*, 11-12.

and Mr. Magoffin went on before us this morning, and we did not see them any more, except for a few moments as we reached camp.[325] Yesterday and today we passed a pretty species of the cactus, being bushlike and as high as a man's head. We saw many horned frogs and large numbers of antelopes, which would stop to gaze at us until we frequently came almost within gunshot, when they would bound off with great fleetness, apparently satisfied that we were enemies. The whole country has more the aspect and marks of a sheep pasture completely eaten out and tramped over than that of a mountain valley far removed from the haunts of civilization. Walter says he saw some mountain sheep at a hundred yards' distance, but we doubted it, though he insisted he had.

About three o'clock we reached the Hole in the Prairie, where we found tolerable water and camped after a march of thirteen miles, our teams being so far behind and so worn out that we found it necessary to stop. While waiting for the wagons to come up, Captain Murphy went out and killed a full-grown antelope close to camp, and one of our teamsters, when they reached us, brought a small one in which he shot on the road. The two were divided amongst the company, and we had a rich bowl, or rather camp kettle, of soup to regale us in the Rocky mountains. The antelopes have been all around camp in great numbers, coming to the water, which is only in two or three holes, no doubt their usual watering place. We have no timber at camp, a species of cactus and a few brush knee-high being the only fuel.

[325] On August 4, Cooke wrote: "We pushed on, over more bad ground, twenty miles to the next water, a mere muddy pond, where we found antelope and elk. After a short nooning, we saw the battalion coming, and Don Santiago [Magoffin] expressing great apprehension of being 'run over by that long legged infantry,' we hastened to depart." *Ibid.*, 12.

But the day is warm, calm, and a little smoky, and we make out to cook, as we frequently have done, by digging pits and burning the brush, cactus, and weeds. We have a chain of mountains on our right, some of which are high conical peaks, and one nearly or directly in front. Mr. Bent[326] (who came up and stopped with us) with a company of rangers who are sent forward to see if any of the enemy are on the other side of the mountains, informs us that those on our right are the Spanish Peaks and the one in front the Ratón. Our mule team was late and the horse team still later getting to camp, and about nine o'clock the general and staff came up and camped with us. A detail of eight men from each company was ordered to leave at four o'clock in the morning and go in advance to open and repair the road where it might require it.

AUGUST 5. We made our usual start about sunup or just after and had a good road to the Purgatoire (about ten miles), a clear, pretty, mountain stream running over a rocky bed, the first we have seen. On its banks and bottom we found a thick growth of black locust, gooseberries, wild cherries, cottonwood, black currants, and several other shrubs and trees, with plenty of weeds and vines. The valley, or bottom land, is narrow but fertile, and its green contrasts strongly with the naked, poor, and dusty hills around, which generally run down within fifty yards of the stream. From this place our road was around the base of the mountains and up the

326 On July 31, 1846, William W. Bent, one of the proprietors of Bent's Fort, offered his services and those of six of his men to Colonel Kearny; but, according to Turner, Bent declined to accept the colonel's terms because the compensation was inadequate. However, on the following day Bent and his men came to an agreement with Kearny, who directed them to accompany the Army of the West and act as a spy party. They performed valuable service between Bent's Fort and Santa Fé, a region with which Bent had been familiar for about twenty years. Turner, Diary, July 31, Aug. 1, 3, 1846, MS., M.H.S.

creek, a distance of ten miles, the country broken and filled with gravel, iron ore, gypsum, sandstone, conglomerate, etc., but seldom in large masses. Our camp is hemmed in by mountains in all directions, except in the direction the creek runs. Except in the bottom, the grass is dry and scarce, and the cactus and low, flat prickly pear are still common. All the ridges are gravelly, hard, smooth, flinty, and sometimes almost quartz-like. We have a spring to supply us with water, and all feel in good spirits, having pure air and wholesome water.

We marched the twenty miles in good season, and our teams came up sooner than yesterday or than we expected, as there were some long and steep hills both to go up and down. One horse gave out and had to be left on the road; he was sent for, however, and brought to camp. General Kearny camps about five miles behind us, and as we came up near our camp we saw Mr. Bent on his way. Just as we reached camp, we overtook the road detail, who had not found many places where their services were needed or where they could do much. The evening was pleasant, and all of both companies enjoyed the fresh, bracing mountain air.

AUGUST 6. The detail to work the road left camp early, and we soon followed, our road leaving the Purgatoire and entering into the broken ridges of the mountains, generally following up some little rivulet nearly to its source. A few miles on our way we crossed a considerable elevation, where the view was rich and magnificent, the whole range of the Rocky mountains with their snow-clad summits being in full view, the valley of the Purgatoire beneath us, and the lofty summit of the Ratón on our left. In fact we are hemmed in on all sides by mountains, and entered a gorge (down which flows a small stream of clear, pure water), which we followed the balance of the day. Everything has changed – the country, game, birds, fish, etc. We saw several of the black- or long-tailed deer, [and] a magpie with red and white on its wings. For the first time since we left Council Grove we have small scrub oaks, and a yellow or whitish willow or cottonwood peculiar to the country, by some called "narrow-leafed cottonwood." [We saw] a little rose similar in appearance to the sweetbrier, with a variegated flower, very sweet. Black currants are common and a species of wild cherry, very astringent; also gooseberries. Pine is the principal growth, though there are several varieties of underbrush. The air is cool, bracing, and pure, but pleasant, our climate evidently having changed. The wagons all came up in good season, and we had a good rest in the afternoon, having marched seventeen miles.

Our camp is at the base of a high peak of the Ratón, where the grass is tolerable and the water very fine. A small branch runs by our camp, and in a little while we caught in it a large mess of mountain trout, which, of course, we enjoyed as a luxury not met with every day. The scenery around is rich, the broken rocky eminences reflecting back the evening sun, and the top of the Ratón towering in the skies and immediately over us. Buffalo heads and elk horns have been common on our road, showing that such animals occasionally wander through these hills and valleys. Some turkeys were seen but none killed by any of the infantry. General Kearny came up in the evening and camped with us; also the engineer corps.[327] All the men appear to have improved

---

[327] On August 6, Lieutenant Emory, of the topographical engineers, wrote: "We commenced the ascent of the Ratón, and, after marching seventeen miles, halted, with the infantry and general staff, within a half mile of the summit

very much since we reached the mountains. Today one of our company, in charge of the guard, was made [to] carry his knapsack for being caught asleep last night as sentinel on post. During the evening in camp we had wrestling, foot races, and more hilarity than the same number of men usually create. Some preferred wandering up the mountain sides, and the spirits of all seemed to have an elasticity suitable to the wild scenery around.

AUGUST 7. From our camp we turned square off to the right, and in a mile and a half found ourselves upon the dividing ridge, where we had another view of the Spanish Peaks, the Rocky mountains (their snow-clad summits reflecting a bright white), the Ratón, the Taos mountains, and probably the Santa Fé. Some peaks in the west appeared very high, the whole country nothing but mountains, the farthest of which is supposed to be from sixty to a hundred miles distant. The descent was gradual and the road free from rock, following a branch about two miles, when it turned to the left, going up a steep and rocky ridge. When on top of the mountain or dividing ridge, we were not more than six or seven miles from where we camped on the Purgatoire, so tortuous and winding had been our road. On the ridge last named considerable work was done by removing rock and other obstructions, the teams, after ascending, having to wait until it was done before they could venture down. However, all arrived safe at the foot, where we again struck the branch we had just left, our road passing into a level open prairie, which we continued in five miles and camped on the bank of the Río Colorado, a branch of the Canadian, and here a clear, cool,

of the pass. Strong parties were sent forward to repair the road, which winds through a picturesque valley, with the Ratón towering to the left." *Daily Union*, Oct. 22, 1846.

pretty stream, with the narrow-leafed cottonwood, willows, etc., along its banks. General Kearny and dragoons passed us in the evening and camped two miles ahead on the same stream.[328] Today we marched eighteen miles, and expect to remain here tomorrow to await the provision teams and draw rations. A private in company A, whose mind has been affected by sickness, wandered away from the company on its march today and has not been seen since. When last noticed, he was leaving the road at the foot of the mountain. There was considerable merriment in camp because the infantry made a road across the mountains for the army – regulars, artillery, and all.

AUGUST 8. By orders we moved our camp two miles down to the general's, where the whole force was concentrated. Our provision returns ending today, we made a requisition, but only got half rations of flour [and] no beans or peas. Instead of pork or bacon we drew part beef (having our choice), deeming it much better on half rations of flour, as we can make soup, which we did this evening, of the best kind.[329] Yesterday and

[328] "Commenced the ascent of the Ratón," recorded Lieutenant Emory on August 7, "which we reach with ease with our wagons; in about 2 miles observed the barometer, and determined the elevation to be 7,000 feet above the sea. From the summit we had a beautiful view of Pike's peak, the Wattah-Yah, and the chain of mountains running south. . . The descent is much more rapid than the ascent; and for the first few miles, through a valley of good burned grass and stagnant water, containing many beautiful flowers, specimens of which were collected. But presently you come to a place where a stream, a branch of the Canadian, has worked its way through the mountains, and the road has to ascend and then descend a rugged spur. Here is where the real difficulties commence, and the road, for three or four miles, is just passable for a wagon. Many of the train were broken in the passage. A few thousand dollars, judiciously expended here, would be an immense saving to the government, if the Santa Fé country is to be permanently occupied." *Ibid.*

[329] On account of the scarcity of provisions, the troops were now placed on half rations. As early as August 7, Lieutenant Emory wrote: "There may be mineral wealth in these mountains, but that must be left to some explorer

today a shower passed around, following the chains of mountains on each side of us. The private of company A lost last night was picked up by Captain McKissack and brought to camp in a wagon. We are again in [a] prairie several miles wide, it being the valley of Red river, and they say our road is now good all the way to Santa Fé. The grass at camp is tolerable, cured on the ground, but not very abundant. We have wood and plenty [of] water. The weather is mild and pleasant and healthy, and we enjoyed it this evening with some of our friends who called to see us. We found hops in great abundance through all the mountains; and there appears to be plenty [of] game near our camp, as the hunters bring it in after being out but a short time.

AUGUST 9. After drawing all the rice in camp, half rations of flour, two fat cattle for beef, six pounds [of] sugar, and thirteen pounds [of] coffee, for the battalion, we broke up camp by direction of the general to make a short march of eleven miles, our road the whole distance being level and good, with mountains on each hand. On our march we saw great numbers of the horned frogs of all sizes and colors. Today antelopes have been seen in great numbers, scarcely ever being out of our sight. Several in company complain of what we call "splint." The shin bone about half way up has a lump upon it, and the leaders are all more or less affected, the swelling sometimes extending to the ankle. It has been common and in several cases bad enough to keep us from marching.

---

not tied to the staff of an army, marching *for life* into an enemy's country. I say for life, for we are, from to-day, on half rations of bread; and although we have meat enough to prevent anything like immediate starvation, we are sufficiently hard-pressed to make it expedient to pounce on Santa Fé, and its stock of provisions, as soon as possible." *Ibid.* See also Turner, Journal, Aug. 9, 1846, MS., M.H.S.

Grass at camp is not only good but very abundant. But we have to dig a well about seven feet for water, which is brackish, and use weeds for fuel or send two or three miles to the mountains, which company A did. The ground is covered with efflorescences of salt, which shows more distinctly than [in] any place we have been. It is low [and] flat and looks like it was marshy in wet weather. Salt is scarce, as we drew but little, and we are forced to use that in the pork barrels. The valley down which we march is from four to ten miles in width, intersected by little streams from breaks in the mountains, along which the land appears good and productive; but the balance is poor, gravelly, and worthless. By direction of the general we took a road which is said to cut off several miles. He himself and the other troops took one leading into the mountains on our right, along which grass was said to be more abundant. As we lay in camp we could see the army *en route* three or four miles off at the foot of the mountain. Showers could be seen all day on one side or the other along the chain of mountains, but it was clear and dry with us. We reached camp about noon.

AUGUST 10. We left camp this morning about sunrise and marched ten miles (with a good road) over [the] prairie to [Vermejo] river, where we found Mr. Bent encamped. He informed us they were making preparations at Santa Fé to meet us, and it seemed to cheer men who had walked 1,000 miles for this purpose. The battalion appeared to think it hard we should go back without one [*i.e.*, a battle], and expressed great anxiety for it to take place. General Kearny's directions would have required us to camp here, but as it was early in the day we determined to go on to where we were to camp the next day, which we did and arrived in good season. Here we found Lieutenant DeCourcy,[330] who had been sent from Bent's Fort to spy the enemy's movements and learn all he could about them. He confirms the news of Mr. Bent that there is some prospect of a fight, and it puts all in a good humor, and we set about making preparations for such an event. The probable force of the Mexicans is variously estimated, but we think we can meet any that will be brought against us. The plain, or rather prairie, over which we have marched today is white with salt in many places – efflorescences, considerably more so than any we have yet seen.

Today we marched twenty-two miles and camped on the Ponil, a small stream with steep banks and willows along them, and here and there a few trees, some of which are about camp. The water is good, and it is three or four miles to the mountains. Before we had our tents pitched, General Kearny and the regulars came up and camped with us. Mr. DeCourcy informs us that there is a Mexican settlement within fifteen miles, which he visited, but all had fled. Taos is sixty miles west. One of our mules died this evening – cause of death unknown. Today I found some rock which would make pretty sets for rings or pins.

330 On July 31, 1846, Colonel Kearny, then at Bent's Fort, ordered Eugene Leitensdorfer, a Santa Fé trader, to proceed "in the direction of Taos" with two Pueblo Indians, in order to distribute copies of his proclamation of July 31 and make friendly overtures to the Pueblo. He directed that Leitensdorfer be accompanied by an escort of a subaltern and twenty men of Doniphan's regiment, and that the party be furnished with provisions for twelve days and with pack animals for the transportation of their baggage. Lieutenant James A. DeCourcy, of the Howard county company, with twenty mounted volunteers were chosen as the escort. After traveling to Taos, Leitensdorfer and DeCourcy's command rejoined the Army of the West on August 10 at Ponil creek. Adjutant Johnston recorded that Leitensdorfer "had not done much for us with the Pueblo Indians." Kearny, Special Orders No. 2, July 31, 1846, Letters Received, MSS., O.F.S., A.G.O.; Johnston, Journal, July 31, Aug. 10, 1846, *ibid.; Daily Union*, Oct. 22, 1846; *Weekly Reveille*, Sept. 14, 1846; *Glasgow News*, Sept. 3, 1846; Hughes, *Doniphan's Expedition*, 59-60.

AUGUST 11. Last night the dragoon guard captured eight prisoners near camp, supposed to be spies. Instead of horses or mules they rode donkeys, and were clustered around a camp fire as we marched through early in the morning, their animals quietly and submissively feeding amongst the horses. They presented anything else but a warlike appearance, and furnished a good deal of amusement to our men, as they passed by.[331] A few miles from camp the road forks, the right going to Taos, which we followed some distance and finding our error, struck across the plain and fell into the right road after crossing the Rayado. Our teams, being in [the] rear, were not delayed much, as we sent back a man to put them right.

Two miles from the Rayado we found a bold, pure spring of icy coldness gushing from the foot of a high mountain, where we stopped until our wagons came up, when it was found that Mr. Matthews of company A had died soon after leaving camp. He is the same [man] who had been lost at the foot of the Ratón.

After a march of fifteen miles we encamped, having to bury the dead, and in the meantime General Kearny and the regulars passed us. We found the grass very good, but [there was] a scarcity of wood and inconvenient to get. Mr. Matthews was buried in the evening with military honors, about a hundred yards west of the

[331] On August 10, Lieutenant Emory wrote: "Five Mexicans were captured by Bent's spy company, who had been sent out to reconnoitre us, with orders to retain all persons passing out of New Mexico. They were mounted on diminutive asses, and cut a ridiculous figure alongside of the thumping big men and horses of the 1st dragoons. Fitzpatrick, our guide, who seldom laughs, became almost convulsed when he turned his well-practised eye upon them." *Daily Union,* Oct. 22, 1846. During the night of August 10, according to Emory, five or six more Mexicans were captured; and on the following day Kearny assembled all of the prisoners together and made them an "admirable speech," declaring, among other things, that he was entering New Mexico as a friend of the people. *Ibid.*

spring on the right of the road. We slaughtered one of our beeves this evening, having plenty of spare time, and the camp again was warmed up with soup. I found plenty of volcanic remains all over the country, amongst which was light pumice stone. There is in all low, wet places a species of grass resembling cane and called "cane grass," which we also found on the Arkansas the other side of the fort and [in] all the intermediate country. It looks like cane but is neither so large nor strong. We have showers on the mountains as usual.

AUGUST 12. Here we struck the mountains again, and immediately after leaving camp, passed through a low gap, or rather over a low ridge, our road strewn with volcanic remains, many massive yet tolerably good. Soon after reaching the summit, we descended into a valley, which we followed a considerable distance, when we crossed into another, the dividing hill being low; and [we] continued on in this way to the Ocate, generally pursuing the valleys (which are prairie) with good roads. We had one short and steep hill leading to a table-land which extends to the Ocate. Just before reaching this stream, we suddenly came upon a deep canyon with rocky and precipitous sides, where we stopped and searched for water but could find none, and [then] went on and about noon found plenty of good water, and General Kearny and all the regulars just leaving camp. Not wishing to be left behind (though the ground was good for camping), after a short stay and replenishing our canteens, we went on, though told that it was a long way to water or any place [where] we could camp. Having already marched nineteen miles, we deliberated about going on, when it was determined we should, Lieutenant Irvine being left to see that our teams were brought up. After leaving the Ocate, we passed over a prairie country diversified with hills and valleys, the low places containing some grass, which the regulars permitted their horses to crop, and the summits rounding off like the swells on the plains.

At sundown we arrived at some holes in the prairie, where we found the general and regulars encamped, the company very much fatigued by the long march, and many falling back upon the wagons. We suffered for water, having marched nineteen miles from the Ocate without finding any, and the road being dusty increased our suffering for the want of it. Having marched thirty-eight miles, we were glad to camp, although we had to go a mile for wood, which we carried and had ready at camp to cook with as soon as our teams came up. Walter being with the teams, the first lieutenant and myself provided for our mess. Just after dark a shower came up and caught us without tents, our wagons not having arrived. And we were all both wet and cold, having nothing to protect us, many not having even their coats, as the day was warm. About eleven o'clock our teams came up, having considerable difficulty to get in, in the darkness, and some having wandered a mile or two from the road. About two o'clock we had such things as we could cook to eat, and then, wet and cold as we were, lay down to take a little rest, which was much needed by all. We are encamped in grass knee-high, and our animals bid fair to do well after the long march of today, which has worsted them a good deal. Water is also abundant and of good quality. In the evening, just before reaching camp, we saw great numbers of antelopes alarmed by the general and regulars who preceded us. At one time we counted seventy or eighty skimming across the prairie to the timber on a high ridge not far off, their curiosity often prompting them to stop and look at us.

AUGUST 13. Notwithstanding the fatigues and hardships of yesterday our company was pretty well this morning after getting a warm breakfast, and General Kearny gave orders for us to remain in camp until noon, and then to march to the Mora, about eight miles. While we lay in camp, the weather was sunny and pleasant, and everything wet was dried. As we are in the enemy's country and chances about even that we shall have a fight, it becomes necessary for us to be on our guard; so an inspection of arms was ordered, and all in camp were soon busy preparing for it before we break up camp. Colonel Doniphan and regiment and the artillery camped at the Ocate last night, and came in sight of us just after we started on our march. When about a mile from camp a thunderstorm came up, and we were wet through and had to march the balance of the day through mud and water. We were at camp some time before our wagons, being delayed and retarded by the mud. A Mexican officer was brought in as a prisoner today and is still in charge of a guard. But the general has released all others, some of whom remain about our camp, seeming to prefer it to any other place. We passed two or three ranches [332] today, the first settlements we have seen,

[332] "A few minutes brought us to the first settlement we had yet seen in 775 miles," recorded Emory on August 13. "The first object I saw, was a pretty Mexican woman, with clean white stockings, who came to me, very cordially shook hands, and asked for tobacco. Fitzpatrick said I was singled out for my large red whiskers; but I was at the head of the party, and *that* was the reason of the honor done me. The next house, and out popped a live American, and soon after, his wife. This was Mr. Boney [Bonney], who has lived here for some time, owns a large number of cattle and horses, which he keeps in defiance of wolves, Indians, and Mexicans. He is a perfect specimen of a generous, open-hearted adventurer, and is in appearance what I have supposed Daniel Boon[e] to have been. He drove his herd of cattle into camp, and picked out the largest and fattest, which he presented to the army. Below, about 2 miles, at the junction of the Moro [Mora] and Sapilla [Sapello], is another American – Mr. Yells [Wells], of North Carolina. He has

miserable-looking places for tenements. Some of the men purchased a pig at the first and brought it to camp in the wagon, others got bread and cheese and milk. It is a new thing to hear a pig squeal in our camp, and [it] looked quite natural. We saw a great many horses and cattle feeding on the prairie, some of which the commissary purchased for the army. We hear of the enemy being in front about twenty miles, which has given new life to all, but we can hear nothing certain as to their numbers or intentions. Colonel Doniphan camps where we did last night. This morning we left a mule at camp unable to get up, having given out completely. Our camp is on the bank of the Mora, after we struck it a second time.

AUGUST 14. We left the Mora by order at seven o'clock, in rear of the regulars and before their train of baggage wagons, and continued in this way about ten miles through the prairie, when a messenger (a lieutenant and three dragoons) from Armijo met the general with a letter,[333] in which he informed us that he would give us battle at the village of [Las] Vegas, eight or nine miles ahead. The general halted in a low place on the high prairie ridge. And we lay by several hours in the hot sun waiting for the artillery and other troops, which

---

been here but six months, and from his gay dress might have been taken for a sergeant of dragoons, with his blue pantaloons with broad gold stripes on the sides, and his jacket trimmed with lace. I bought butter of him at 4 bits the pound." *Ibid.* See also *Southwest Historical Series,* I, 74.

[333] This letter was Armijo's reply to Kearny's communication of August 1, which had been delivered by Captain Cooke. The Mexican dragoons, according to one of Kearny's officers, were "dressed in a roundabout and pants of light blue cloth, similar to our own dragoons, with a red stripe down the outer seam of the pants. They all wore large Mexican hats; there was a Lieutenant, Sergeant and two privates. They rode small horses. The Lieutenant had a sabre; the others were armed with carbines and lances. They made a very respectable appearance, but such soldiers cannot fight U.S. Dragoons." *Daily Missouri Republican,* Sept. 24, 1846.

finally came up, and we continued our march in the same order, the country being prairie all the way. As we approached [Las] Vegas, we saw large flocks of sheep and goats amongst the hills, and all the population out to see the army come up. As we are now all together for the first time, we make an imposing show, enough to alarm people less timid than the Mexicans. And this, no doubt, was partly the general's object in waiting for us, expecting the news would be spread abroad that our force was greater than it really is, the number of teams adding greatly to the display. We descended a bluff, rocky and tolerably steep, into the bottom, which we followed down a mile and a half and encamped on the creek, with grass plentiful and the running water brackish.

Many Spaniards showed themselves both about town[334] and wherever they could have a good view of us, and as soon as we encamped they were all amongst us with green corn, cheese, chickens, etc., to sell, which found a ready market.[335] We appear to have taken the country by surprise. Such a thing as our army, so well provided with everything, they never dreamed of; and if they expected invasion at all, they thought it would be by such a force as the Texan-Santa Fé expedition. They look with amazement at our arms and accoutrements, our horses and equipage, our provision trains, baggage and ammunition wagons, and show a disposi-

334 Las Vegas. One of Kearny's officers wrote: "From white men, who reside here, we learn, that the Governor exercises the most despotic sway over the common people, aided by the priests. . . What a change will be effected among these people when they are emancipated. If Gen. Kearney succeeds in this expedition without inflicting any pain, he will be the greatest man that has ever been in New Mexico." *Ibid.*

335 Sergeant William Clark Kennerly, of company A, light artillery, Missouri volunteers, stated: "The poorer natives were glad to trade with us and seemed to bear no malice for Kearny's conquest." William C. Kennerly, Recollections of our War with Mexico, MS., M.H.S.

tion to submit quietly to a fate which they cannot avert. An order was issued that no injury should be done either to the persons or property of individuals, and in the evening the general complimented our battalion as being the only troops that had obeyed it.[336] Armijo's messenger informed us that Captain Cooke started back on his return yesterday morning. We, of course, have not learned the result of his mission.

The country has become more open, but is poor and rocky except immediately on the streams, where we find corn, wheat, and other products growing. No portion is cultivated except the bottoms, and they are constantly watered, the water being carried by trenches all over them and as high on the hillsides as possible. The town presents a ruinous and dilapidated appearance,[337] and no doubt has seen better days, the incursions and marauding of the Indians having completely destroyed any enterprise the people ever had. Their flocks are permitted to degenerate, their houses to molder, and their farms to go to decay, having no protection against the Comanche, the Ute, the Pawnee, and other tribes who frequently make inroads upon them, drive off their stock, and carry their women into captivity.

Today we marched about eighteen miles, and our camp is on a pretty, green grass bottom, just below town,

336 An officer wrote that Kearny had given strict orders to keep the army's animals out of the extensive fields of corn and wheat; "yet some did get in, and some damage was done. The Gen. told the Alcalde that he had used every precaution to prevent 'any interference with their crops,' yet 'they had sustained some loss.' He told him to examine the fields and ascertain what the damage was to each man, to send him a statement of it to Santa Fé, and that full compensation should be paid them. They seemed delighted with this exemplification of equal justice – a thing not dreamed of in New Mexico, under the rule of Armijo." *Daily Missouri Republican,* Sept. 24, 1846.

337 "The village, at a short distance, looked like an extensive brick-kiln," recorded Emory on August 14. *Daily Union,* Oct. 22, 1846.

which is in full view. Armijo is not here, and we have no further news of him, the whole ending in braggadocio, as Mexican threats or promises usually do. We have no timber except pine and cedar, and no great abundance of them convenient to camp. All are in fine spirits at once more reaching the habitations of mankind, where we can procure a few articles to break the monotonous life we have led for nearly two months, and at the prospect of a speedy settlement of all our hopes and fears.

AUGUST 15. We left camp just after sunrise and entered the town of [Las] Vegas, where General Kearny assembled the citizens and after addressing them in a long speech, administered the oath of allegiance to the principal citizens. The people were clad in the peculiar custom of the country, both the men and women of a shabby appearance, and contrasted strongly with our Anglo-saxon dress, manners, complexion, and general looks. Instead of the black-eyed Spanish woman, we found ourselves amongst a swarthy, copper-colored, half-Indian race, the most of them not much better-looking than the Indian squaws upon our frontier. All were much disappointed at the poor appearance of the people, as well as [at] the sterility of the soil generally, and began to realize fully the stories we had heard of the low condition, ignorance, and want of spirit which was characteristic of the country.

After the general had concluded his conference, we were formed in order of battle immediately in rear of town, the regulars in front, the infantry next, it being reported that the enemy was posted in a gap in the mountains two miles ahead. After marching in this order about a mile, the regulars were ordered to charge through the gap, where the pass is very narrow, and the infantry to scale the mountain, a high, steep, and rocky eminence, which they soon accomplished with great zeal, expecting a fight every moment. But when they reached the top, there was no enemy there, nor had there been, the whole being intended to try the troops. When the regulars in the valley below first saw us, they thought we were Mexicans fleeing, but they soon found their mistake; and in the meantime we descended and had a good laugh over the sham fight. Captain Stevenson's [338] company of mounted volunteers were dismounted by General Kearny, and crossed with us, but not being accustomed to the infantry service, could not get over such a place so well as we did. Had the Mexicans really been there and held on to the place, they could have given us a good deal of trouble, as nature has made it a strong place.

After halting awhile to rest in a pretty grove of pines and cedars, after the race across the mountain, the whole army took up its line of march, very much disappointed because there had been no fight. We have left the prairies and entered upon a broken and timbered country, the soil in the hills and mountains having a red color and in some places a Spanish brown, which gives it a singular and poor appearance. The timber is all pine or cedar, and the soil filled with gypsum, or, as it is most commonly called, isinglass, which glitters in the sun like diamonds or precious metals. All kinds of rock are filled with it – flint, sandstone, etc.; and, of course, they are of

[338] John Dunlap Stevenson was born in Staunton, Virginia, June 8, 1821. Migrating to Missouri during the early forties, he settled at Union, Franklin county, in 1843. He was captain of company E (Franklin county), Missouri mounted volunteers, who were mustered into service at Fort Leavenworth, June 27, 1846. He served with distinction in the Union army during the Civil war, and died in St. Louis, January 22, 1897. Virginia Stevenson, Life of John Dunlap Stevenson, Stevenson MSS., M.H.S.; Heitman, *Historical Register*, I, 923; Connelley, *Doniphan's Expedition*, 135-136, 550.

every shade and color – striped, speckled, black, white, etc. – and many very pretty and new to men who have never been out here. Captain Stevenson with his company marched a few miles with us, but not being able to withstand the fatigues as men inured to it as we were, fell back and remounted their horses by permission from the general, glad to escape from the foot service. Santa Fé is about fifty miles distant, and we have large flocks of sheep and goats at all the ranches. We also procured cheese from goat's milk, which they make in great abundance, and which I found good. But as they are too dirty to suit our taste, we have denied ourselves this luxury, except when hungry enough to eat anything. Today we also procured green corn, onions, and mutton, all good and palatable. Captain Cooke [339] met us at a little town [340] five miles from camp, and from his account we despair of getting a fight. The people through this section appear well disposed and generally to have remained at home.

---

[339] Philip St. George Cooke was born at or near Leesburg, Virginia, June 13, 1809. After graduating from the United States Military academy in 1827, he was promoted in the army to second lieutenant in the Sixth infantry. On March 4, 1833, he was transferred to the First dragoons with the rank of first lieutenant, and on May 31, 1835, was commissioned captain. He had extensive military experience on the frontier. In 1829 he was a member of Major Riley's detachment of infantry which escorted Santa Fé traders from western Missouri to the Arkansas river and return; in 1843 he was in command of a similar expedition, which disarmed Snively's band of Texans; and in 1845 he served in Kearny's expedition to the South pass. Meanwhile, he had been stationed at various western posts, such as Jefferson Barracks, Fort Crawford, Fort Snelling, Fort Leavenworth, Fort Gibson, and Fort Wayne. Not long after reaching Santa Fé in 1846, he was placed in command of the Mormon battalion, which opened a wagon road through southern New Mexico during the latter part of that year. He died at Detroit, March 20, 1895. A more extensive biography of Cooke will be given in volume VII of this series. Cullum, *Biographical Register,* I, 317-318; "A Journal of the Santa Fé Trail" (William E. Connelley, ed.), *Mississippi Valley Historical Review,* XII, 73; Thomas M. Spaulding, "Philip St. George Cooke," *Dictionary of American Biography,* IV, 389.

[340] Tecolote. Cooke, *Conquest of New Mexico and California,* 34.

Today we marched seventeen miles and camped at the San Miguel spring,[341] with wood and water plentiful and grass sufficient. Two horses gave out today and were left on the road. We are now fairly in the settlements, villages and ranches being found wherever there is water.

AUGUST 16. This morning we left camp in good spirits and in a few hours reached San Miguel, where the general addressed the people in a speech which had great effect. He told them that he came not to make war except on those who resisted, that he came to claim the country as a portion of Texas, and that all who submitted should be protected in their persons and property; that his force was sufficient for any purpose, and that other troops were following him; that the people should be protected against the Indians; and that under his government the rich and poor would fare alike, etc.; after which he administered the oath of allegiance to the alcalde and dismissed them, directing that the same laws should govern them for the present, but in the name of the United States.[342]

---

[341] This is an error. The army camped at Bernal spring, or Ojo Bernal, a short distance east of San Miguel. *Ibid.;* Johnston, Journal, Aug. 15, 1846, Letters Received, MSS., O.F.S., A.G.O.

[342] "Marched to San Miguel," recorded Lieutenant Emory on August 16, "where the general assembled the people, and gave them much the same harangue as at the Vegos [Las Vegas]; but in swearing the poor old alcalde there was great difficulty. His honor hesitated, faltered, looked at the priest, who held down his head and refused to respond to his inquiring looks. But it had to go down; the general was pertinacious. As we were ascending the ladder, the priest – a famous man in this country; famous for his love of cards, women, and wine – stopped the general to engage him in a discussion on the merits of the question of invasion. He said a great deal that was exceedingly silly and out of place. The general told him so very sharply before all his people. Sinner, as he is, his hold upon his flock is firm and unyielding. The repartee of the general floored him completely, and made some of his poor deluded flock look aghast. He had previously invited the general to his quarters. Being in our route, we halted. The general told him that he and

The town is not much better-looking than those we came through, but is a little larger, the interior of the houses presenting rather a neater appearance and more comfort. Except the narrow strip immediately on the creek, the country is too poor for anything except sheep, goats, and asses. The people bring in quantities of provisions, which the men readily purchase as they are on half rations, and we now have abundance to eat. The system of irrigation prevails throughout all New Mexico, the climate being too dry without it to produce corn and the little they raise. They take great pains to conduct the water over every place possible to carry it, and by opening the trenches can completely flood their patches and fields.

After a considerable stay the bugles sounded, and we went on and camped off the road (grass being scarce) at least half a mile from water, having marched about eighteen miles. When our teams came up, another man of company A was found dead in a wagon. There is considerable excitement in camp about Armijo, some thinking he will yet give us a fight. We received intelligence today that General Kearny has received his commission, as such, having heretofore acted as colonel. We now call him by his proper title. It came with some officers by way of Bent's Fort.[343] The corn so far has been low and

all his brotherhood were laboring under a great mistake with *regard* to the *intentions* of the American government in respect to his religion; that there was not the least *intention* of disturbing it, or any of its rights and privileges; but if he found any of them stirring up the people to rebellion, he would not let the priest's robe stand between the offender and the rope. This, by the way, he mentioned in his speech to the people, while the priest was made to stand by him in full view of the mass below. His reverence saw the sort of person he had to deal with, and disclaimed any mischievous intentions. This through, he displayed his Taos brandy, which we drank. The general cracked several jokes with him, and finally took leave, by a cordial embrace and mutual assurance of friendship." *Daily Union,* Oct. 23, 1846.

[343] See footnote 186. Early on the morning of August 15, Kearny received

not very productive, but we have a field near our camp this evening which would be no discredit to "the States." The guard left an ox on the road today, unable to bring him up. Our camp is around the base of a hill, which is prairie half way up, the other portion being a pretty grove of pines and cedars. A picket guard from the infantry was ordered to be posted on its summit, and I, as officer of the day, went up after night to examine the ground and attend to it. There I had a most lovely sight, the camp fires extending in the shape of a half-moon around its base at least a mile and a half, the whole army reposing in perfect security, and the busy hum of voices coming up as if from a crowded city.

I purchased some pine nuts today, the first we have seen, and found them oily and not unpalatable. The country is very broken and is nothing but a succession of ridges or hills, our road generally being on top of them and extremely good considering the general topography and aspect of the country. A chain of mountains is on our left, around which we have marched, its sides strongly marked by the different colored soils, red or a Spanish brown prevailing. The strata of rock in them are almost invariably horizontal, divided by seams deeply colored and apparently mineral at a distance, which makes them look in some places as if the pencil of art had been at work upon them. Occasionally we pass through small glades or prairie, the grass thin and dry, but most usually our road is through pine forests containing several varieties of this tree.

AUGUST 17. The private of company A who died yes-

---

his brigadier-general's commission from Major Thomas Swords, chief quartermaster of the Army of the West, and Lieutenant Jeremy F. Gilmer, chief engineer of the Army of the West, who had just arrived from Fort Leavenworth. Turner, Diary, Aug. 15, 1846, MS., M.H.S.; *House Ex. Docs.*, 30 cong., 1 sess., no. 41, p. 27; Cullum, *Biographical Register*, I, 350, 574-575.

terday, whose name was Euton, was buried this morning before breakfast near camp with military honors. After a march of fourteen miles over a country similar to that passed over yesterday, we came to the old deserted Indian town of Pecos, and turning to the right went down to the creek or river of Pecos and encamped on the hillside immediately adjoining the bottom. Last night the son of General Salazar was taken prisoner [while] approaching camp, and is still detained. His fate depends upon the truth of his story, which is that Armijo has fled and his troops [have] been disbanded.[344] We have heard this before, but Spanish treachery is so well understood that we have not given it full credit until this evening. Spaniards have been coming in and meeting us all day, and since noon all doubts have been removed, and from the general down its truth is recognized. The war in this section has ended, all submitting to our authority, and it is hard to tell whether the news has been joyously or sorrowfully received. They generally appear well satisfied, and Armijo gets curses on all sides for cowardice and his tyranny. It is said he has gone to Albuquerque.[345] The road is open to Santa Fé, and we shall camp there tomorrow night. . .

[344] On August 17 one of Kearny's officers wrote: "Our picket guard took a prisoner, the son of the noted Salazar, well remembered by the Texian prisoners for his cruelties to them. He stated that the Mexican army had left the Cannon [Cañon] and gone home. The Gen. told him he would keep him a prisoner, and if he found that he had told him falsely, he would hang him. We soon met others from Santa Fé, who congratulated the Gen. on his arrival in the country, and their deliverance from the tyrannical rule of Armijo." *Daily Missouri Republican,* Sept. 24, 1846. See also Connelley, *Doniphan's Expedition,* 60.

[345] Governor Armijo, accompanied by sixty men, fled southward by way of Galisteo, and by August 20 reached the town of El Manzano, about forty miles southeast of Albuquerque. On that date he wrote the following letter to Colonel Mauricio Ugarte, comandante general of the department of Chihuahua, who was then marching to the aid of New Mexico: "At ten o'clock

It sprinkled rain today, and from appearances has evidently rained hard lately. Thunderstorms continue to go round, following the mountains. This morning, by order of Captain McKissack, we left four head of horses at camp, and one ox was left on the road, the guard not being able to get him to camp. We spent a pleasant evening with W. P. Hall, H. Wilkinson, and Benjamin Bean, with whom we talked until a late hour about home, friends, the march, our troubles, etc. The use of a meadow and other grounds was purchased, and all of our stock put upon good grass.

AUGUST 18. A general order [346] was read at the head of the company declaring the country annexed to the United States as a part of Texas, [and] prohibiting any bad treatment of the citizens or molesting them or injuring their property in any way; so that after a march of 1,000 miles we still find ourselves in the limits of our widely-extended Union. It rained very hard last night.

on the evening of the 19th instant I received your official letter of the 13th, dated at Los Alamitos. I am filled with joy to see the enthusiasm with which you and your subordinates have offered to aid me and defend this part of the Mexican Republic; but I am very sorry to inform you of the circumstances in which I find myself. At present I am in the town of El Manzano, accompanied by a company of sixty men, including officers and troops from this department and from other regions – among them, the worthy and loyal Brevet Captain Don Antonio Sena, also Brevet Lieutenant-colonel Don Francisco Martínez, and Lieutenant Don Gaspar Ortiz. These are the only troops of this department of New Mexico who have been willing to follow me until we meet with troops of the supreme government. All the other soldiers have turned against me under the pretext which I will make known to you when I see you. With respect to the people in this department, I believe that in general they are pro-American. For these reasons I have had to retreat from the capital of Santa Fé, where the United States flag is at present raised. The number of troops found in the said capital does not exceed three thousand, nor is it less than twenty-five hundred. I know this beyond question. By tomorrow I shall have the pleasure of arriving where you are and shall make known to you the details and motives I had for retreating from the territory." Armijo to Ugarte, Aug. 20, 1846, *Diario Oficial,* Sept. 10, 1846.

[346] Order No. 13, Aug. 17, 1846. See appendix.

This morning [it] is cloudy and raining a little occasionally. I left camp early, before the company, and came by Pecos, where I wandered amongst its ruins until forced to leave and join them [*i.e.,* the company] on their march. With great reluctance I left a place venerable from its antiquity and rendered interesting by tradition, as I had not had sufficient time to examine all that remains of this place, once the abode of a dense population, now a desert.

In about four miles we came to the mouth of San Miguel pass, a deep canyon with lofty mountains on each side and [with] barely room enough generally for a single wagon, large rocks [being] heaped in confusion all along each side of our way. We passed on through it, a distance of seven or eight miles, and at the west end found some timber cut down and a few attempts made at fortification, which the enemy had abandoned the day before. It is a place of great natural strength and could easily be defended by a few men against a whole army, as we have to pass down the canyon, with timber and rock all around affording a natural breastwork. Cannon at the mouth can sweep the whole road, as it is almost impossible even for infantry to ascend the precipitous sides of the mountain and attack in the rear, the only way to dislodge troops determined to hold their ground. After passing through and looking back, we were not more astonished that it should be abandoned than glad that the Mexicans who were here yesterday had fled in confusion and disorder and returned to their homes to await events. From information obtained in various ways, it is pretty well ascertained that there were about 3,000 men (not soldiers) at the pass day before yesterday, and that they disagreed amongst themselves, had a fight, and broke up in a row, Armijo with the artillery and some regulars taking the road to the south.[347]

We continued to march rapidly on to Santa Fé, all anxious to see a place about which they had heard so much, our road being over a broken country, poor, and covered with pines. We saw large flocks of sheep and goats in the mountains, which we pass at a low gap, and met several of our friends from Santa Fé, some who ventured in yesterday. After a long march of twenty-

[347] Writing from Fray Cristóbal on August 23, 1846, Colonel Mauricio Ugarte, in command of a detachment of Chihuahua troops marching to the aid of Armijo, made the following report of conditions in New Mexico during the invasion of the Army of the West: "Report of the most notable events which took place in New Mexico since the arrival of the invading army. On August 14, General Armijo had gathered about two thousand men of all classes of people at the entrance to Pecos canyon, among whom were two hundred and sixty regulars and seven pieces of artillery with two carts of park. On the 15th a dispute arose between the chiefs of the auxiliary forces and the general over various opinions respecting the defense. The result of this was the disbanding of the forces to their homes and the retirement of the general with the soldiers and artillery to Galisteo. The *presidiales* abandoned him, and he, after spiking seven cannon, entered the Sierra del Manzano with only sixty men of the Second and Third regular cavalry. The great majority of the people of New Mexico attribute the loss of the department to General Armijo and vice versa. On the 16th the army occupied Santa Fé. It is commanded by Colonel Karene [Kearny], and comprises three thousand men and sixteen pieces of artillery. Six days later the caravan will arrive, which contains a million pesos in merchandise, escorted by one thousand men, including one hundred Zuaves. The American flag was raised in the plaza of Santa Fé. James Magoffin is the governor. After the installation of the government, detachments of from two to three hundred men left by different routes; it is not known with what object. The clergy, all the political and judicial authorities, and the troops who went over to them solemnly swore obedience to the new government. Henry Connelly wrote a letter to General Armijo inviting him in the name of the new government to return to Santa Fé to occupy his [former] position, offering him all sorts of guarantees, which he refused. It seems that a detachment of six hundred dragoons is coming to establish itself in the last settlement to prevent all persons from leaving the department. The usurpers spread propaganda through all the towns that they will respect lives and property, customs and religion, and finally that there will be an era of happiness. From the village of Tomé up, there is intolerable espionage; not a word can be spoken against the Americans." Ugarte to Cuilty, Aug. 23, 1846, *Diario Oficial,* Sept. 10, 1846.

eight miles we found ourselves on the high ground overlooking town, where we had to wait at least one hour for the artillery to come up. They finally made their appearance; and [with] the regulars in front [and] the infantry next we proceeded to take possession of it [*i.e.*, Santa Fé], the artillery remaining on top of the hill. But a few citizens showed themselves, many having fled to the mountains; and we marched into the plaza and ran up the Stars and Stripes from the top of the Palace, the artillery firing a salute of thirteen guns, when we all returned to the hill and encamped, it being dark by this time. No person came out to meet us, no troops were embodied, and there was not the least show or appearance of resistance in any way.[348]

The appearance of [the] town was shabby, without either taste or a show of wealth – no gardens that deserved the name, the fields all unenclosed, the people poor and beggarly, and nothing to pay us for our long

348 Lieutenant Elliott, of the Laclede Rangers, described the army's entrance into Santa Fé: "Our march into the city, I have already told you, was extremely warlike, with drawn sabres and daggers in every look. From around corners, men, with surly countenances and downcast looks, regarded us with watchfulness, if not terror; and black eyes looked through latticed windows at our column of cavaliers, some gleaming with pleasure, and others filled with tears. Strange, indeed, must have been the feelings of the citizens, when an invading army was thus entering their home – themselves used only to look upon soldiers as plagues, sent to eat out their substance, burn, ravage and destroy – all the future of their destiny vague and uncertain – their new rulers strangers to their manners, language and habits, and, as they had been taught to believe, enemies to the only religion they have ever known. It was humiliating, too, to find their city thus entered, without a gun having been fired in its defence; and we thought humbled, mortified pride, was indicated in the expression of more than one swarthy face. As the American flag was raised, and the cannon boomed its glorious national salute from the hill, the pent-up emotions of many of the women could be suppressed no longer, and a sigh of commiseration, even for causeless distress, escaped from many a manly breast, as the wail of grief arose above the din of our horses' tread, and reached our ears from the depth of the gloomy-looking buildings on every hand." *Weekly Reveille,* Sept. 28, 1846.

march. The valley is narrow and the only cultivated ground, and that is made to produce as much by irrigation as [by] its natural fertility. To add to our disappointments, our teams are all behind, and we have a fair prospect of going without supper and of having no blankets. And as the night is dark and timber a long way off, our situation is far from being comfortable. The Mexicans bring a few things to camp, but as yet they are shy and not prepared to supply the wants of 1,800 men and as many horses. There is no grass near us, and our stock is badly provided for, the mounted men grumbling a good deal. Our ox team finally came an hour or two in the night, and we made out to get along. The army generally is in the same fix we are, but all bear it cheerfully as there is now some prospect of easier times and better fare. The roads have been muddy nearly all day, which made walking laborious; and the company are very much fatigued, many scarcely able to get along. Water is inconvenient, and we have to burn the tops of green cedars to keep a fire.

ENCAMPED IN SANTA FÉ

ENCAMPED IN SANTA FÉ

General Remarks. Santa Fé, August 18. On the morning of August 18, 1846, Santa Fé was declared by General Kearny to be a part and parcel of the United States, and an order to that effect was read to the army; and in the evening of the same day it made its entrance into town after a long march.

We learned that most of the citizens had fled (a great many to the mountains), expecting harsh treatment if they remained. Yet we found a considerable population, and a town scattered over a large area, of a foreign aspect in all respects, and, in its external appearance, not very inviting from the high ground on the Independence road. The houses are all, without exception, of adobe – rough, and of a dingy, clay color, which gives them more the appearance of brickkilns than houses. Some of the streets are tolerably wide and roomy but they are generally narrow and not always straight. Corn, wheat, and other products of the country are found growing throughout its entire limits; and a stranger is very apt to imagine it smaller than it really is, extending, as it does, a considerable distance up and down the creek, and covering the entire bottom, at its widest place nearly a mile wide. It is exceedingly well provided with water, which is conveyed in trenches all over the place to irrigate their fields and gardens. Besides, [there are] several large, fine springs in the very heart of it.

The interior of their houses is neat but generally almost destitute of the kind of furniture usually found in American dwellings. Instead of chairs they have a mud wall elevated the proper height above the floor [and] covered with a carpet or blankets of native manufacture for a seat, forming a kind of settee. The floors are dirt, the wealthy only using carpets. The fireplaces are small and illy-contrived, and the ceilings high, the only timber about it [*i.e.,* the house] being the doors and windows (which are as few as possible), and the joist to support the roof, which is flat, covered with dirt three or four feet, and almost invariably with a parapet wall all around. The people lack that neatness and show of wealth, that taste and refinement which we left in "the States," a few only having a genteel appearance. The women are bold and not overloaded with modesty; nor are there at this time many pretty ones to be seen. . .

The people are civil and well disposed, not being able to resist the force brought against them. But they are shy and far from receiving us generally as deliverers, though the leading and principal men so regard us and no doubt will influence the balance and bring them to the same state of mind. They are very much exasperated at Armijo and threaten his life if he returns, now that they can find protection against his tyranny.

The Pueblo Indians, a fine, hardy, robust-looking set, with bows and arrows and Indian dress, have been in to tender their submission. They have a tradition amongst them that their deliverers from Spanish oppression would come from the east, and our army is looked upon by them as fulfilling a prophecy long hoped and expected. Mr. Gregg, in his book, speaks of such a tradition,[349] and it no doubt exists and is calculated to make them our warmest friends.

Instead of wagons the people have clumsy truck

[349] Gregg, *op. cit.,* XX, 57.

wheels made out of large cottonwoods, so rude and unwieldy that they are but little used, mules and asses answering all purposes of transportation, on which they pack everything. To our camp they bring wood, green corn blades, meats, etc., packed on the back of one of these diminutive and submissive little things. This affords a good deal of amusement to the men, as they generally return astride of their haunches, their feet dangling, and *el burro* answering to the licks of a stick, as they have no bridles or anything except the same weapon, which both drives and guides them. Cattle are scarce about town, and the few hogs we have seen are little, runty things, picketed out, and led to water as they require it. The products are corn, wheat, and a few vegetables. The corn is small but bears an ear of respectable size, the grain generally colored and speckled such as is sometimes found in "the States," but more particularly amongst the Indians. Many call it "squaw corn." The wheat is short but well headed and of good weight, the bread being sweet and white when bolted. Unbolted meal is most commonly used, which is said to be healthy but is not very palatable to men who have been used to American flour. The corn is very green, and harvest [has] not yet begun. They bring roasting ears to camp.

There are several churches, [constructed] of the same material [as] the other houses are, the principal one being east of the plaza. They make but a sorry showing to men who have just left a country containing so many edifices of great beauty and costly finish dedicated to the worship of God. To make amends for this, they are loaded with bells, as many as five being on the main church.

AUGUST 19.[350] Today we remained in camp outside of

[350] The second section of Gibson's journal, which covers the period from

town, immediately on the brow of the hill, the mounted volunteers on the right, the regulars in the center, the artillery on the left, and the infantry, being nearer town than the others, in front of the regulars. As only a few of the teams reached camp last night, many having given out on the road, the morning was spent in procuring something to eat, the men having had nothing since yesterday morning except what they could procure from the Mexicans, who are badly provided to feed a starving army. It was afternoon before the teams came up, having camped twelve or thirteen miles out, and the men suffered some privations, having neither tents nor blankets last night. Some complaints were made, but after their hunger was appeased they were jolly and satisfied, all being well again. At nine o'clock General Kearny made a speech to the people and took possession of the government offices, making such appointments as were necessary, the officers taking the oath of allegiance to the United States and entering upon the discharge of their duties. The general established his quarters in the Palace, occupying, together with the government offices, the entire block of buildings on the west side of the plaza. It has been determined to erect a flagstaff in the center of the plaza, to bear the Stars and Stripes as the emblem of our dominion, and a detail of two men from company B was ordered and furnished to assist in its construction.

The dragoons were moved from camp to quarters in town near the plaza, and Lieutenant Eastin [351] and my-

August 19 to November 29, 1846, is entitled: "Journal of Proceedings at Santa Fé in the Summer and Fall of 1846 by Geo. R. Gibson, Second Lieutenant Infantry Company B Mo. Vol. from the occupation by Genl. Kearny down to November 29, 1847[6], with remarks on the country, its inhabitants, productions, customs, and manners, climate, etc."

[351] Lucian J. Eastin, of Jefferson City, Missouri, was a second lieutenant

self were sent to see the general in relation to ours, when he told us to send down Captain Angney to select such as would suit and report to the quartermaster. The general was in fine spirits, took us through the Palace, and introduced us to the ballroom, as well as [to] the private chamber of the governor's lady. The ballroom is a large, long room, with a dirt floor, and the panels of the interior doors [are] made of bull or buffalo hide, tanned and painted so as to resemble wood. There are various other rooms besides the antechamber, which has the lady's private apartment at one end and the ballroom immediately back of it and parallel to it. The office of [the] Secretary of State is on the east side, and the guard room and prison on the west end of the block. The rear contains kitchens, bake ovens, and ground for a garden, the whole being roomy, convenient, and suitable to the dignity of a governor in New Mexico. Some parts of the building appear to be made bomb proof or so to be intended, but it would hardly be a defense against American arms. Many parts of the building are in a state of decay and have been neglected for some time, especially the apartments near the *calabozo*. The walls are all thick, and it contains as few doors and windows as possible. A delegation of Pueblo Indians waited upon the general while we were present, others having been in before. There were ten or twelve, a fine-looking set of men, who formed a semicircle around him, Mr. Robidou interpreting. They appeared satisfied and pleased at their reception.

The town is crowded with Indians and soldiers, and the grogshops do a thriving business. Heavy showers of rain can be seen following the different mountain chains,

in the Cole county infantry. *Jefferson Inquirer,* Nov. 17, 1846; Connelley, *Doniphan's Expedition,* 566.

but we have none here. Those on the east are close, as we camp at the base of the mountain. A few nectarines and a good many melons were brought to camp today, besides green corn, milk, bread, nuts, blankets, wood, etc., in abundance. We make quite a respectable showing since our wagons came, and we have stretched our tents all in a line in view of town. The nights are pleasantly cool, and through the day it is warm but not oppressive. It is reported that Armijo is not far from town and that he will surrender in a few days, but it does not receive much credit. No movement has been made against him and most probably will not be.

AUGUST 20. I spent the morning writing letters; and our two captains went to look for quarters, and when they returned we were ordered to be ready to move into them at three o'clock. Just as we were ready to do so, a severe thunderstorm came up, and all in camp except ourselves were wet, and we were delayed some time. It cleared off finally, the sun shining out, and we broke up camp and marched into town, where we have quarters clean, neat, and comfortable but too small for the number of men. They are a few doors from the southeast corner of the plaza, in the very heart of the place and on the street leading from it [*i.e.,* the plaza] to the principal church. The messes have all been broken up, and cooks for the whole company detailed. McCormack and Curry [352] are detailed to assist in getting out the timbers and erecting the flagstaff. Company A had none. The principal priest returned this evening, having fled to the mountains. He is a fat, jolly fellow, bets high at monte, loves good liquor, and attends all the *fandangos* of the respectable

352 Andrew McCormack and John Curry were privates in the Platte county infantry.

people or public places.[353] General Kearny gives a ball tomorrow night, and we received invitations this evening. Change of diet has produced its usual effects upon me and all the company.

AUGUST 21. This morning all were busy cleaning and preparing the quarters for a winter residence. Melons, plums, and other things have been offered in abundance, and many of the men were sick last night, which we attributed to dissipation and change of diet.

The ball to be given by the general was postponed, and in place of it we had a *fandango* at Mr. Pruett's, the only hotel in the place.[354] As it was the first, the officers generally attended from curiosity. But there was nothing to interest us except a Spanish dance, which afforded some entertainment from its novelty and singularity. It

353 "The same afternoon [August 20]," recorded Lieutenant Emory, "just as twilight had closed, the vicar of the department, a huge lump of fat, who had fled with Armijo, came puffing into town, and soon presented himself to the general. The interview was amusing. His holiness was accompanied by two young priests: one of them showed the highest state of alarm and agitation. The vicar assured the general he had been persuaded to run off by the women of his family. The general told him, sharply, he thought it would have been much more in keeping with his holy office to stand by his flock, and not desert them in the hour of trouble, than listen to the unreasonable fears of two women. He then told the general that at another time he would give him the real reason for running away on the approach of the American army." *Daily Union*, Oct. 23, 1846.

354 Benjamin Pruett, of Jackson county, Missouri, a Santa Fé trader, opened a tavern, or hotel, in Santa Fé during the summer of 1846. On August 18, Lieutenant Elliott, of the Laclede Rangers, wrote: "Here was my good friend, Frank McManus, a trader to Chihuahua, who piloted me, at 10 o'clock, into an eating house, kept by an American, named Priest [Pruett], who, with a neat, good-looking wife, had been trying for a month past to make a fortune in Santa Fé, by keeping a hotel! He came out from the States this spring, and really sets quite a respectable table, round which are placed the oddest-looking pine chairs that ever eyes were set upon. On the table he actually had *castors* – real castors, with pepper and mustard, and such like, reminding me, like the church of San Miguel, of home and a high state of civilization!" *Weekly Reveille*, Sept. 28, 1846. See also *Southwest Historical Series*, I, 139.

is neither waltz [nor] cotillion, nor like any of ours [*i.e.*, dances], but seems to be a mixture of all. Beginning like a country dance, it changes to a kind of Indian swing and ends with a waltz. It is said to be of great antiquity and to be in part Indian, which it no doubt is. The women were far from handsome or what in "the States" would be called modest, but I have since found that the most decent and respectable were not there. Their dress was plain after the American fashion, without collars, shawls, or handkerchiefs, and if taken as a fair sample of Santa Féans does not speak well for them. The supper was not so good as we generally get at a farmer's house, though we had fried chicken, hashed beef, and boiled and baked mutton. The coffee was not good, and they had neither butter nor delicacies of any kind except sponge cake, which was delicious and received the general praise of the company as the best they ever saw. The officers of the army and a few citizens only were invited. As we could not speak Spanish nor they English, we made rather a poor showing in conversation; in fact, there was none, as it is unfashionable for men to sit amongst or talk to the women. But few women attended, some having fled to the mountains, and others not yet being willing to submit to the American yoke.[355]

[355] Lieutenant Kribben gave the following description of this *fandango:* "Day before yesterday the Mexican aristocracy gave a ball for the officers of the army. I was there, in company with several officers of our battalion, in order to make the acquaintance of the town's élite. On entering the hall (N.B. a barn, like all the houses) a cloud of smoke met me. On arriving inside, I saw some twenty-five women sitting cross-legged on couches rather like divans and smoking *cigaretos*. The officers of the regular army were nearly all there. You may imagine us in this society, since none of us spoke Spanish and none of the women either English or French. Everyone smoked, and we, on our side, laughed at the comical situation we were in. But nothing could disturb the women's cold composure. We soon began to dance, mostly waltzes, but in five-eighths time and slow as a minuet. The orchestra consisted of two violins, a singer who sighed out the melody after the instruments, and

Three or four pieces of artillery have been found about twenty-five miles below and brought in, one a very fine one taken from the Texans.[356] All hopes of Armijo returning have been abandoned. He is on his way to Chihuahua.

AUGUST 22. A detail of one lieutenant, one sergeant, two corporals, and twenty-two privates was ordered from our battalion to mount guard tomorrow on the plaza, this being the first time we were called upon to furnish a general guard. I was detailed as the lieutenant, and it no doubt will be continued, each one being called

---

a five double-stringed guitar quite unlike the German variety. One smoked while dancing and, when one was tired, simply left the Doña to look after herself. Then the lady would take her *rebozo* (a kind of mantilla generally thrown over her head and shoulders and made of cotton, though among the better classes sometimes of silk or satin) over her head, would take a fresh maize leaf from an etui, tobacco from a pouch she usually had with her, would roll it, and then get onto her seat without further ceremony and light up her *cigareto*. The priests, who are of the people, share all their vices and virtues. They are generally present at *fandangos* and pay their compliments to the ladies like other christians, and get disgustingly tipsy. In fact a priest present at this affair collapsed from drunkenness while dancing. They picked him up and took him to the door, where he eased his heart by a simple operation and then went home. The music has a very individual character and must be beautiful when well-played. By the way, they only know about twelve melodies here, and since neither priest nor verger sings at Mass nor anywhere else, the *fandango* virtuosos play there the same melodies as the night before, only in adagio tempo. This is quite in keeping with the naïve simplicity of the people." *Täglicher Anzeiger des Westens,* Sept. 26, 1846.

356 On August 20, 1846, Captain Woldemar Fischer, of the German company of light artillery, captured some Mexican cannons at Galisteo, where Armijo had abandoned them while retreating southward. These pieces of ordnance, according to Lieutenant Kribben, were three bronze four-pounders cast in Barcelona in 1758, and a four-pounder howitzer. *Täglicher Anzeiger des Westens,* Sept. 28, 1846; *Weekly Reveille,* Sept. 28, 1846. Captain Cooke asserted that nine cannons were captured, one of which was marked: "Barcelona, 1778." Cooke, *Conquest of New Mexico and California,* 42. Hughes stated that seven cannons were taken from the Mexicans, one being a piece which Armijo had captured from the Texans in 1841 – "a 6-pounder made of brass." Connelley, *Doniphan's Expedition,* 65. On August 23, Ugarte wrote that Armijo had spiked seven pieces of artillery at Galisteo. Cuilty to the Governor of Chihuahua, Aug. 29, 1846, *Diario Oficial,* Sept. 10, 1846.

on in turn. The weather is mild and pleasant, rather bordering on the cool, and the men are better and in fine spirits fiddling, dancing, laughing, etc., when not on drill, which we have twice a day, having commenced yesterday. Harpst and Kuychenthal now act as corporals in place of Thurman and McGuire resigned.

AUGUST 23. Being officer of the guard, I could not visit church, where it is fair to presume the best of the population would be found. But I understand ladies more genteel than any we have heretofore seen, attended. The general with his staff, and many officers were there, with crowds of Spaniards and soldiers. After mass the music – two violins and a guitar – escorted the general to the Palace, a great crowd following, where he had to address a few remarks to them to get shut of them. I am told it is the practice after church for the music to go round town, all following who hear it, playing a lively air, and thus winding up the religious ceremonies of the Sabbath with fiddling and dancing.[357] As this was our first Sunday in Santa Fé, I expected some rioting, but the day passed off quietly and orderly, and I was not troubled with prisoners.

Captain Murphy received an order to go with fifty men about eight miles in the country and take some military stores said to be secreted, said to consist of two wagonloads of powder. He is to leave at eight o'clock tomorrow. It is strange to see what familiarity the Span-

[357] Captain Cooke, who attended the church services, wrote: "On our first Sunday the bells invited us to worship. I went to the parochial church: although built of adobes, it is sufficiently lofty, and has two steeples, or towers, in which hang three or four bells. With the usual wax images, it is adorned with numerous paintings – one or two of some merit. There was some music, of violin and triangle, and no spoken service. The streets and shops were thronged, and nothing indicated there that it was the Lord's day." Cooke, *Conquest of New Mexico and California*, 43-44.

ish children take with the goats and sheep, running out to meet them in the evenings as they are driven home, hugging and holding on to the old nannies, which they take with the greatest kindness and as expected. It is a common practice for the Mexican women to carry their earthen jars on their heads, having it balanced with great tact, and walking along at their usual gait. I have even seen small children, not over eight or ten years old, perfect adepts at it.

I had a striking instance of the tyranny and oppression under which the Santa Féans have labored, and [of] one of their peculiar legal proceedings. The sentinel on post at the *calabozo* was instructed to permit no person to enter and converse with the prisoners, several of whom were confined. About dark a Spaniard presented himself and said he was sent to jail (for something) by the alcalde. But as there was no person with him and he had no written direction to deliver himself up, the sentinel called on me to know what to do, the Spaniard being offended at a refusal to be received. On inquiry I found it was usual for the alcalde to order to prison and for the person under sentence to go and deliver himself up, without warrant or officer, and for the jailor to receive and confine him. I told him I had nothing to do with it, and that he and the alcalde and jailor might settle it as they pleased. And he went to see this dignitary in high dudgeon, which was the last I heard about it. Whether he came and hunted up the jailor and suffered the penalty of the law or whether he concluded that it was better living out of doors, I never took the trouble to learn.

AUGUST 24. The detail of fifty men were ready to march at eight o'clock and had actually started when news came that the Spaniards themselves were bringing in the stores, and their march was countermanded. The day is very pleasant, and some of the troops have been ordered to commence the fieldworks today on the hill northeast of town. It is to consist of a battery and breastwork, with two blockhouses, a magazine, a storehouse, and quarters for some troops.[358] The only kind of broom

[358] On August 19, 1846, Kearny ordered Lieutenant Emory, of the topographical engineers, and Lieutenant Gilmer, chief engineer of the Army of the West, to make a reconnaissance of Santa Fé and select a site for a fort. Two days later Emory and Gilmer recommended that the post be located on a hill six hundred and sixty-four yards northeast of the plaza, and on August 22 submitted a complete plan of the fort to Kearny, who approved it. A small force of troops started construction work on August 24, but three days afterward the number employed was increased to a hundred. Each soldier who labored ten or more consecutive days received a compensation of eighteen cents a day in addition to his regular pay. On August 31 some thirty Mexican brick masons were hired to erect the adobe work. The fort was constructed under the superintendence of Lieutenant Gilmer. On September 15 or 16, 1846, Kearny named the post "Fort Marcy," in honor of the Secretary of War, William L. Marcy. It was not completed until 1847. Writing from Santa Fé during the latter part of August, 1846, Emory stated: "The site selected [for the fort], and marked on the maps, is within 600 yards of the heart of the town, and is from 60 to 100 feet above it. The *contour* of the ground is unfavorable for the *trace* of a regular work; but being the only point which commands the entire town, and which is itself commanded by no other, we did not hesitate to recommend it. The recommendation was approved by the general, who viewed it in person. On the 22d we submitted a complete plan of the work, which was also approved, and a copy of which will hereafter be forwarded to the department. It is computed for a garrison of 280 men. Its irregular shape is the natural consequence of the ground; and, estimating its merits, due consideration must be given to the objects in erecting it. It is to be a magazine of ammunition, and a citadel in case of extremities, into which a few troops can retreat, and hold at bay, until help arrives, a large number of an opposing force. But the chief object which its imposing position will doubtless achieve is the moral effect over a feeble and distracted race, who are now, since our capture of their artillery, without a single gun. Their own guns will be chiefly used to garrison the fort; and with them every house in Santa Fé could be levelled on the least appearance of revolt." *Daily Union,* Oct. 23, 1846. See also Kearny, Order No. 23, Sept. 15, 1846, Letters Received, MSS., O.F.S., A.G.O.; Marcellus B. Edwards to Joseph D. Edwards, Aug. 23, 1846, Mexican War MSS., M.H.S.; *House Ex. Docs.,* 30 cong., 1 sess., no. 60, pp. 172-175; *Saint Louis Daily Union,* Sept. 15, 1846; *Weekly American,* Nov. 5, 1846; Hughes, *Doniphan's Expedition,* 122-123.

used here is made by tying together a bunch of long grass peculiar to the country, which answers the purpose very well and is rather neat and pretty. Colonel Rich informs me that the mail which is to leave tomorrow now contains 997 letters and packages.

AUGUST 25. A general order was read this morning requiring all persons to submit peaceably to the new order of things, stating that General Kearny would act as governor until new regulations could be made, and that any citizen who attempted revolt would be treated as a traitor. The express left this morning, conveying the important news to our friends that Santa Fé was annexed to the Union and without firing a gun. Orders were issued for some troops to visit Taos, California, and the country below, but none specified, and there is great dissatisfaction about half rations and some uneasiness at the prospect of its getting worse. The infantry and artillery remain here. Our invitations to the party at the general's were renewed, and it comes off next Thursday evening.

AUGUST 26. There is a great deal of murmuring at half rations and the prospect of its continuance. The mounted volunteers are not willing to venture to California in the jaded condition of their animals and with a short allowance of provisions; and as the order for two companies specifies no particular ones, all take an interest in it, as they are liable to be called on. A small printing press was brought from Taos, the type badly pied and but little. Workmen are sorting and distributing it, and trying to put the office in a condition to print the public documents, proclamations, orders by the governor, etc. Being a Spanish concern, there are no "W"s, but they probably can use the capital "M." [359] Great

[359] John T. Hughes also stated that the press had Spanish types, which

uneasiness is experienced lest we should all become lousy. The whole town is infested by them, and some have already been found in the army. Our quarters are

included no "W"s. Hughes, *Doniphan's Expedition,* 120-121. However, in 1929, Douglas C. McMurtrie, typographic historian, demonstrated that the press which Kearny found in New Mexico in 1846 did have "W"s, and that the fonts were probably English rather than Spanish. McMurtrie, "The History of Early Printing in New Mexico," *New Mexico Historical Review,* IV, 371, 383, 388-389. But how and when was this press brought to New Mexico? Writing in 1844, Josiah Gregg asserted that New Mexico's only press was transported across the plains from the United States in 1834. Since Gregg was a member of the trading caravan in the latter year, and since he always wrote with great accuracy, his statement is probably correct. Another member of the caravan in 1834 was Edward Charless, a printer by trade and at that time one of the proprietors of the St. Louis *Missouri Republican;* but whether he transported the press to Santa Fé has not been ascertained. During September or early in October, 1846, Lieutenant Lucian J. Eastin of the Cole county infantry, a printer formerly associated with the *Jefferson Inquirer* of Jefferson City, Missouri, was placed in charge of the printing establishment in Santa Fé. On September 2, 1846, he described the press as follows: "Enclosed I send you [editor of the *Jefferson Inquirer*] a proclamation issued by Gen. Kearny, which was printed here [Santa Fé]. The press is a very small affair of royal size – Ramage patent, with iron bed and iron platten [platen]. The type are old, of small pica size – and not sufficient to print a paper – barely enough to print the orders of Gen. K." *Jefferson Inquirer,* Oct. 13, 1846. After reading Eastin's letter, the editor of the St. Louis *Weekly Reveille* (October 19, 1846) wrote: "Here is a glorious incident in the history of this war for old Adam Ramage. He doubtless never dreamed that a press of his patent would work off a *Yankee* proclamation in the governmental palace of an American foe!" Adam Ramage, the inventor of the Ramage press, was a native of Scotland who had migrated to Philadelphia during the latter part of the eighteenth century, where he made a number of improvements in the hand press then in use. "He substituted," according to Baker, "an iron bed and platen for the wood and stone that had been in use so long and built a much better machine, though still small in size. He used a triple-thread, rapid-motion screw that greatly shortened the pull, and his press was much admired in his day. Even as late as 1885 a number of them were in use as proof presses. They were usually about cap size (13x16)." Daniel Baker, *Platen Printing Presses* (Chicago, 1918), 3. See also Isaiah Thomas, *The History of Printing in America* (Albany, 1874), I, 36; *Missouri Republican,* Aug. 26, 1834, May 7, 1879; *Jefferson Inquirer,* Nov. 17, 1846; Gregg, *op. cit.,* XIX, 331-332; Scharf, *History of Saint Louis City and County,* I, 909; Connelley, *Doniphan's Expedition,* 65, 72.

amongst the cleanest in the place, and if any escape we should, though one of our men on examination was found to have plenty on his head.

AUGUST 27. I took a walk with the first lieutenant over the upper part of the city, which I enjoyed, following the creek, the clear, pure water rippling over its rocky bed, and carried in trenches high on the hillsides, with branches through their fields to irrigate them. All the wheat I saw was large, plump, and clean, and would make the best of seed. We passed several little tube mills, the only kind they have, the shaft turning the millstone, which is concave, the bottom one being convex. The only machinery is a wheel, shaft, millstones, and hopper to make the flour we daily eat. As far as we could see, the private houses are comfortable within, and by their construction well adapted to the climate, which is very dry. The walls are solid, and with a little care will keep out vermin of all kinds, which otherwise would be exceedingly troublesome. The plan of having an interior court affords protection against both heat and cold, and is a pleasant and retired place to lounge. In our peregrinations we found some of the women shy, but others the reverse. Perhaps their shyness was owing to a disgusting practice, which is very common, of painting the face like Indians. It is said to whiten the skin. In this condition they present a most frightful appearance, as if their whole face was sore or covered by erysipelas. Their gardens are universally poor, peas being the principal thing I have seen in them. We returned by way of the hill on which the fortifications are going up and found Lieutenant Gilmer, who has the superintendence, very kind and ready to show us every attention possible. We found a detail of twenty men from our battalion assisting in the work, which is unusually heavy for fieldworks. The orders for 900 men to march tomorrow have been countermanded.

AUGUST 28. They have a large white onion here in great abundance, of a mild and pleasant flavor. It is grown from seed, transplanted, and as it grows, the dirt taken from around it.

The general's ball came off last night and was fine for the country. It was a new thing for plain republicans to revel in a palace, which, if not Montezuma's, is claimed by the aborigines as a portion of the dominions over which he swayed his scepter. The rooms were decorated with the different flags of the army, some of which were very pretty and, as the inscriptions gave us to understand, were the work of the fair hands of the patriot mothers and daughters of Missouri. They commenced assembling about nine o'clock, and dancing soon followed. The time for going to *fandangos* is regulated by the church bells, very few attending before they ring. The general and staff, and some of the officers belonging to the regular army were conspicuous by their dress. The crowd was great – at least four or five hundred. Amongst them [was] the principal priest, who received great attention from the general, who no doubt sought this opportunity to satisfy the Church, the great lever in Mexico by which all important transactions are effected. Some of the women were richly dressed and all genteelly. A few were good-looking if not handsome. As a general thing their forms are much better than the women in "the States." In their dress there was nothing different from what we meet with at home, unless it be the absence in most cases of collars or anything about their necks. A few wore satin dresses and rich shawls. The supper was good, as good as the country and place could afford, the liquors from El Paso, or [the] Pass as [it is] usually called. The dancing was a mixture of Spanish and American, in which all seemed to take equal interest and to get along equally well, and continued until a late hour. The wall near the center of the room had painted on it the general handing a Mexican the constitution with the word *libertad* beneath, the design and execution of which was very good; and the effect was heightened by having the flag which floats daily on the plaza tastefully hung around it. Back in the distance was the plough, the cross, and a cannon, the whole being both appropriate and neat.[360]

AUGUST 29. The weather continues to be delightful. [It is] dry here but with almost daily showers on the mountains, and is just about the temperature one would desire. There is a good deal of talk about the ball at the general's, and all are better satisfied, the conduct of the women not being so objectionable nor the want of mod-

360 Captain Cooke described Kearny's ball as follows: "Yesterday the 27th, the General, or Governor, gave a ball to all the officers, and to citizens generally in the government house; it was a political, or conciliatory affair, and we put the best face on it. The women are comely, – remarkable for smallness of hands and feet; as usual in such states of society, they seem superior to the man; but nowhere else is chastity less valued or expected. There was an attempt at cotilions; but the natives are very Germans for waltzing – and they possess musical ears as well. Their favorite, called appropriately the cuna (cradle) is peculiar; it is a waltz; but the couple stand face to face; the gentleman encircles his partner's waist with both arms; the lady's similarly disposed, complete the sides of the cradle which is not bottomless, for both parties lean well back as they swing around. There were men present in colored cotton trowsers secured by leathern belts, and jackets, but they danced well. The American merchants were of course, very genteelly represented; there were twenty or thirty of them. The supper was good, particularly in cake. The fiddlers accompanied their music at times by verses, sung in a high nasal key. I was surprised, but amused to hear one of our captains join in this; – and he could waltz them all blind; – but we got him from the navy. The ball went off harmoniously, and quite pleasantly, considering the extravagant variety in its make up. But we did not feel particular – out here." Cooke, *Conquest of New Mexico and California,* 49-50.

esty quite so conspicuous as at Mr. Pruett's. C. Perry arrived today in advance of his wagons and spent the evening and night with us. We sat up until late talking about home, what has transpired in the last two months, and the various incidents of our march. Only those who have experienced it know the pleasure of meeting an old acquaintance a thousand miles from home in a strange land. As he left soon after we did, he brought but little news and no papers or letters.

The people here take great pains to ornament their bridles and saddles, many having massive silver plate curiously and ingeniously worked. The stirrups and cantles also have skins attached to them both for use and ornament, almost covering their mules and horses. The future movements of the troops furnish a subject for conversation, as it is determined to make an expedition with nearly all the troops to the lower part of the territory. Melons are abundant but not very good. The cantaloupes are fine, and a few peaches and grapes are in [the] market. The New Mexicans work their oxen by the horns, and the yoke is a very rude thing, lashed to their head with rawhide thongs. Yet it seems to answer the purpose, and the oxen are obedient. I have not seen oxen worked except to drag timber, which they do by cutting a hole in one end of the stick, to which a strong rope or rawhide is attached and the other end fastened to the yoke. A further detail for the fort was ordered from our battalion, and an order that all on the hill should have full rations, which they have not got to furnish. The people almost universally take their siesta. But few can be seen for an hour or two after dinner, and they are the market people stretched along the plaza (where marketing is sold), some asleep and all drowsy and lazy. It is no uncommon thing to see women asleep on the sidewalks, their chattering stopped, and in the place of anxious looks, heavy eyelids. All found here at this time of day have some kind of marketing for sale, and they are a dirty, filthy set, more like lazzaroni than any other species of the human family.

AUGUST 30. I attended the principal church, which was crowded with citizens and soldiers, amongst the last the general and his staff. The music was good, consisting of two violins and a guitar, the same we have at the *fandangos,* and we only had mass – no preaching. Many ladies, genteelly dressed, attended, who sit *à la mode* Turkish on the floor or kneel in devotion, there being only two or three benches in the whole chapel. The building itself, like all others, is adobe, large, and in the shape of a cross, with heavy cornice around the ceiling or roof, and round, smooth logs at short distances for joists. It looks much weather-beaten in the interior, many of the picture frames having rotted and come to pieces. The walls are very rough, and with the dust settled on them no doubt look more ancient than their antiquity would justify. On the east side are three windows, and a door from what I supposed was a confessional. The altar is decorated with looking-glasses and other trinkets of a very common kind, and is fitted out more to suit Indian taste than according to our notions. The pulpit is plain, and the floor of rough-split pine timber, far from looking well, though durable and answering the purpose. All the workmanship, finish, and furnishing is of the roughest kind, far behind anything in "the States" and only equalled by the Indians. The building is about a hundred feet long, and the ceiling about twenty-five feet high, with a gallery for the music over the west end, which is the main entrance.[361]

361 "To-day we went to church, in great state," recorded Lieutenant Emory

Two ladies appeared on the plaza in bonnets and attracted great attention, as they are the first and only ones we have seen, the women using the *rebozos,* or scarfs, entirely.

AUGUST 31. The dragoons all left yesterday for the grazing camp, twenty-seven miles afoot, where they are to be mustered for pay. Some are to return as soon as this is done. The train of ammunition wagons in charge of Lieutenant Warner came up today; so we are safe on this account. The weather continues fine, and we were mustered and inspected for two months' pay. A proclamation has been issued abolishing the stamp on paper, which was heavy.[362] Hon. Willard P. Hall, with Colonel

on August 30, 1846. "The governor's seat, a large well-stuffed chair, covered with crimson, was occupied by the general. The house was crowded with an attentive audience, of men and women; but not a word was uttered from the pulpit by the priest, who kept his back to the audience, the whole time uttering prayers. The band – the identical one used at the *fandango* – played the same tunes as at the dance, without intermission. Except the governor's, and one row of benches, there were no seats in the church. Each woman dropped on her knees, on the bare floor, as she entered; and only changed this position for that on her seat, at long intervals, announced by the tinkle of a small bell. The interior of the church was decorated with some fifty crosses, a great number of the most miserable paintings, and wax figures and looking-glasses, trimmed with pieces of tinsel. The priest, who was a very grave, respectable looking person, of fair complexion, commenced the service by sprinkling holy water over the congregation. When abreast of the general, he extended his silver water-spout, and gave him a handful. When a favorite air would be struck, the young women – those that we had recognised as figuring at the *fandango,* counted their beads, tossed their heads, and crossed themselves, at the time of the music. Though not a word was uttered, the whole service was grave and impressive; and I thought it was the very religion for the people present; and much more decent and worthy of God's temple, than many of the ranting, howling discourses we have at home. All appeared to have just left their work to come to church. There was no fine dressing or personal display, that will not be seen on week days. Indeed, on returning from church, we found all the stores open, and the market women selling their melons and plums, as usual." *Daily Union,* Oct. 23, 1846.

[362] On August 29, 1846, Kearny issued the following order: "From this day so much of the law, hitherto in force in New Mexico, which requires that *stamped paper* shall be used in certain transactions, is abolished." *House Ex. Docs.,* 30 cong., 1 sess., no. 60, p. 173.

Doniphan, has been appointed to revise the Territorial laws. Many are oppressive and tyrannical, and an entire new code will have to be framed. The tax on *fandangos* is increased from 50¢ to $1.50, and a fine of $5 in case of violation. Chickens can be purchased at twelve and a half cents apiece, but are scarce. The apples are small, sweet, and not good, but abundant. I have not seen such a thing as a turkey; and hogs are scarce, small, runty, and tied or picketed up, led to water, and poorly fed. There is plenty of goat's milk in [the] market, and the little I tried I found sweet and palatable, I fancied better than cow's [milk]. But [as] it is all so dirty, we prefer going without [it] except when we can get cow's [milk], which we sometimes do from an old man who brings it to our quarters. It is astonishing to see what loads of anything the little donkeys carry. They will put as much on six as a common two-horse wagon will carry; yet they go along with ease and safety.

SEPTEMBER 1. The troops are busy preparing to leave on the expedition which is to be made below. Various reports are in circulation: that troops have come up from Chihuahua, that Armijo is at the head of 5,000 men, etc., but none of them receive any credit here. Yet General Kearny goes prepared for any state of things. The infantry remains. The general says they must guard this post. The general expects to be absent about two weeks.

Although Santa Fé presents a forbidding aspect as you approach it on the Independence road, the very reverse is the case on the opposite side. One of the most lovely and varied views, in a country abounding in scenery, is from the fort. I have scarcely ever met with anything so rich and pleasing. The town has quite a businesslike and city appearance. The plaza is in full view, and considerable regularity shows itself in the town. The mountains close by are not only high but broken, and those on the west are amongst the highest we have met with. Like all mountain ranges they present a varied aspect, which is increased by the valley of Santa Fé and its principal settlements. The Taos mountains are visible in the north, and the whole country is broken and elevated.

SEPTEMBER 2. Nine hundred troops [363] under the command of General Kearny left yesterday and today for the country below, and only the fractions of companies remain, except the infantry. Colonel Doniphan is now in command here,[364] and the absence of so many troops has not the effect which might have been anticipated; yet it is both seen and felt. For dinner we had rice pudding, mutton pie, roast mutton, and some other things. The first no doubt is a new thing in this country, but Walter did the thing right. The weather continues delightful, as fine as heart could wish it.

All the floors in Santa Fé are dirt, even the one in the Palace, and only a few of the wealthy have them carpeted. Yet in this climate they do exceedingly well, the structure of the houses rendering it in a great degree unnecessary. Besides, lumber is high, from three to four dollars per hundred, and has to be obtained by whipsawing. The general has ordered the machinery of a mill, which is expected out this fall, and they are preparing to have everything ready for it when it comes. It is much needed, as we have great difficulty to get

---

363 About seven hundred mounted troops. *Ibid.*

364 On August 30, 1846, Kearny issued the following order: "Colonel Doniphan, being now engaged on highly important business, in this City, will remain in command of all the Troops left in this City." Kearny, Order No. 20, Aug. 30, 1846, Letters Received, MSS., O.F.S., A.G.O.

stuff for bunks or even to make a rude bedstead for ourselves. We still have to lie on the floor, on the same bedding we used on the prairie.

SEPTEMBER 3. Now, while nearly all the troops are away, our whole battalion is on duty, some at the fort, some as general guard on the plaza, some working on the flagstaff, some at the printing office and hospital, and some at home. The general's proclamation has been printed in both languages and placarded at all the most public places, and distributed not only here but throughout all the territory. Taking a walk last night, I found many of the Santa Féans, men, women, and children, sleeping in the street in front of their houses. This appears to be a common thing either to avoid vermin which infest many of their houses in this climate, or because it is equally as pleasant as the house and gives them free circulation of air instead of the confined atmosphere of their rooms, with only one window, as most are.

SEPTEMBER 4. A report reached here last night that Paredes had retaken Matamoras and that General Kearny was retreating, all of which is totally unfounded. The many rumors afloat have an injurious effect, as they keep the people of New Mexico in constant alarm and prevent many from visiting town to give in their adhesion to the new order of things. Last night some commenced packing up their things, preparatory to leaving. Yet there was not a particle of foundation for their fears, and everything in the conduct of the army went to inspire confidence. The acting governor has issued a proclamation, or order, for the return of all arms in the hands of the disbanded Mexican soldiery as being the property of the United States, and prohibiting their sale. Three days are allowed to return them. I purchased some fine grapes in [the] market, but have not been able to learn their name or whether they are indigenous or not; but they resemble the Catawba.

For dinner we had roast mutton, peach pie, custard pie, and rich and juicy grapes, which we all did full justice to, our appetites being sharp at the sight of such rich viands to which we had been totally unaccustomed for two months, and which I suspect could not be found in another house in Santa Fé. They were all prepared by Walter, and our health being good, we enjoyed it as much as men a thousand miles from family and friends could be expected. Proposals have been issued and placarded about town to supply the troops stationed here this winter with beef and mutton twice a week until next June, supposed to require eight hundred pounds each time and to be alternately beef and mutton.

SEPTEMBER 5. For dinner we had apple and custard pies, with other things, and all enjoyed them. Yesterday the grazing party heard cannon firing in the direction of Albuquerque, supposed to be General Kearny firing a salute, as he reached there about that time. An express came from him this morning by which we learn all was quiet and no armed force of any kind in the field. Lieutenant Johnston [365] returned today from Taos and reports everything quiet in that quarter. In looking over the papers in the secretary's office, Doctor Waldo and myself found a letter [366] dated July 1, 1846, from General Ugarte to Governor Armijo, in which he says he is directed to open a correspondence with him and that it is necessary to check the Americans who will make an attack on Santa Fé or Chihuahua. He further says he

365 On September 1, Captain Johnston, of the First dragoons, had left Santa Fé for Taos in order to obtain information about the best route to California. Turner, Diary, Sept. 1, 1846, MS., M.H.S.

366 See appendix.

has 500 dragoons and can have the same number of infantry to march to his assistance at a moment's warning. He promises to lay down his life for his country and ends with the exclamation, "God and Liberty." This is the same officer who was in command at El Paso when we came here, and [who] deserted his post and ran when he heard it. A set of sawmill irons nearly complete were found today in Mr. Álvarez's store, our former enterprising and accomplished consul. They were brought out by him some years since to engage in milling, but the unstable condition of the public mind deterred him from the undertaking. They may now be found of great benefit. The adobe work to be done at the fort was commenced today, Spaniards both making and laying the sundried brick.[367]

SEPTEMBER 6. No such a thing as a potato is to be found, and we miss them as much as the sons of the "Emerald Isle" could. The dryness of the climate, it seems, is the reason why they are not cultivated. Perhaps it could be done by irrigation. There were two *fandangos:* one at Pruett's, to which most went for a short time. The crowd, however, was of too motley a character to suit our taste, and we left, having taken no part in

367 Writing from Santa Fé on September 1, 1846, Lieutenant Gilmer stated: "Some five or six days ago, I commenced a small field-work (garrison 300 men) on a point completely commanding the town, and I am now pushing the excavations and embankments as rapidly as possible, with a force of 100 men, this being the number which the commanding general has detailed for the purpose. These 100 men, if they work well, may be able to complete the fort in some 20 to 25 days. We have at present but a small supply of entrenching tools, and it will be some days before any additional picks or shovels can reach here. In addition to the field-work already commenced, I propose to construct a kind of block-house in the rear of the fort, which will increase the strength of our position, and furnish quarters for some 80 or 90 men. Gen. Kearny has sanctioned the above plan of defence, and ordered the quartermaster to furnish the materials required." *Daily Picayune,* Nov. 6, 1846.

the amusements of the evening. The weather continues very pleasant, but the nights a little cooler than they have been.

SEPTEMBER 7. The flagstaff in the plaza was raised this forenoon, but the flag will not be run up until General Kearny returns, which is expected to be about Friday. Gregg's description of the dress of the women of New Mexico is accurate and just as well as everything else in his book. It is equally so of the men and their horse trappings when they wish to be fine. The two principal chiefs of the Taos Indians were here today to see the general. They told Colonel Doniphan that their people were pleased at the manner they were treated, that they came down to get something to hunt with, [and] that about thirty miles above them (north) the grass was good and [there was] but little snow in the winter. The colonel told them that as soon as the general returned, some companies would be sent up, and they could then get such things as they wanted, if not before; that if the Navajo would not keep peace with them, he would go and make war on them, and they must show him the road; that he wanted them to stay at home, cultivate their grounds, and raise all the stock they could, and they should be protected. They seemed pleased and satisfied and said they would do as desired. They number about 200 of the bravest men in Mexico. Doctor Waldo, who interpreted, told me the Navajo were about 1,000 warriors, but the two chiefs said they were as numerous as the Mexicans, and that their country was poorer than the Ratón and valleys this side.

Mr. Perry's teams all arrived safe, and their loads were discharged. Mr. Weston and [Mr.] Baker came with them and stop with us; so that our mess consists of the captain, first lieutenant, myself, Perry, Billingsby,

Abel, Ross, Somers, Shorten, Weston and Baker, Walter, and Albert, a German boy.

SEPTEMBER 8. Grapes in abundance appear in the market, and, with custard pie, we have them for dinner every day. The weather continues pleasant but if anything a shade cooler than it has been. The town is dull and time drags along heavily, but we hope for something to give new life when the general returns, which will be soon.

SEPTEMBER 11. The weather continues pleasant, but indicative of the approach of autumn in the clearness of the atmosphere and brilliant tints of the setting sun, with a slight coolness of the evenings. General Kearny returned this evening, and the flag was run up the new staff in the center of the plaza, and a salute of thirteen guns fired. It was unfurled amidst the cheers of Americans and Spaniards, and gloriously waved as the rays of a mild, setting sun were shed upon it. It is a beautiful shaft and banner a hundred feet high, towering far above the town, and the most conspicuous thing in or near the place and visible in every direction. The general found everything well below:[368] fruit plentiful, a country much finer than this, and the people more as we expected to find them. It is harvest time, and it would amuse our farmers to see their [*i.e.,* the Mexicans'] short hooks twelve inches long and the slow process of reaping. Scarcely a stalk, though, is left, as they take pains to glean as they proceed. The wheat is all spring wheat, large, plump, and white, and when well ground makes excellent bread. It is both bald and bearded. The trains of commissary teams (twenty-two) which we have so

[368] Kearny reported to the adjutant-general that the natives were "highly satisfied and contented with the change of government." *House Ex. Docs.,* 30 cong., 1 sess., no. 60, p. 174.

long expected arrived, and, for the present, we have plenty [of] provisions – sugar, coffee, molasses, beans, flour, vinegar, etc.

SEPTEMBER 13. A report has just reached here that Paredes was arrested by his troops and the government revolutionized, the Santa Anna party having acquired the ascendancy. Gaming is a vice very common at Santa Fé and throughout all New Mexico. Houses are licensed for monte, and every grogshop is a notorious gambling place where frequently all classes resort. Nothing is more common than to find large crowds on Sunday collected on the side of the plaza where marketing is sold, engaged in different games of cards. Gaming is the only amusement I have yet seen or heard of, except a billiard room, and all classes from the priest down are passionately fond of it. Bullfights have long been out of date in this section, and cockfighting seldom occurs – not since we came. The stores and shops are all kept open Sunday, and it appears to be a fashionable day to go shopping after church hours.

The church [369] on the south side of the plaza appears to have been erected at an early day and is becoming antiquated. It is not now used but undergoing repair, a new roof having been put on, and the interior protected from the weather. It is government property, and a sentinel is posted in front of it to prevent persons from running in and abusing it. There is nothing in the interior but a back to the altar, cast from plaster of Paris, consisting of various Catholic pictorial representations. It extends nearly to the roof, is massive, well done, and beautiful. The steps and platform for the altar are of the same material; also the pulpit, which still remains en-

[369] *La castrense,* or the military chapel. See *Southwest Historical Series,* I, 94-95.

tire. In front of the building there is also some of the same workmanship and material. Except these, there is nothing but bones in the recesses – the relics of departed Saints or mementos of the earthly victories of the cross over the infidel and savage. There are inscriptions on each side as follows:

Á DEVOCÍON EL SEÑOR DN. FRAN. ANT. MARTIN DEL VALLE, GOB- ERNADOR Y CAPN. GEN. IDES[?] TEREINO[?]	Y DE SU ESPOSA DA. MARÍA IGNACIA MARTÍNEZ DE UGARTE AÑO DE 1761

which I translate as follows:

IN MEMORY OF SEÑOR DON FRANCISCO ANTONIO MARTIN DEL VALLE, GOV- ERNOR AND CAPTAIN GENERAL OF THE EARTH[?]	AND OF HIS WIFE DOÑA MARÍA IGNACIA MARTÍNEZ DE UGARTE 1761

SEPTEMBER 14. This morning I called on the general to make my report as officer of the day, when he invited me in to take breakfast with him, which I accepted. He told me we should remain here this winter and that he would consult the civil authorities in relation to gambling on or near the plaza. In excavating for the magazine at the fort, they dug up a great many coffins and bones. It is said to have been the American graveyard. The ground is exceedingly dry and is mixed with ashes, charcoal, etc., as far down as they have gone, five or six feet. All that remained were the bones and some of the coffins, except one skeleton which had on whiskers perfectly, but they only clung to the bone and fell off when touched. Captain Murphy and [Lieutenant] Eastin are detailed to superintend the workmen at the fort.[370] They

[370] In a letter dated Santa Fé, Texas, September 16, 1846, Lieutenant Gilmer described the progress of construction at Fort Marcy: "Since the date of my

have eighty men, twenty of whom are from our battalion. They expect to be on duty three days, when they will be relieved.

SEPTEMBER 15. Today an order [was] issued for two companies of Colonel Doniphan's regiment to visit the Ute country and for three others to go below about Albuquerque to watch the Navajo. They start on Friday next. The troops who were in the lower part of the territory say they saw large flocks of ducks, geese, and swans on the Río Grande, and plenty of fish. There is no such thing as money in the army, and the day will be celebrated when a paymaster presents himself in his official capacity. When below, the men had to use their brass buttons as currency, trading them to the Indians for grapes, melons, fruit, etc. They are valued highly, and a button would buy more than twenty-five cents of the articles generally offered. The general received the most flattering treatment when below, some of the towns exhibiting fireworks, theater, etc. Armijo's wife was at his brother's, where the general and Captain Turner, his adjutant, called to see her. She is represented as being a good-looking woman and rather cheerful.[371] She

last I have been busy laying out the different parts of the field work now under construction near the town, and urging forward the excavations and embankments. The work progresses much slower, however, notwithstanding my exertions, than it should. The system first adopted in making the details was bad, and caused much delay. The whole number of men for labor was made up of small detachments from the numerous commands composing the 'Army of the West,' and these detachments were sent to the site of the fort under corporals and sergeants, who were inefficient in all, and would frequently arrive an hour, or even more, after the time appointed for commencing work. By making strong representation to Gen. Kearny in regard to the matter, a few days ago, I have induced him to order a change; and a captain and lieutenant are now daily detailed to command the troops laboring on the fort." *Daily Picayune,* Nov. 12, 1846.

371 The English traveler, George F. Ruxton, who saw Señora Armijo on December 17, 1846, described her as a "comely dame of forty, with the remains of considerable beauty, but quite passée." Ruxton, *Adventures in Mexico and the Rocky Mountains,* 186.

lives in some style and has every convenience common to the country. Armijo's brother said he had received a letter from him, and that he wrote he was coming up next month with 4,000 men; but he [*i.e.,* Armijo's brother] said he had no idea he [*i.e.,* Armijo] could do so. Some of the towns below are represented as delightful, the walls all around crowned with cactus to guard against intruders, and the vineyards and peach orchards within, as fine and beautiful.

SEPTEMBER 17. This morning an express with the mail left for "the States" and is expected to reach Independence in twenty-four days. Colonel Ruff[372] has tendered his resignation, which is accepted, and he returns to the United States to accept a captaincy in the new regiment of dragoons in place of General B. M. Hughes. Today, for the first time, I found myself riding out. I directed my course over the hills north of town. But after following a road which led me up the ravines a considerable distance, without finding anything to interest me, I struck across the summits of the hills and

372 Charles Frederick Ruff was born at Philadelphia in 1818. He was graduated from the United States Military academy on July 1, 1838, when he was promoted in the army to second lieutenant in the First dragoons. He served at Fort Leavenworth, Liberty Arsenal, Fort Atkinson, and Fort Sandford. Resigning from the army on December 31, 1843, he settled at Liberty, Missouri, where he practiced law until 1846. At the outbreak of the Mexican war he enlisted as a private in the Clay county volunteers, and on June 18, 1846, was elected lieutenant-colonel of Doniphan's regiment. Among the troops he had the reputation of being a strict disciplinarian, although his wife stated that "he really was tender hearted by disposition." On September 17, 1846, he resigned his commission in the Army of the West in order to accept the appointment as captain in the Mounted rifles. He left Santa Fé on September 27 and arrived at Fort Leavenworth on October 30. After a varied military career he retired from active service on March 30, 1864. He was professor of military science at the University of Pennsylvania from July 3, 1868, to February 21, 1870. He died at his home in Philadelphia, October 1, 1885. V. Mott Porter, Reminiscences of Mrs. Annie E. Ruff, Ruff MSS., M.H.S.; *Daily Missouri Republican,* Nov. 7, 1846; Cullum, *Biographical Register,* I, 570-571, III, 129; Heitman, *Historical Register,* I, 850.

crossed a mile below town, where I found some Spaniards in the bottom harvesting wheat, which was both short and thin. They permit it to become very ripe, and any their rude hooks leave they pull with their hands as they go along, scarcely leaving a stalk. I saw some standing in other fields, green and not fit to cut for two weeks. M. L. Hardin received his discharge for inability to do a soldier's duty, being subject to fits. Captain Hudson has authority from General Kearny to receive volunteers from the mounted companies to be formed into a company, to go to California with Captain Allen and the Mormons. Some of our men wish to go, but Captain Murphy would not consent. Captain Fischer is ordered to pursue some Navajo charged with driving off the stock of Mr. Pruett of this place and to bring them back.

SEPTEMBER 18. Last night Captain Stevenson shot one of his men,[373] and today an investigation took place which exonerated him from all blame, having done it in self-defense. This morning Captain Jackson was elected lieutenant-colonel to fill the vacancy occasioned by the resignation of Colonel Ruff. The candidates were Jackson, Gilpin, and Reid. Reid found he would not be elected and withdrew, and all his men went over to Jackson.[374] Otherwise, Gilpin would have been elected.

[373] "A very lamentable circumstance occurred at 9 P.M.," recorded Hughes on September 17. "An aged man, Wm. Bray, of the Franklin Company, being in liquor, & raving about in camp, made an attempt to rush upon Captain Stephenson; the latter drew a pistol & snapped at him twice. Mr. Bray still rushed on him with his knife drawn – the Capt. shot him through the breast – he fell dead with the knife clenched fast in his hand – Mr. Bray was an old soldier, was in the battle at New Orleans, was a man of family, was 63 years old, & now lies buried on the hill to the north of Santa Fé in the American Burying Ground." Connelley, *Doniphan's Expedition,* 70, 72.

[374] Congreve Jackson, captain of the Howard county volunteers. *Ibid.,* 556, 559.

The three companies of Colonel Doniphan's regiment under the command of Colonel Jackson, destined for the country beyond Albuquerque and bordering on the Navajo country, are leaving, and Major Gilpin with two companies leaves tomorrow for the Ute country.

SEPTEMBER 19. We surrendered our rooms to the company and took others on the same street, east of the company quarters, which we find more pleasant and suitable. It is now understood that Colonel Doniphan with his regiment goes to Chihuahua as soon as Colonel Price arrives and he can get off.

SEPTEMBER 20. In the forenoon the general attended church, or rather mass, as usual, and the chapel was crowded. I saw some pretty women, who seemed to be the only devout persons in church. A seat has been provided for the general, cushioned and covered with red cloth. This evening an express came in from Colonel Price, bringing the intelligence that Captain Allen [375] was dead and his [*i.e.,* Price's] command in need of provisions. They all come the Cimarrón route except Captain Morin's and Captain Giddings's companies, which two last should now be here. They came by Bent's Fort. A trader has since arrived who says that Colonel Price ought to be here in six or seven days and that they were on one-third rations. We have pies, both grape and custard, and Walter also gave us soup and boiled and baked mutton for dinner, as we entertained Lieutenant DeCourcy. We find it much better to buy the sheep alive and have it slaughtered, as we are then sure not to eat goat's meat, which we have been buying in [the] market for a fortnight as sheep and found not so good.

[375] Captain James Allen, of the First dragoons, a native of Ohio, died at Fort Leavenworth on August 23, 1846. *Daily Missouri Republican,* Aug. 31, 1846.

They have a strange custom for burying children, which, I am told, prevails throughout Mexico. It [*i.e.,* the corpse] is dressed up with a cross upon its breast and is carried (without any coffin) to church on a kind of handbarrow or platform, generally by little girls, escorted by the same music used upon all occasions, a fiddle and guitar playing a lively tune. We had one [*i.e.,* a funeral] today, and the same tune was played which I have heard at their *fandangos,* not half a dozen following in the procession. The whole seems to be more of rejoicing than mourning. Various appointments have been made, Mr. Charles Bent for governor, amongst others. They generally give satisfaction and have been well received.[376] John Abel is quite sick today. Captain Murphy and myself are on a general court-martial to meet tomorrow

[376] On September 22, 1846, Kearny made the following appointments for the government of the Territory of New Mexico: Charles Bent, governor; Donaciano Vigil, secretary of the territory; Richard Dallam, marshal; Francis P. Blair, United States district attorney; Charles Blumner, treasurer; Eugene Leitensdorfer, auditor of public accounts; and Joab Houghton, Antonio José Otero, and Charles Beaubien, judges of the superior court. *House Ex. Docs.,* 30 cong., 1 sess., no. 60, p. 176. Some soldiers criticized several of these appointments. Writing from Santa Fé on October 25, 1846, one volunteer asserted: "The appointment of Governor, so far as I can judge, seems to have produced a good deal of dissatisfaction. I have heard many of them say (and some of them intelligent men) that he has been the instigator of those rebellions among the Indians, with which they have been so long troubled. This seems to be a very common impression among them, I cannot say how justly." *Missouri Statesman,* Dec. 25, 1846. On September 24, 1846, Lieutenant Kribben wrote: "All the nominations, with but few exceptions, show the primitive state of things here. I need only mention that all the judges of the Superior Court together do not possess the legal knowledge of a justice of the peace in St. Louis. They know as much of the nature of law as they do of the law of nature, and have applied the latter in the course of their lives largely to eating, drinking, and trade. However, the matter has its good side. The laws we have here are in English; and, since the President of the court, Mr. Otero, knows no English, and the Solicitor General, Mr. Blair, no Spanish, the arguments and 'opinions of the court,' if ever published, will never give rise to complications." *Täglicher Anzeiger des Westens,* Nov. 16, 1846.

for the trial of offenders.[377] Some Ute had a council with the general, and they left him, not altogether satisfied, as he threatened to make them behave. . .

SEPTEMBER 22. Today Captain Fischer returned with about fifty Navajo, who had a council with the general, the result of which I did not learn. This evening about dark a hard rain blew up, the first we have had since August 20.

SEPTEMBER 24. The high peaks of the mountains northeast of town are covered with snow, which glitters as the rays of the morning sun strike them. From their perfectly white appearance, the snow must be at least several inches deep. We had a hard rain here last night, but it has scarcely effected any change in the temperature of the weather – at all events so little that we find it comfortable enough without fire. These mountains are said to have snow and ice generally about their summits. The court-martial adjourned today after acting on the case for which they were convened. The merchants gave General Kearny a *fandango* at the *Palacio* last night, but none of us attended except the first lieutenant. King's train of commissary teams drove in this morning, having

377 On September 19, 1846, Kearny issued the following order: "The General commanding has much regretted to see such a want of discipline & insubordination as exists in most of the companies of the Mo. Mounted Vols. From this time a change for the better should be effected, & all officers, particularly company commanders, should more closely attend to their duties, & see that the men under them properly perform what is expected from soldiers in the service of the U. States. Officers must not think, that the object of the Government in sending them into the field, is, to make interest with those under their command, so that they may secure their votes either at home or abroad: but that they are commissioned to perform certain high duties for the advancement of the glory of our country; & such duties can only be performed by exacting rigid discipline & subordination from all under their command. An army is a mob of the worst kind, unless properly governed & restrained." Kearny, Order No. 28, Sept. 19, 1846, Letters Received, MSS., O.F.S., A.G.O.

left Fort Leavenworth July 7. He says the teams hired to come to Bent's Fort had all turned back, having first discharged their loads, and that he knows of fifty doing so.

SEPTEMBER 25. Today about noon General Kearny left for California, and Colonel Doniphan is now in command. There is considerable sickness not only in our company but with all the troops here. Some have chills which they brought with them; some with what Doctor De Camp says is called in Missouri "winter fever"; and many with tonsilitis, a disease affecting the men something like mumps.

SEPTEMBER 28. Lieutenant Abert arrived yesterday from Bent's Fort and says that two companies of Price's regiment reached there before he left, and that a hundred wagonloads of provisions had been stored away, the teamsters returning to the United States. The nights are cool, very much like October weather in "the States," but without frost, and the days warm and pleasant. Out of doors, fire is comfortable at night but is not yet required in the houses. The people of the United States are greatly behind the Mexicans in making cornstalk sugar, as it is a very common thing both here and farther south. The Santa Féans are now employed at it, the process being very simple. They take the young stalks, beat and mash them up with malls in large troughs, then press them in a press such as we generally have at cider mills, and boil the juice in kettles. Today I saw the process in all its different stages in three or four places in the upper part of town. The sugar is pleasant and put up in cakes with corn shucks, and for a long time was mistaken by us for maple sugar brought from Chihuahua.

SEPTEMBER 29. Colonel Price and Major Spalding

reached here last night, but they bring no news. The troops[378] will be in, in two or three days.

OCTOBER 1. Today Captain Morin came up in advance of his company, which escorts a train of commissary teams from Bent's Fort. He brings a report that negotiations for peace are on foot and that orders have [been] issued accordingly to the commanding general in the South. I visited the men in the mountains from our company who are getting out mill timbers, and had a pleasant ride, and a hearty dinner at their camp. I saw no game except a prairie rabbit and [a] squirrel, and Spaniards with wood, which they bring in eight or nine miles on their donkeys.

OCTOBER 2. Four companies of Colonel Price's command came up, and after marching into the plaza returned and camped where we did, on the hill that overlooks town. They are a fine-looking set of men, and their horses generally are in good order. They brought one howitzer in with them. The companies were under [the] command of Major Edmonson.

OCTOBER 3. Major Spalding,[379] the paymaster, commenced paying off the officers today, not having money sufficient to pay the men. It seems they have only brought out a small portion of specie, expecting to be able to sell Treasury drafts to the traders, in which they are disappointed, the traders not yet having reached Chihuahua. Great complaints are made, as the paper is

378 The Second regiment of Missouri mounted volunteers, in command of Colonel Sterling Price, reached Santa Fé during the latter part of September and the early part of October.

379 Dunham Spalding, a native of New York, was made additional paymaster of volunteers on June 3, 1846. In company with Major Walker, chief paymaster of the Army of the West, he left Jefferson Barracks for Fort Leavenworth on July 28, and journeyed thence to Santa Fé, arriving there in advance of Walker on September 28. He died on May 25, 1848. *Daily Missouri Republican,* July 29, 1846; Heitman, *Historical Register,* I, 908.

almost worthless here, and the army can procure nothing without the cash. Provisions are scarce, and everything obtained from the sutler [is] dear; so that without money their wages are soon exhausted. What will be done is hard to divine, but it seems impossible for a payment to be made for a long time. And some actually suffer for the want of it, particularly those unwell who can procure nothing to suit the fastidious taste of such. We have loaned to the company all the money we could raise, and shall have to go without, ourselves, unless some funds can be obtained from the paymaster.[380] The governor

[380] On June 14, 1846, Major Walker, chief paymaster of the Army of the West, then stationed at Jefferson Barracks, wrote a letter to Colonel Kearny inquiring what amount and kind of money he should obtain to pay the soldiers of the Santa Fé expedition. Replying a week later, the colonel advised that as much gold as practicable be obtained, that next to gold, Treasury drafts were the most desirable, that only a small quantity of notes of the Bank of Missouri be secured, and that some dimes and half dimes be included for small change. Kearny also stated that he could give Walker no definite estimate of the total amount of money necessary, since this sum would depend upon the size of the expedition and upon the length of its service outside of the United States, facts which had not as yet been positively determined. On July 28, Walker, accompanied by Spalding, left Jefferson Barracks and arrived at Santa Fé on October 7, Spalding having been sent ahead with the funds. The currency which Walker brought from St. Louis consisted of about $20,000 in gold, some Treasury drafts of small denominations, a few notes of the Bank of Missouri, and small change. But this amount of money was totally inadequate to pay all the officers and men in the Army of the West. Besides, the drafts and notes were not acceptable as a medium of exchange in New Mexico. "It turns out," asserted the *Daily Missouri Republican* (November 11, 1846), "that these Treasury drafts will not go any better in Santa Fé than they do here [St. Louis], if so well, and the notes of the Bank are in worse odor. The Mexicans will not sell any thing whatever for Treasury drafts (they don't like Uncle Sam's promises) or for Missouri notes. Every thing they have to sell must be paid for in specie, or they will not sell at all. The general trade of the country has been so broken up by the war and the delay of the traders on the route, that they have not the specie (if they had the inclination) to exchange for these drafts; consequently, the Government officers can do nothing with them, except, in a few instances, when the sutler or some American trader, chooses to take them at a large shave." See also Turner to Walker, June 21, 1846, Kearny Letter Book, MS., M.H.S.; *Daily Missouri Republican,* July 29, 1846; *Jefferson Inquirer,* Nov. 17, 1846.

has passed an order directing all stores to be closed to-morrow, and the church bells have been ringing all evening on account of it. Such an order was much needed, as there was not the least observance of the day by anybody – so little that it could easily be mistaken for any other day of the week. It is reported that some Navajo Indians recently made an incursion upon San Miguel and drove off a large flock of sheep. But the Spaniards are such notorious liars that little credit is given to what they say.

OCTOBER 5. General Kearny directed Lieutenant Gilmer to explore the head of this little stream and see what connection there was between it and the lake which is said to exist in the mountains; and this morning he left for that purpose, as the season was getting late. Captain Murphy, with R. Groomes, accompanied him, and they expect to be absent three or four days.

OCTOBER 7. As soon as Colonel Price arrived, an express was sent to General Kearny, which returned last night, having left the general a hundred and seventy-five miles from this place. It brought an order for Colonel Doniphan to march with his regiment against the Navajo and make war on them, and then to proceed south and join General Wool;[381] also an order authorizing Colonel Price to follow him to California with not exceeding 500 men as soon as the Mormons leave, who are to have an outfit first. Captain Cooke is placed in command of the Mormons and has returned to assume it. Colonel Doniphan says if he can get pack animals he will take our company along to the Navajo country, but as there is great difficulty in procuring them, we are apprehensive we shall remain, much against our inclination. We had a hard rain last night, and the mountains

[381] See appendix.

northeast of town are covered with snow a second time this fall, and the weather is chilly compared to what we have had. Another of Colonel Price's companies arrived yesterday, and several more are expected today. Doctor Penn, who has received an appointment at St. Louis, leaves with a mail, and Mr. Thurman of our company goes as one of the escort. Sealey, a private in company A, died last night at the hospital, and was buried this evening with military honors. He is the fourth who has died since we left Fort Leavenworth, Robinson, who was left sick at Bent's Fort, having died there.

OCTOBER 8. Lieutenant Gilmer and Captain Murphy returned from the mountains yesterday and report the snow on them about three inches deep. They found the wheat perfectly green in some of the valleys about ten miles up, the strawberries in bloom and some just ripe, and altogether as many climates in the short distance of eighteen miles as the world will perhaps afford anywhere. They represent the lake as a small affair, a hundred and fifty yards long and seventy-five wide, the head of this stream, and a canyon with precipitous and rocky sides running in the shape of a horseshoe into the heart of the mountain. The country is filled with chasms, ledges of rock, and precipices in many places, presenting impossible barriers; and the summits of the mountain [are] covered with balsam firs [and] with long and velvetlike moss, which gives a dreary appearance and hiding place for the few pheasants or grouse that frequent these lonely places. The inclemency of the weather caused them to hurry home. And they say they could catch no fish in the lake but saw some of a singular appearance, the fins [being found] where the legs of other animals are. They saw scarcely no game, but indications [were] plentiful that bears were in abundance.

Major Walker, the paymaster, arrived last night, and also a letter mail, but [there was] nothing for me except a few papers. I received a letter, though, from Mrs. Gibson by one of the sutler's teams, the first I have had for a long time. This made me wish I was where I could enjoy the comforts and happiness of a domestic fireside, which only those who have tasted of it know how to estimate. Major Walker brought no specie, and the army and public are all much dissatisfied at the simpleness of our rulers who thus permit the soldiers, or rather force them, to go six months when they should be paid every two. Mr. Billingsby returns to Missouri with Doctor Penn and gave me a cordial shake as he started off. I wished I had to accompany him in, as he accompanied us out. Harris, of our company, has the scurvy badly, and I am told it is common in the army. The cause cannot be salt provisions, for we have had none. The weather has become quite cool, and frost makes its appearance about the water, but the atmosphere is too dry for it to be general. The most disagreeable sight, as well as the object of greatest commiseration, in Santa Fé is an old, demented woman who is said once to have been the wealthiest individual in New Mexico. She is constantly wandering about the streets in filth and rags, begging for something to eat, and devouring the castaway rinds of melons like a hog. She is a nuisance to the public, and perhaps verifies the old saw, *quem deus vult perdere priusquam dementat.*[382] I have seen many objects of pity but never one whose history, if written out, would be so full either of interest or instruction.

OCTOBER 9. The necessity of specie is so great that it has been determined to send to St. Louis for $100,000,

[382] Whom god wishes to destroy he first makes mad.

and Captain Murphy is detailed to go after it.[383] He left us this morning with a pack mule, expecting to overtake the mail which left on the seventh with one wagon and an escort. He expects to return between Christmas and the middle of January, before which time the troops cannot be paid off. That the trip will be a severe one cannot be doubted, and at that season of the year it may be productive of suffering incalculable.[384] The Mormons

[383] Writing to the Secretary of War on October 20, 1846, Colonel Doniphan described the conditions in New Mexico which led to the dispatch of Captain Murphy to St. Louis: "The army has been greatly embarrassed for want of specie funds. The Qr. Master has been required to furnish large supplies of mules for transportation & has had no available means; the same remark applies to all the Departments; the Paymasters, Majors Walker, Spaulding and Cloud, bringing comparatively nothing with them but checks. Although most of the men would have received these checks – yet, as they would have depreciated immediately, we deemed that the wishes & views of the Government would be better carried out by making no payments to privates except in gold & silver. Heretofore this currency [*i.e.,* checks] was greatly sought after in this Country, but such is not the case at present. The want of all intercourse with Chihuahua and other southern provinces, & the inability of traders to carry goods into them, or bring specie out, has rendered it impossible to convert any sort of paper into specie here. This Territory is poor, and the money is confined to a few American traders – who I regret to say are generally Americans only in name. They are Mexicans in feeling, & Jews in principle – and the few drafts that were attempted to be cashed for the Qr. Mrs. Department, they were the first to depreciate; & although they are making some remittances, they ask from 10 to 25 per cent to make an exchange alike accomodating to them & us. The Spaniards will not touch checks; but this is not strange. After a consultation with Major Walker and others, it was deemed proper to send an express to St. Louis for $100,000. I sent a Captain for it. He will get proper transportation at Leavenworth and be back by the first of January. I feel assured that in this our views meet the approbation of the Administration." Doniphan to Marcy, Oct. 20, 1846, Letters Received, MSS., O.F.S., A.G.O.

[384] Accompanied by three men, Captain Murphy made a rapid journey across the plains, reaching Westport, Missouri, on November 3 and St. Louis five days later. In the latter city he obtained $100,000 or $120,000 in gold from the Bank of Missouri and departed for Fort Leavenworth as soon as possible. Leaving that post with an escort of about twenty men on December 5, he made a winter trip over the prairies, arriving in Santa Fé about the middle or latter part of January, 1847. *Daily Missouri Republican,* Nov. 9, 11, Dec. 17, 1846, Feb. 19, 1847; *St. Louis Daily New Era,* Nov. 14, 1846; *Weekly Tribune,* Nov. 21, 1846; *Weekly Reveille,* Apr. 5, 1847.

in charge of Lieutenant Smith arrived and attracted great attention. They are well drilled, a shabby-looking set, and camped northeast of town with Major Edmonson's command. The women and children generally and a large body are behind, only about three hundred coming in today. A large mail came in today, but [there was] nothing for me except the letter of August 14, mentioned yesterday as received, which I got this morning.

OCTOBER 11. Colonel Mitchell's command arrived yesterday and made a good showing, both horses and men, the former being in pretty good order and condition. And all the remaining companies, except Captain Morin's, came in today. It rained hard yesterday and the night before, but the weather is otherwise pleasant and tolerably warm, notwithstanding the snow on the mountains. The town is crowded with soldiers, and all are anxious to get away, each one wishing to be the first. Some prefer an expedition to California, and some south, and all are fearful they will not get to go where they wish. Mr. Fitzpatrick, who went as one of General Kearny's guides, returned today in company with an express from California.[385] He brought us intelligence that the Californias were revolutionized, Colonel Frémont acting as governor, and that General Kearny had ordered back all the troops with him except a hundred, whom he took and proceeded on his way to the Pacific.

385 Fitzpatrick brought important dispatches from California, which Kit Carson had delivered to Kearny on October 6. Fitzpatrick left Santa Fé on October 14, reached St. Louis on November 15, and two days later departed for Washington, D. C. The St. Louis *Weekly Reveille* (November 23, 1846) stated: "Few would think, who look at this plain, unassuming mountaineer, that for years his pathway has been through the wild and dangerous regions which lie towards the Pacific. Among the wild tribes of the west he is well known, and none more respected – this may be attributed to the fact that he is cool in danger, kind in his intercourse, and cautious in his movements." See also *Daily Missouri Republican*, Nov. 16, 1846; *House Ex. Docs.*, 30 cong., 1 sess., no. 41, pp. 53, 572.

OCTOBER 12. Captain Hudson has given up his expedition to California, and the men have all returned to their respective companies. A train of commissary teams in charge of Captain Morin's company came up, and two other trains are close behind. Santa Fé is now more like an American than [a] Mexican town, and I cannot go out without meeting an acquaintance from Platte. Many have called to see us, and we are quite at home, having so many of our friends around us. Of course, there was a great shaking of hands and numberless inquiries of men who left Missouri some time after we did. Santa Fé is completely eaten out – scarcely a red pepper is to be found in [the] market. The remainder of the Mormons came up, and when the wagons containing the women stopped at the plaza, all the Mexican women near went up and shook hands with them, apparently both rejoiced and surprised to see them. The kindness and hospitality of the women throughout Mexico is proverbial, and in this instance the burst of feeling was as cordial and warm as a greeting of old friends and acquaintances after a long separation. I saw one very pretty Mormon girl who seemed highly pleased at her reception in Santa Fé and received the Mexicans with as bland a smile as they could have wished. The day Captain Murphy left, John Abel and all at the store left us, and now there is no one in our mess except the first lieutenant and myself and Walter, the servant.

OCTOBER 13. The weather continues cool and bracing, and the sick generally are better. However, frost has not yet shown itself except immediately about the water, but the men camped at the fort say the water in their buckets froze across. About fifty Ute Indians came in and held a council with Colonel Doniphan. They were brought by Major Gilpin, who has been in their country with his command. They are large, robust-looking men, but inferior, I thought, to the Delaware and Shawnee; and such was the general impression. Nor had they that rich Indian costume which I have seen in all the tribes bordering Missouri. Their horses were small but well proportioned, and no doubt were admirably adapted to their habits and pursuits, being both quick and fleet, with powers of endurance. They entered into a treaty, and peace now exists between them and New Mexico.[386]

OCTOBER 14. Mr. Perie, a private of our company who has been sick since we reached Santa Fé, died at the hospital this morning of a pulmonary disease. He had an attack of the same disease about two years since and thought he had recovered, but about the time we reached here he relapsed, after performing the march, having complained but little on the whole route. He was both a good man and good soldier, and his death was much regretted by the company and all who knew him. He had the best medical advice and every attention which could be shown him. This evening he was buried with military honors on the hill near the fort, where all the soldiers are interred, and is almost immediately under the guns of Fort Marcy. His last moments were easy, and he left us with the same tranquil mind which he displayed through life. He now reposes, the evening and morning gun unheard by him, for the great day when Heaven's artillery shall wake the dead to be marshaled for their final doom. There is a general court-martial now in session, and the first lieutenant has preferred

[386] In a letter to the Secretary of War on October 20, 1846, Doniphan wrote: "I am pleased to inform the department that, on the 15th Inst. we closed the war with the Eutaws by a treaty which I doubt not will be lasting. One half of my Regiment under Major Gilpin penetrated their Country 200 miles to the Rocky Mountains; and the principal chiefs came in." Doniphan to Marcy, Oct. 20, 1846, Letters Received, MSS., O.F.S., A.G.O.

charges against Sergeant Aull, who is to be tried by it.

OCTOBER 15. The weather has moderated, and we have one of the most lovely mornings which it has been my good fortune to enjoy. There is great anxiety about subsistence, and we are endeavoring to get away to the south for this and other reasons, with some prospect of success. All the army is now up except the regiment of infantry, and we have not yet heard from them. Companies from Colonel Price's and Colonel Willock's commands have been leaving to relieve Colonel Jackson and Major Gilpin, who march against the Navajo. This evening, with Mr. Giddings, I called upon the priest, who received us kindly, and [we] found him agreeable. He is the fat, jolly fellow mentioned in a preceding page, and talks as if he snuffed to excess or was burdened with his flesh.

OCTOBER 16. Anxious to visit the Navajo country, I solicited Colonel Doniphan to permit me to accompany him in his contemplated expedition against them, but he declined doing so and said the company could not spare any more officers from duty. As their country is in a measure unexplored, and represented to be very broken and picturesque, I was in hopes I could visit it, but all chance seems to be gone for such a trip. Our company furnishes details for almost everything that has been done since we reached here. A large party has been camped in the mountains, getting out timbers for the fort and mill. Another party is camped at the fort, consisting of carpenters, masons, and their assistants. We have one at the blacksmith shop, one at the printing office, two at the hospital, and some procuring wood for the company, besides the guard at quarters and our regular guard on the plaza. All these have kept the men constantly on duty, so that frequently every man was at something, and sometimes [there were] not enough [men] to answer the details made upon us. Many of our men have been sick, which I attribute to sleeping on the dirt floors. They are sprinkled to be swept, and consequently are kept cold and damp, producing a return of ague and some cases of fever. Arrangements have been made by the first lieutenant to procure bunks, and I think their health will be greatly promoted by it, if not entirely restored.

On our route we often passed what are miscalled "dog towns," never dreaming that we were on our way to one that would far eclipse them all. If Santa Fé could boast of nothing else it might lay claim to the appellation of "biggest dog town in the Union," for if ever the canine species infested a place, they do this. When we first reached here, they literally had possession of the streets, the plaza, and the suburbs, and enough can still be found to make a respectable dog town. But between kicks and cuffs and sabres and bayonets, they have been considerably thinned. Nor are they such dogs as one can feel disposed to pick acquaintance with; none of your well-fed mastiff's frank and open countenance, but a kind of sneaking, wolfish cur that carries his head down as if he was afraid to look you in the face or had been caught at some mean trick – one that sneaks off when [a person] boldly advances upon him. Such they are generally, but to give variety to their nightly concerts they keep a stock of all kinds of feists that have a treble note by no means pleasant. The whole valley for miles is made to ring with their yelps as far as can be heard, first one commencing below and then another above town, all between answering and keeping up a perpetual bark from sundown to sunrise. Much has been said about Mexican shepherd dogs, and they have some which deserve all the notice given them. But about here they have only a few which are not lank, lean, ill-fed, and ill-tempered, without any pretensions to the claims set up for them. Good shepherd dogs must be valuable, for our men camped at the fort tell me they see wolves there almost every morning, thus making their approaches, as it were, into the very town, notwithstanding their dogs and the fuss they keep.

One of the few entertainments we have is the artillery band at tattoo, who play several tunes every evening between the calls. To hear the martial notes of a bugle [on] a clear, calm, lovely evening is always soul stirring, but to have three or four good musicians in a land destitute of taste or rational amusements nightly play some old and favorite air, when one's mind is running upon home, friends, and the many luxuries and enjoyments we have deprived ourselves of, is certainly a pleasure of no small consequence, and especially when we have but little prospect of getting away soon from a place we are all tired of. When I was weary and fatigued on the march across the plains and heard the bugle call the hour for rest, I thought it a glorious sound stealing over the dreary waste. But long habit and the many pleasant associations it brings to mind, make it doubly dear now, and one of the few enjoyments I have in Santa Fé is the music. While the Mormons were camped above us, the drum and fife gave a more warlike tone and supplied a desideratum on many occasions. But nothing produces that quiescent state of the mind like the bugle, with its full rich notes, when well and skillfully handled.

October 19. An American who came out as teamster for the quartermaster was found dead on the Independence road in the outskirts of town, and two Mexicans have been arrested for his murder. He was beaten to death with rocks, his head and body most shockingly mangled, his pockets turned wrong side out, and his watch gone. The watch was found on one of the prisoners, and the proof against them is said to be strong. Of course, such an occurrence produced great excitement in the army, and fed the fire of animosity kindled in our bosoms against them for the low condition and vices which prevail. But there has been no breach of good order, nor even any threats, the whole matter being left to take the due course of law. Should a similar occurrence, though, take place, there would be danger of an explosion, as there is no good feeling for the native population. The green-eyed monster is said to have been the cause of the murder. But as the man was only paid off that day (yesterday), and having evidently robbed him of his watch and perhaps [his] money, as none was found about him, the probability is that it was only a pretext to be used in case of detection.[387]

A report is current that 1,200 or 2,000 Mexican troops from Sonora are at the Pass,[388] and that they have captured the goods of the traders who went below to await the taking of Chihuahua by General Wool. We have had plenty [of] ice for several nights, and it is quite cool, but dry as usual, and the days pleasant – October weather. Frost only appears near the water, as the atmosphere is too dry to produce this sanitary visitor. Colonel Doniphan's regiment have been leaving for several days, and the last broke up camp today and took up the line of march southward, except a few who are compelled by their duties to remain. They first visit the Navajo country and then go south to join General Wool.

387 The murdered teamster's name was Robinson. *Weekly Reveille,* Dec. 21, 1846.

388 El Paso del Norte.

A more ragamuffin-looking set than the Mormons it would be hard to find out of New Mexico, and they will just suit [as] men and women for this latitude. From the officers down I could see nothing like a genteel-looking man, all having a shabby appearance, and most generally bad countenances. Some of their women went to a Spanish *fandango,* and it was hard to tell which had the advantage of the other, the Mormon or the Mexican. Some of them left yesterday, and the remainder today, about ninety returning to Bent's Fort to winter and cross over at the South pass in the spring.[389] The others strike the Pacific at the nearest point, where government transports will be provided to carry them up to California. They left without noise or confusion, and I watched them from Fort Marcy as they slowly gained in distance until they were entirely lost to view. Their departure has considerably thinned the town, but we still have more troops than are needed at this point, as they only create confusion and disturbance. "The States" have lost nothing by the Mormon emigration, and California gains as little, for the state of Illinois makes a good bargain to get shut of them at any cost.

OCTOBER 20. Mr. Campbell arrived from "the States" and brought us intelligence that ten infantry companies were at Fort Leavenworth ready to leave, and that they are now probably thirty days out. Major Sumner, Lieu-

[389] Captain Cooke, who assumed command of the Mormon battalion on October 13, 1846, described it as follows: "It was enlisted too much by families; some were too old, – some feeble, and some too young; it was embarrassed by many women; it was undisciplined; it was much worn by travelling on foot, and marching from Nauvoo, Illinois; their clothing was very scant; – there was no money to pay them, – or clothing to issue. . . A small party with families, had been sent from Arkansas crossing up the river, to winter at a small settlement close to the mountains, called Pueblo. The battalion was now [*i.e.,* about October 18] inspected, and eighty-six men found inefficient, were ordered, under two officers, with nearly all the women, to go to the same point." Cooke, *Conquest of New Mexico and California,* 91.

tenant Love, and Lieutenant Stanton returned to Fort Leavenworth, the former to take his command in the Second regiment [of] dragoons, the second to recruit, and the last to take the regimental papers. The report now is that some of the traders have been imprisoned and their goods taken. If so, it is believed here to be by a marauding party, plunder being their only object. Our company suffer many privations for the want of wood, and have just cause of complaint on this score. The teams furnished by the quartermaster are old, broken-down oxen that frequently give out, and at best only make one load a day, as it has to be hauled six or seven miles. In consequence, their meals are very irregular, and it is oftentimes annoying, and when they get wood it is green and makes but a poor fire. How we will do when winter sets in with all its rigors, can be better imagined than described, unless some improvement is effected. The first lieutenant has been complaining, with the hope that something would be done; but as yet there is no change, and we all complain but to no purpose. The quartermaster says he has no better teams and that he cannot procure forage to feed teams.

OCTOBER 21. A report has been industriously circulated this morning that the Spaniards were to have attempted [a] revolt last night by cutting off the officers, producing confusion, and then seizing upon the artillery and magazine. No credit is given to it, notwithstanding it is countenanced by some men of influence who reside here. It is said to come from the Mexican women, who disclosed the plot. But the best informed lay it at the doors of a few men who have been reaping a rich harvest from the soldiers, and who adopt this plan to retain a large force at this point. Whether their fears are real or pretended, the effect is injurious both to the people and troops, as they serve to keep up a hatred or contempt which should be kept down, now that they are our fellow citizens.

For the past three days I have been on duty superintending the work at the fort and found it more pleasant than I anticipated, but by no means agreeable on account of the dust. This evening a storm blew up, and between rain, hail, and dust, it was not only impossible to work but even to see. The effect was to cool the air and drive us home a little before our time. The blockhouse is to be adobe, with walls six feet thick, and was marked off today by Lieutenant Gilmer, the breastwork for the batteries and ditch being nearly completed. At the depth of seven or eight feet the earth seems never to have been wet, and is more like an ash heap than anything else, except near the surface, where it is gravelly and hard. They continue to dig up human skeletons, which are scattered all over the hill. There is a tradition that the Indians and Spaniards fought a battle at this place, but I can learn nothing certain about it.

OCTOBER 23. It is cloudy, cold, and has every appearance of visiting us with a snowstorm; yet the early morn was clear, warm, and delightful. The court, in the case of Sergeant Aull, found him guilty and sentenced him to forfeit one month's pay. The first lieutenant has procured bedticks and straw for the company, and it is hoped their health will now improve. Men are detailed to get out the lumber and timbers for bunks, when they will at least be more comfortable.

OCTOBER 24. Though nearly seven thousand feet above the ocean, Santa Fé is blessed with a climate singularly mild, equable, and salubrious, and what is most strange, is surrounded by mountains of considerable elevation.

It has been snowing on both sides of us for twenty-four hours. And one can hardly realize the fact (but "seeing is believing") that it should be so mild and temperate, and withal sunny, in the midst of snows; yet such is the case. This evening sundown was magnificent, a heavy dark cloud resting on the mountains in the northwest, evidently discharging a fleecy covering on them. And in the southwest we had as rich a sunset as an Italian sky could boast, with its gold and purple colors intermingling and as finely displayed as the fancy ever painted or could wish. It looked strange to see winter in one part of the heavens and summer in another. When you turn to take a view in the opposite direction, you have the snowy mountains, their white summits reflecting back the rays of the sun in strange contrast with the country around us, where summer still lingers, as if loath to leave us. In a conversation with the commissary I learn that it is impossible to procure feed within fifty miles for the cattle belonging to this department, the whole country being literally eaten up. And the impression is becoming strong that all the troops except one or two companies will have to leave this post on this account, as we can neither keep beef cattle, oxen, or mules, and consequently will have no wood or fresh meat.

OCTOBER 25. Armijo left in such a hurry that his state coach fell into our hands and is still here, a curious specimen of Mexican taste and workmanship. The body rests upon two large pieces of timber firmly secured on the axles, which are wide apart, making it both heavy and unwieldy. In front it is ornamented with gilt work, and, when new, was no doubt very grand and imposing in the eyes of his dutiful subjects. What will be its fate I know not – perhaps to carry Governor Bent and his successors to different parts of this valley; for, as to going out of it, no one in his senses would risk his neck in such a clumsy and crazy affair.

I have not been well for several days – perhaps the effect of a good appetite and not sufficient exercise. So I put myself on short rations of bread and water, and this evening tried the remedy so efficacious on the prairies – a box of sardines. The medicine, if not so active as a bolus, is at least more easily taken, quite as pleasant, and probably as judiciously administered. We have had a fine, clear, warm day, but a few nebulous clouds have been resting all the time on the mountain tops as low down as the snow line, produced no doubt in the same way the well-known Magellan clouds are. The first lieutenant and myself visited Captain Morin's company, who leave tomorrow for Red river and will not likely be here again this winter. They were all busy fixing gears and preparing for the march. As we returned, the artillery band had just given a call for retreat and were entertaining the town with some music, which, dull as the place is, gave some life to the scene for a few moments. The Hon. Joab Houghton has ordered a special term of the circuit court for Santa Fé to be held the first Tuesday in December next for the trial of all criminals who may be brought before it.

OCTOBER 28. For the first time we have had a little snow today. But the weather is by no means unpleasant, neither windy nor cold. Corn meal is scarce and is worth $5 a *fanega,* which is about two and a half bushels. The commissary purchases flour at $4.50 per bushel, and mutton at $1.50 a carcass, butchered and dressed. Melons are still abundant in [the] market, and *piñones* in any quantity. Wood is worth two bits a jack load, and the quartermaster allows ten loads to make a cord, but it is not enough. This would make wood worth about $2.50 per cord, but you cannot procure it for less than nearly double this amount. I learn that the quartermaster is offering $80 per thousand for lumber and cannot procure it at this price. Bacon is selling at 40¢ per pound, and fresh pork at 18¾¢, and good brandy at $10 per gallon.

All of the volunteers have expressed the greatest anxiety to get out of the country, and each one is trying to devise some plan to be ordered south, which is regarded as tantamount to it. Without any warfare except Indian, and that only the semblance of one, and without employment except the drudgeries at the fort and other places, and surrounded by poverty and ignorance, they naturally begin to be very anxious to change their condition. Our schemes to be ordered south have all fallen through, and we fear that Santa Fé will find us here next spring. Without books, society, or amusements, we would gladly exchange the mud houses of Santa Fé for a log cabin in "the States." On Monday a letter was received from Captain Burgwin, requesting Colonel Doniphan with his regiment to come down immediately, as the enemy were threatening to plunder the traders; and another [letter] from Colonel Owens [390] confirms the

[390] In a letter dated Valverde, October 20, 1846, Samuel C. Owens wrote his wife: "I wrote you from opposite Socorro, some two weeks ago. Since then, we have come on to this place. We have sent an express consisting of Doct. Connelly, Mcmanis & Doan. James Magoffin went ahead of them, and was Robd of every thing that he had, between Doña Anna and the El Paso. At this last place, on Mr. Magoffin's arrival he was detained as a prisoner. On the arrival of our express at El Paso they also were taken as prisoners, and all of them have been sent to Chihuahua. All intercourse is cut off between Chihuahua and this department, and when we will get any news from there god only Knows. At any Rate we do not look for any before Wool captures that City. The prospect for the traders are gloomy. Their expenses have been so enormous, that it must eat up all the proffits, and at present there is no Knowing when those expenses will cease." Owens to his wife, Oct. 20, 1846, Owens MSS., Jacksonville, Fla.

news. This has thrown the whole army into commotion, all requesting to be ordered on the expedition, as several hundred troops were said to be collecting within four days' march of the traders. Our chance seems slim, but we still have a lingering hope that something will transpire to call us from the mud walls and dusty streets of Santa Fé. Colonel Doniphan left on Tuesday, and Colonel Price is now in command of this post, Colonel Doniphan still being in command in New Mexico. The first lieutenant has been on duty at the fort since Monday.

OCTOBER 31. The snow line has been gradually extending down from the summits of the mountains until this morning it reaches their base, and it is cold and wintry. In addition to the officer drill, we are hereafter to have a dress parade at least every Sunday. The artillery now have one every evening. This morning James Smith, one of our company, died suddenly from measles. He was one of our best and most estimable men, and the event is regretted by all. This evening he was buried at the fort with military honors. Captain Thompson, of [the] First dragoons, arrived from Fort Leavenworth and brought news that the infantry regiment at that place was disbanded by orders from Washington.

NOVEMBER 1. The mountains in all directions have snow on them, yet the day is [as] warm and pleasant as May. A report has reached us via Chihuahua that General Taylor had attacked the Mexicans in their intrenchments at Monterrey, which he carried after considerable loss, the Mexican general being killed, and that General Wool was approaching Chihuahua, which, it was thought, he would reach before 3,500 Mexicans from Sonora could get into the place. Governor Bent thinks there is some foundation for the rumors, but as yet they want confirmation. The news about the infantry regiment has quieted all alarms about provisions, and it is now thought we shall have enough to subsist upon. The greatest difficulty yet exists about procuring forage, and we cannot get teams sufficient to carry on the work at the fort, much less for other purposes. The stock is all poor and unable to bring in a decent load of wood, and the men often suffer for the want of fuel.

NOVEMBER 3. I was officer of the guard on Sunday and again today, and had some amusement at the effect of the late orders. When the gun fires, they can be seen running in all directions, the monte tables are deserted, and the merry *fandango* is no longer heard. The night is beautiful and clear, the full moon shedding its mild rays upon a quiet and peaceful town, and the stillness [is] only interrupted by the tread of the sentinels, the rattling of their arms, or the reliefs going on post. Occasionally a sentinel is heard calling for the corporal of the guard, having taken a prisoner, some unlucky individual who is caught straying from home or returning from a gambling house. But such occurrences are very rare, as all have a dread of the guardhouse and calaboose. They tell a good story on Captain Fischer, who, [on] Saturday night, sent his baker into town for bread, where the guard took him prisoner and lodged him in the guardroom. The captain waited, but his baker did not come, and he came out himself to see what was the matter, fearing all was not right. And the first sentinel he came to took him prisoner, not having the right countersign, and he was also sent to the guardroom, where he found his baker. After explanations the officer of the guard released him, it appearing the countersign had become public and [had] been changed. There was a *fandango* opposite our quarters Saturday night, and when they came out to go home they found a sentinel posted at the door, who refused egress. The consequence was [that] the men and women all preferred spending the night [there] to going to the guardroom; and [they] were only permitted to come out at reveille, which they did, vowing it was the last *fandango* they would be caught at after ten o'clock.

Yesterday was All Saints' Day, and they commenced ringing bells at daybreak and continued it until noon. Everything in the shape of [a] bell, big and little, cracked and sound, was brought into requisition, and they kept up a constant clattering as if the salvation of souls depended on their ringing. A mail arrived this evening but, much to my disappointment, there was nothing for me, not even a newspaper. Neither did it bring any news except what we have had from some other source.

NOVEMBER 4. This morning I purchased from some Pueblo Indians a *tilma* for Mrs. Gibson, made of buffalo hair and handsomely embroidered around the edges. It is a fine specimen of native manufacture. What the cause of the late orders is, or under whose influences they have been framed and advised, I cannot learn, but their operation is far from beneficial. Colonel Price's own regiment and Colonel Willock's battalion complain loudly, as they furnish the picket guards and patrols, the artillery and infantry making up the plaza guard. The citizens openly express their dissatisfaction for depriving them of their pleasures and amusements, and all condemn the plan of giving the military the supremacy over the civil authorities. There is still snow on all the mountains, but down here we have sunny, pleasant weather. A young Spaniard who was a cadet at one of the Chihuahua military schools died, and was buried yesterday with military honors, Major Clark furnishing an escort from the artillery. The procession was unusually large and respectable, headed by the priest in his robes in the usual Catholic style, the first time I have seen him heading a funeral. There is a curious house bird here of the swallow species. At a little distance it has a brown appearance, but when examined is found to be nearly a mixture of red and gray. There are great numbers about the houses, which they serve to enliven. When we first came, we found a swallow pretty much like the river bird of this species in "the States," but they have all left. The former is probably a species of redbird and has a chirp very much like the female redbird.

The army complains of the adjutant's office for the irregularity in making details, and the infantry in particular have just cause, as they do more than any other corps and always have. The mounted troops are without discipline or order and only swell our numbers, eat rations, and kick up rows. Of course, all duties which can be are imposed upon the artillery and infantry, as they inspire more confidence, particularly in guard duties.

NOVEMBER 5. I am on duty at the fort today, and as I returned from dinner found the sun and heat oppressive, and perspiration free. I was not up long and had not yet set the men to work before a dark and threatening cloud was seen in the southwest, and from its rapid approaches and the muttering thunder we had indications not to be mistaken that we had better seek a shelter. This we barely had time to do before the most violent storm of wind and hail blew over us that we have had at any time. After nearly covering the ground with hail, it commenced snowing and eased off raining, the sun finally coming out bright and warm as usual, though the mountains are white with snow, almost into the very town. It was a day in which summer and winter appeared hand in glove, thunder, snow, dust, and mud all intermingling, the evening being as fine as we have after a spring shower. The accession of snow on the mountains is very apparent. I visited all the sick and found them generally better, except Mulkey. I went to see Surrat, who has been at the hospital some time as attendant, and who has been sick himself for several weeks without my knowledge. I found him better and convalescent.

Eggs are worth twenty-five cents a dozen, and [are] very scarce and hard to get. The commissary now issues one ration to each of the officers, and charges transportation from Missouri for all bought over and above this. It may not be credited, but I saw a Jew betting on monte, and I am told he is a constant frequenter of the tables and generally wins. He seemed to bet liberally and to throw out his gold like a most accomplished blackleg. Here they have no such thing as professional gamblers, for all classes are addicted to this vice, and there is nothing disreputable about it. The picket guard is suspended for the present, and in lieu we have a spy company.

NOVEMBER 7. The day has been warm, clear, and pleasant, and all enjoyed it. The fort is so far completed that it could be occupied in case of necessity, only a portion of the ditch having to be finished. The blockhouse and quarters go up slowly for the want of teams, and it is now doubtful whether they will be finished this winter, though the foundation is laid.[391] Every day at

[391] On November 1, 1846, Lieutenant Gilmer wrote: "The fort now constructing, under my direction, for the defence of this post, is situated on a commanding point to the north-east of the town, and at a distance of 664 yards from the centre of the Plaza, which is about the *point blank* range of a six-pounder. The work is a 'Star Fort,' and the plan is constructed within the sides of an irregular hexagonal polygon, each face having the dimensions

ten o'clock a cannon is fired for the officers to meet on the plaza for drill, and many complain loudly about exposing them to the men, as they are not so good on parade as the privates of the artillery and infantry. The artillery has been moved to the plaza and makes a most formidable park. There are 2 twenty-four-pounder howitzers, 4 nine-pounder cannon, 4 six-pounder cannon, 2 twelve-pounder howitzers, 11 four-pounder howitzers, [and] 2 four-pounder cannon (Mexican), making a total of 25 and extending across the plaza, besides several yet at the artillery quarters. One of the fine brass six-pounders is the Texan piece, the Lone Star and M. B. Lamar's name upon it; and [it] is superior to any six-pounder we brought out. All except some of the six-pounders are brass.

Yesterday Walter stole the first lieutenant's purse and about $10, and he had him in the calaboose last night.

---

necessary to adapt it to the accidents of the ground which forms the site. The batteries are on the fronts, which give the most direct fires upon the town and valley of Santa Fé, and the avenues of approach. The parapets are of sufficient extent to furnish space for mounting seventeen cannon, and still afford long lines for musketry. The work has a relief of seventeen feet; that is, the top of the parapet is seventeen feet above the bottom of the ditch, the ditch being eight feet deep. The fort is of a more permanent character than is usual in the construction of field works. The revetments of the interior and exterior slopes, and of the embrasures, are made of sun-dried brick, which, in the climate of New Mexico, are much more durable than sods, fascines or gabions. All the heavy excavations and embankments are now completed, and the work is in a condition to make a good defence, should any emergency require us to fight for our position. A garrison of 350 American soldiers will be able to hold the place against any Mexican force *ten* times their number. It is proposed to build a powder magazine and store house within the fort, the former of which is now partially constructed, and may be completed in a few days. The barracks for a small garrison will be in a square defensive building, situated on a point in advance of the north-east face of the work, and at a distance of about sixty yards from it. This defensive building is partly erected, and, should the weather of the present month prove favorable for the prosecution of the work, it will be finished this fall." *Weekly Reveille,* Jan. 18, 1847.

This morning he brought him up to the kitchen and went out a few minutes, and in the meantime Walter absconded through the window, and we are without a cook. I purchased a fine specimen of gypsum from a Spaniard, which he said he got about eight leagues west, in the Navajo country. With an ax he had taken out a large block eighteen inches long and as many wide, [and] three or four inches thick. It is unusually clear and pure, and was intended for window glass, which he said they made by dipping it in warm water and then separating it in thin laminae.

NOVEMBER 9. Great numbers of the troops have the measles, and they prove fatal to many, the least exposure prostrating them; and the consequence is that many are alarmed. The general health of the country is not good, as many Spaniards are laid up. The measles are in our company, and we have about twenty on the sick report, and some very bad. The picket guard caused so many complaints that it has been suspended, and the whole converted into a general guard for the plaza, quarters, etc. I wrote to Mrs. Gibson today and promised Jimmy a pair of Spanish spurs and [a] *serape,* and Mrs. Gibson a *tilma* and [a] *colcha.* A great many reports are in circulation, none of which receive any general credit: one that a large body of the enemy are marching up from the lower country; [and] one that General Kearny has been cut off by troops from Sonora and taken prisoner. But they are from Spaniards and will not be credited. We now have a dress parade every evening at four o'clock, in addition to three drills a day.[392]

[392] In a letter dated Santa Fé, November 14, 1846, a volunteer described the daily routine of a soldier: "The time drags heavily along; the reveille summons the men at daylight to attend roll call, when the details are made for the business of the day; in our company, consisting of eight for guard, three for work on the fort, three for fatigue duty in the camp, and three for bringing

NOVEMBER 10. Thomas Mulkey, a private of our company, died last night, and was buried with military honors this evening. Measles was supposed to be his disease. A train of commissary teams arrived today, and others are following close behind. We have a report that General Kearny has been cut off by troops from Sonora and taken prisoner, but it receives no credit. Yet the constant circulation of such rumors keeps the public mind and that of the troops in a feverish and excited state. The Mexicans believe everything, and no reasoning will convince them of any absurdity or impossibility.

NOVEMBER 11. John Groomes, a private of our company who had been confined with the measles in quarters near the fort, was removed to the hospital after becoming very bad, and died there today. He was one of our best men. And there being six deaths yesterday and five today, the public mind is excited, and there exists considerable uneasiness lest we lose a great many this winter.[393] He was buried today with military honors, and

wood. Guard is mounted at nine, and the relieve stands two hours each in every six hours. The city being under martial law after 10 o'clock at night, no one is allowed to stir abroad without the countersign, so the men find no amusement in the numerous *fandangos* in the neighborhood without making a tour in the guard house. At 8 o'clock [A.M.], call for drill is sounded. At ten, the officers drill; at four in the afternoon the men are again drilled, and then paraded on the Public Square, when batallion orders, etc., are read, and again the old bugle is blown at 9 o'clock at night, to summon the men again to roll call, which terminates the business of the day, and the boys are at liberty to get into their blankets." *St. Louis Daily New Era,* Jan. 1, 1847.

393 During October and November, 1846, considerable sickness prevailed among the troops encamped in Santa Fé. The principal diseases were measles, dysentery, and typhus fever, which were often fatal. A number of houses were commandeered and transformed into hospitals, where the sick were under the care of army physicians. The dead were interred at the new American cemetery near Fort Marcy, sometimes as many as five and eight being buried on one day. There were so many deaths that the soldiers became indifferent to the fate of their comrades. "Tis a sad thing," wrote one volunteer, "thus to see so many brave and good men drop off far from their kindred and

richly deserved all of our respect and consideration. The principal disease is measles, and many citizens are suffering from the same cause, three hundred, as I hear from report, being now on the sick list. The weather is warm and pleasant, and it is expected there will be some improvement after they have all had the measles. Captain Thompson, of the First dragoons, is to give us lessons in the sabre exercise, etc., and we are all pleased to have one to perform this duty who can do it so well.

NOVEMBER 15. It has been snowing all morning and is now three inches deep. It comes down in large flakes, and is unusually beautiful from the absence of wind, and size of the flakes. Petitions have been handed Colonel Price from all of us to grant an order for the election of major in our battalion, and should it be done Captain Angney will probably be elected, as he has made a good officer, and one who deserves promotion. A mail leaves tomorrow for "the States," and I wrote to Mrs. Gibson. Lumber is so scarce that the quartermaster has to use wagon bodies to make coffins. Yesterday I procured another servant, Joe, and our dinner today has been better than we have had for some time.

NOVEMBER 18. An order for Lieutenant-colonel Mitchell to proceed to Chihuahua was promulgated yesterday, and will be found on the next page,[394] and all

---

homes with no kind friend or relative to watch over and soothe them in their sickness or to comfort or solace them in the hour of death. The dead here have but few mourners; there are but few tears shed over the soldiers grave. A rude coffin is fixed up for his remains, he is wrapped in his blanket – he is escorted to his burial place by a few soldiers, three rounds are fired over him, and all sorrow and grief for his death, if any there be, is buried in the grave that contains him." *Missouri Statesman,* Jan. 1, 1847. See also *Weekly Reveille,* Dec. 21, 1846, Jan. 4, 11, 1847; *St. Louis Daily New Era,* Jan. 1, 1847; *Daily Missouri Republican,* Jan. 1, 1847; *Jefferson Inquirer,* Jan. 5, 1847; *Weekly Tribune,* Jan. 2, 1847; Connelley, *Doniphan's Expedition,* 77.

[394] See appendix.

are anxious to know who accompanies him. The snow is now three inches deep and it has been still falling today, and we have cold winter weather. The general health of the army has been bad, the measles carrying off numbers, but there is some abatement and prospect of improvement. Today I purchased a robe for Jimmy, from a friend, a merchant of the place. And our new servant gave us a present in the shape of bacon and cabbage for dinner, which is the only one we have had since our departure from Missouri. Commissary trains are coming up every day, and we have provisions in abundance.

NOVEMBER 21. I met Colonel Mitchell today, and saw him again this evening, when he told me I would be taken with him. Of course, I feel rejoiced [395] at leaving a place like Santa Fé and joining the expedition, though it may prove hazardous and severe at this season of the year. We have theater tonight, and all are going to try and spend one pleasant evening. There are some fears about General Wool, as we have no news whatever from him or Chihuahua. A messenger from Armijo's brother with letters to the ex-governor was captured by the regulars, and it makes some talk. He was disclosing our situation and recommending him to come up with a force, as we were much scattered (so I am told). Armijo has been in custody but was released from some cause.

NOVEMBER 22. Last night the theater went off well, and was attended by such a large crowd that there was great inconvenience on this account. The *vicario* was present, as well as many of the best women, all of whom enjoyed it and were much pleased. The tragedy was

[395] Many troops, tired of living in Santa Fé, were anxious to get into active service. "I am heartily sick and tired of Santa Fé," recorded one soldier on November 14, 1846, "and the glory of *serving my country*, etc., might all go to the very ——, if I could once more sit down to a good dinner in St. Louis." *Weekly Reveille*, Jan. 11, 1847.

"Pizarro," all the characters of which were remarkably well sustained, particularly Alonzo, Rolla, and Pizarro. The afterpiece was "Bombastes Furioso" and produced no little merriment, but the Ethiopians created roars of applause. The prologue was original and good – nay in some parts very fine – and whoever the author of it and [of] some sallies of wit, deserves great credit. One thing that pleased much was in the Negro performance, when the question was asked why a lady's bustle was like Missouri volunteers, and answered: "Because it is filled with bran" – alluding to Taos flour, which is unbolted and unpopular in the army.[396]

Commissary trains arrive daily, and Mr. Culver informs me that there are 500 dead oxen between this and

[396] In October some of the volunteers organized a dramatic association, which gave its first performance about the middle of November. Lieutenant Elliott described its activities: "A large room in the palace had been granted by Governor Bent for the use of a Thespian Company, organized mainly by some of the Laclede Rangers, under the direction of the projector, Bernard McSorley, still [1883] a citizen of St. Louis. McSorley was stage manager, and star actor. Under his direction scenes were painted and the 'sala' fitted up in a manner that would have made Sol. Smith leap for joy in his itinerant days, when he sometimes had to use big potatoes for candlesticks in his row of tallow footlights. The play on the first night was Pizarro in Peru, or the Death of Rolla, and was well sustained to a 'crowded house.' McSorley was a splendid Pizarro, and conquered the audience as if they were real Peruvians. Elvira was done by Edward W. Shands, and Cora by Wm. Jamieson, of the Rangers, both in appropriate female costume, doing their best to look the characters as well as act them. After the tragedy came negro minstrels, led by James W. Leal of the Rangers, who afterwards suffered so terrible a death in Taos. As we had at times to use unbolted flour, made from native wheat in the rude native mills, one of the conundrums was – 'Why are the volunteers like ladies' bustles?' – and the answer – ''case they're stuffed with bran!' The Mexican ladies were much amused at the idea of 'hombres' (men) acting feminine characters, and said it might do in the 'Teatro,' but would not answer so well in the 'casa,' or dwelling." Elliott, *Notes Taken in Sixty Years,* 250. See also *Täglicher Anzeiger des Westens,* Jan. 4, Feb. 20, 1847; *Weekly Reveille,* Dec. 21, 1846; *Daily Missouri Republican,* Jan. 1, 1847; Edwards, *A Campaign in New Mexico with Colonel Doniphan,* 70-71.

the Mora, and that there are nearly 200 teams to come in from the same place, besides 200 more between that and Bent's Fort; and at the latter place [and] from the Mora here, there is no grass, and cattle die for the want of feed. This evening I received orders to report for duty to Colonel Mitchell, and having done so, was informed that I would act as assistant quartermaster for his expedition south. Of course, I shall have some disagreeable duty to perform but greatly prefer it to life in Santa Fé, and consider myself fortunate to be selected in any capacity for the trip. I am now hunting up forage, tents, camp equipage, oxen, mules, wagons, etc. Captain Cooke, we learn, has been compelled to turn his course for the want of transportation and to march on El Paso, where he will give battle with the Mormons or have what he wants. General Wool, it is reported, is within a hundred and fifty [miles] of Chihuahua and has been for a month, but we cannot believe the story. I visited Colonel Price with Doctor Nangle in relation to the attempts to get up a revolt, and found that he had been informed of it previously. The precise day I cannot give, but it was about this time. The colonel expressed his satisfaction and informed us he would attend to the matter. Our information, it may be proper to say, was not definite enough to enable him to act openly and take decided measures for its arrest. But subsequent events have proved the correctness of Doctor Nangle's suspicions.

NOVEMBER 29. Having been put on detached service and received orders to act as assistant quartermaster and commissary for Lieutenant-colonel D. D. Mitchell's escort, I have been busily occupied receiving provisions and everything belonging to these two departments, and today started two ox teams in advance loaded with provisions. Dawson, of our company, died yesterday and was buried today.

Mexican Weights and Measures. A *fanega* contains 12 *almuds,* and is nearly equal to two and a half bushels. Two *costals* make a *fanega.* A *costal* is a sack one and a fourth *varas* long and three-fourths of a *vara* wide. In some parts the *almud* is heaped, and in others they strike it; but it amounts to about the same thing, as they use a larger measure where they strike it. A *vara* is three inches shorter than our yard. A *frasco* is about three quarts. The weights and measures in New Mexico and generally wherever I have been are badly regulated, uncertain, and without uniformity. Corn in the ear is measured by the *costal* [and] shelled by the *almud* or *fanega.* Two *costals,* though, are not equal to a *fanega* of shelled corn. One hundred and forty-four pounds are supposed to make a *fanega* of flour, etc., but it will not do it.

THE MARCH TO EL PASO DEL NORTE

THE MARCH TO EL PASO DEL NORTE

DECEMBER 4.[397] The company, on account of the scarcity of forage, having (with all the baggage and stores) been sent forward in detachments as they were ready, I found myself the last of the escort, and about noon on December 4 bid good-bye to a place we were anxious to leave. Our road was down the Río Chiquito, a poor, barren country without the least thing to give interest. And as there was no one with me but my servant, I found the road tedious and irksome. At dark we came up with our last wagon, stalled in a branch and unable to proceed farther. They had sent to camp for assistance – about two miles. But after considerable delay we succeeded in getting it up the hill and after night reached camp, where we all lay down and slept soundly without tents or cover except our blankets, though the ground was covered with snow and the weather quite cool and no timber near. Colonel Mitchell stopped at Delgado Ranch,[398] and our camp was on the creek, fifteen miles distant from Santa Fé. As the evening sun set, I could not help but admire the gorgeous dress in which its last

397 The third section of Gibson's journal, which covers the period from December 4, 1846, to January, 1847, is entitled: "Geo. R. Gibson's Diary of the March from Santa Fé by Lt. Col. D. D. Mitchel in the Month of December 1846 to El Passo Del Norte to open a communication with Chihuahua 1846."

398 Susan Shelby Magoffin, who camped at this ranch on October 7, 1846, described it as "a little farm, called a rancho – rather a poor place, only a little corn, beans, and an abundance of *chile verde* [green pepper], a few goats, sheep and jacks." Magoffin, *Down the Santa Fé Trail and into Mexico* (Drumm, ed.), 150.

rays were shrouded, and thought of Kendall [399] and his book, of home and friends, and [of] our hazardous expedition. At camp we found Lieutenant Sproul and others who had preceded us, all in fine spirits but suffering for the want of wood, provisions, and camp equipage, which was scattered through the wagons as it best could be put in.

DECEMBER 5. On the fifth, after a hard day's march and great trouble with our teams, we reached San Felipe on the Río Grande, eighteen miles from camp. Our road was generally bad from sand, and the men with us had to spend half of their time at the wheels, the wagons having, in addition to other things, a large quantity of corn in them, as there is neither grass nor corn to be had for any price this side of Albuquerque. Consequently it was some time after dark before we reached camp, the night being very dark, windy, and cold. San Felipe is a small Pueblo town,[400] [and] the people and country poor but picturesque. One very pretty butte stands a short distance this side, and the precipitous bluffs of the river make a handsome appearance. As you look back, the country seems to be formed into steps; and such is

399 See George W. Kendall, *Narrative of an Expedition across the Great South-Western Prairies, from Texas to Santa Fé* (London, 1845), I, 389-400.

400 San Felipe, a Keres Indian pueblo on the west side of the Río Grande, is located near Thornton station on the Atchison, Topeka and Santa Fé railroad. On March 6, 1807, when Lieutenant Pike passed the pueblo, a wooden bridge of eight arches spanned the Río Grande at that point; but on October 10, 1846, when Lieutenant Abert arrived there, the bridge had been "entirely swept away." San Felipe is still occupied by Keres Indians. *House Ex. Docs.*, 30 cong., 1 sess., no. 41, pp. 461-462; Thomas Falconer, *Letters and Notes on the Texan Santa Fé Expedition 1841-1842* (F. W. Hodge, ed., New York, 1930), 93; *The Expeditions of Zebulon Montgomery Pike* (Elliott Coues, ed., New York, 1895), II, 616-617; Earle R. Forrest, *Missions and Pueblos of the Old Southwest* (Cleveland, 1929), 123-127; Adolph F. Bandelier, "Documentary History of the Río Grande Pueblos, New Mexico," *New Mexico Historical Review*, V, 334-335.

the case, as we have been rapidly descending from Santa Fé, which is considerably higher than the river and is really in an elevated valley. On our left are the Placer mountains filled with the precious metals, distant six or seven miles – perhaps ten – though it does not look to be five, owing to the purity of the atmosphere in these elevated regions. They are now nearly covered with snow, as well as all others that are visible. There is nothing marked in their appearance at this distance; nor are they so elevated as many others we can see. Yet they are celebrated and no doubt will soon become more so. We purchased plenty of wood and some fodder from an Indian, and altogether did very well after reaching camp, except that we have not yet been able to find all of our camp equipage in the confused state it was put in. Every morning we are busy regulating our loads, and have made considerable improvements already.

DECEMBER 6. Today we marched twelve miles down the valley of the Río Grande, our road being tolerably good. In six miles we overtook Lieutenant Todd and the principal part of the escort, who left several days before. Their provisions were exhausted, and, of course, our arrival was gladly hailed by them. After deliberating some time, it was determined to go on six miles to Sandía, where it was thought we could procure something, and the next day reach Albuquerque, Colonel Mitchell having today gone in advance to the latter place. In our march we passed several pretty places and some large ranches surrounded with vineyards and fruit trees, being the first places we had seen in New Mexico where any comfort seemed to reign, or industry and plenty were to be found. Sandía [401] is a small Pueblo

[401] Sandía, a Tigua Indian pueblo on the east side of the Río Grande, is

town with fruit trees and vineyards around and in it, the people retaining the appearance, dress, and characteristics of this race. They had plenty of wood and forage, which I procured on reasonable terms. And for the first time we had our tents up and a little comfort in camp, the evening being very cold and chilly. Our road is around the Placer mountains, the valley of the river being several miles wide and almost destitute of timber, as well as the mountains. But the improved appearance of the houses and people gives some interest to our march. We are now all together except Lieutenant Kribben and the detail from Captain Fischer's company, which will have to follow and join us, should it come at all, about which there are great doubts.[402]

DECEMBER 7. This morning we found ourselves buried in snow four inches deep which had fallen in the night, and [it was] a cold, dreary, wintry morning.[403] But our

located at Alameda station on the Atchison, Topeka and Santa Fé railroad. On September 5, 1846, Emory described Sandía as "an Indian town, on a sandbank, at the base of a high mountain of the same name." *Daily Union,* Nov. 5, 1846. See also *"Noticias que da Juan Candelaria Vecino de Esta Villa de San Francisco Xauier de Alburquerque"* (Isador Armijo, translator), *New Mexico Historical Review,* IV, 280-282; Charles Wilson Hackett, "The Location of the Tigua Pueblos of Alameda, Puaray, and Sandía in 1680-81," *Old Santa Fé,* II, 381-391; *The Expeditions of Zebulon Montgomery Pike* (Coues, ed.), II, 618-619; Falconer, *Letters and Notes on the Texan Santa Fé Expedition 1841-1842* (Hodge, ed.), 57; Forrest, *Missions and Pueblos of the Old Southwest,* 127-128.

402 Lieutenant Kribben, in command of ten men of Captain Fischer's artillery company, left Santa Fé on December 5 or 6 and joined the Chihuahua Rangers on December 10. *Täglicher Anzeiger des Westens,* Feb. 22, 23, Apr. 10, 1847.

403 "Rising early this morning to prepare breakfast," recorded Richardson on December 7, "I found the snow four inches deep, and still snowing very fast." *Journal of William H. Richardson,* 40-41. Edwards wrote: "One morning [December 7], on waking, I raised my head, which caused a quantity of snow that had fallen during the night to get into my neck, giving me a sudden cold bath. On looking about, I could only see the rounded forms of my companions lying under the snow." Edwards, *A Campaign in New Mexico with Colonel Doniphan,* 72.

animals had plenty of corn and fodder, and we took the road as soon as possible. Before starting, I descended by a trapdoor from the top into one of the Indian houses to procure a receipt, and I found it warm and comfortable and well supplied. Yet the strange way of getting into them made it interesting. You reach the roof by a ladder, which is easily pulled up, and the inmates are fortified. It is a common thing and is done for fear of attack. After a march of sixteen miles, we came to Albuquerque,[404] a place of more beauty than Santa Fé. And here we found 225 men of the First regiment [of] dragoons and shook hands with many acquaintances, amongst others Captain Grier, whose late exploit amongst a marauding party of Navajo has made considerable talk. He showed me an arrow which struck his saddle blanket, but my time did not permit me to remain long, and I did not learn all the particulars. While on the march this morning, the mountain on our left, with its crags and precipices, presented a most magnificent appearance, the snow and morning sun bringing them in bold relief. Its summit and base [were] both enveloped in a dense, heavy, white cloud. It presented all the desolation, barrenness, and dreary waste of a high northern latitude, and made me think of Norway and her mountains of ice and snow in winter. The valley has widened out and now is a low, uneven bottom covered with sand hills and irrigating canals and occasionally a volcanic pile. Geese are abundant, and some few have been killed, but the weather is too cold for sport.

The evening is windy and cold, and wood [is] scarce,

404 "Albuquerque," noted Wislizenus on July 12, 1846, "is a town as large as Santa Fé, stretched for several miles along the left bank of the Río del Norte, and if not handsomer, is at least not a worse looking place than the capital." Wislizenus, *Memoir of a Tour to Northern Mexico,* 33. See also *Southwest Historical Series,* I, 113.

as it has to be hauled twenty-five miles from the valleys in the interior of the mountains. The men have suffered considerably for the want of good tents and plenty of wood, but at the usual hour all was quiet in camp, and [they] seemed to be tolerably comfortable. And I visited my friend, Lieutenant Ingalls, with whom I exchanged a glass, and where I found all the officers in a great glee. There being two roads to Valverde, one of which crosses the river here, it has been determined to pursue the latter, as there is said to be a prospect of procuring forage, beef, etc., on it, and it is better for wagons. At this place we procured corn and fodder sufficient for our present wants. But as these articles, for one reason, cannot be hauled well, and for another are very dear, we purchase what we can day by day. And it is productive of great trouble to me, running all over every place we enter before I can find what we require. When found I have great trouble to purchase it, as I cannot speak the language. But my interpreter seems to understand them well and after some delay usually succeeds.

DECEMBER 8. Our tents, being wet yesterday, are frozen stiff this morning, and we have to remain in camp until the morning sun thaws them; and [also] partly because it is too cold to drive our animals across the river. We finally got off and doubled our teams to cross the river, the first attempting it without [doubling] and causing us a good deal of trouble. We were delayed there, and kept back [some] more by the sandiness of the roads, our road being down the river bottoms. But about dark we reached Isleta, an Indian village, and as usual procured forage and fuel by purchase,[405] there

[405] However, Richardson asserted that on December 8 forage was taken from the Mexicans. He wrote: "We had six small ears of corn for our horses, and no fodder. I went to the Quarter Master and was informed by him that

Indian Church at Isleta, New Mexico
From a photograph taken in 1867

being no such thing as grass or timber near us, or even in sight. We marched fourteen miles after a hard day's work, and at dark camped in the town – a cold, windy, stormy evening. Just before reaching Isleta,[406] we overtook our ox teams with provisions, which, it was hoped, were still several days in our advance. They had made short marches in consequence of the weather, the want of feed, and heavy loads. In sight of camp we passed an ox which had given out and lay down in the road, and learned another had died the night previous. They are all pretty well used up and may cause us great trouble. Today we passed Major Edmonson's command encamped a mile or two from the road, and saw the Stars and Stripes afloat long before we came opposite, which put new life in our little force and served to cheer them up.

The corn we purchased at Albuquerque was from the priest, a close trader and shrewd man, who gave me a glass of the best Pass brandy I have found. And here the priest is also the great trader and most important functionary, and of course we go to him for everything

the Mexicans had refused to sell us any thing. I cut some buttons from a uniform jacket, and with them tried to purchase food for my horse, but I was refused every where. I sat down and made out a requisition, and with several others went to their large stacks, ten feet high, which we ascended, and threw down a large turn for each. We succeeded in coming off with our booty, and in a few minutes, we were in bed. We were not disturbed in conscience in the least, being fully covered by the axiom, 'necessity knows no law.' " *Journal of William H. Richardson,* 41.

406 Isleta, a Tigua Indian pueblo on the west side of the Río Grande, is about twelve miles south of Albuquerque. On July 19, 1846, Wislizenus wrote: "Our night camp was at the foot of some sand hills, nearly opposite to a pueblo on the other side, called *Isleta*. The small village, with its church, green fields, and cluster of cotton and orchard trees, looks quite picturesque in the desert around us." Wislizenus, *Memoir of a Tour to Northern Mexico,* 35. See also Hackett, "The Location of the Tigua Pueblos of Alameda, Puaray, and Sandía in 1680-81," *Old Santa Fé,* II, 381-391; Forrest, *Missions and Pueblos of the Old Southwest,* 151-155.

wanted. My mess now consists of Lieutenant Sproul, Lieutenant Todd, myself, Mr. Barnes my interpreter and guide, and Lang my servant. And we all took a room in an Indian house, where we spread our blankets and had a comfortable night's rest in spite of the cold and wind. As yet we can hear nothing of Colonel Doniphan and think he must be on his march to the south. We passed some provision teams for him the first day out from Santa Fé, and I fear they will not get up as they are badly provided with feed for their animals. The colonel stopped with the priest, the most important personage, but a low, vulgar fellow, and he [*i.e.,* the colonel] left him and took quarters at another house. Captain Thompson, of the First regiment of dragoons, accompanies us and belongs to Colonel Mitchell's mess.

DECEMBER 9. After a march of nine miles we camped at Los Lunas, where we found Wooster and Major Spalding, paymaster. There was but one individual here who had corn, and I was forced to press it into the service,[407] which created considerable excitement amongst the population; but all was finally adjusted and peace restored. I also purchased wood, fodder, etc., the former being very scarce, yet I procured enough. Meat of no kind was to be had; so we use our rations of salt pork. It continues very cold and windy, but the men complain not.

DECEMBER 10. Two of our men were sent back this

[407] Richardson described how the detachment commandeered corn at Los Lunas: "Our interpreter was sent to procure forage for the horses, but he returned with the news that none could be had. Our Captain told the Sergeant to go up with a file of soldiers and *take* what was wanting. He formed a line of twenty men, I among them, and marched off with our Orderly at the head, and second Sergeant, with the bags to put the corn in. At the door of the house, we were ordered to halt. The lock was broken, and we entered, filled our sacks and packed them down to the camp." *Journal of William H. Richardson,* 41-42.

morning in consequence of sickness. And I had some trouble paying for wood which the men had taken from corrals, etc., near us. All being settled for in the shape of damages, we made an early start notwithstanding the cold, and marched twelve miles to Belen, which we reached in good season and found a rather pretty place, camping immediately back of the church. Here, as usual, we found the priest the big man of the town, for he had whiskey, corn, and goods to sell, besides furnishing entertainment to the colonel. Before we broke up camp this morning a Mexican stopped at one of our camp fires to warm, on his way to Tomé for the priest of that place, to visit (as he said) the Indian town of Isleta, the priest's child of the latter place being about to die. Thus they live openly with often more than one woman, and nothing is thought amiss. We found here, as at all other places, the priest provided with a spiritual wife or two, who lived with him and acted as mistress. Lieutenant Kribben joined us this evening, having come down the river on the other side and espied us from Tomé while on our march.[408] He brought with him the detachment from Captain Fischer's company, and also the news that Lieutenant Hinton passed through Tomé on express to Santa Fé for Captain Weightman's company of artillery, which was good news to us. Major Spalding, who accompanied us thus far, immediately returned to Santa Fé in hopes he would also be ordered south. In a few days more we shall join Colonel Doniphan and know what is to be done. We found chickens and eggs at this place, and I procured mutton enough to issue one ration to the company, but could find no beef.

DECEMBER 11. I left camp early with Mr. Barnes, my

408 Lieutenant Kribben's detachment crossed to the west side of the Río Grande at Los Lunas. *Täglicher Anzeiger des Westens,* Apr. 10, 1847.

interpreter, in advance of the company and continued down the river bottoms, with nothing to relieve the monotony except stopping at every ranch to purchase cattle, mules, corn, fodder, wood, etc., where we always created great terror amongst the children and caused yelping amongst the dogs, every place having its full quota. In fourteen miles we came to San Sabinal, where we waited for the company, having procured wood, corn, and fodder. As yet we find no beef, which I need much, and tomorrow I shall go ahead again in hopes we can procure some and also oxen, one of my teams having broken down. Here we took quarters in a house, as at Isleta, and found it very comfortable.

DECEMBER 12. We had a good road today, and rather warm and pleasant weather. We met a detachment from Colonel Doniphan's camp going to Tomé for 1,000 sheep. They informed us he was at Valverde, and that Major Gilpin with 200 or 300 men was about to leave for Doña Ana. Except [for] this, they had no news, and after a march of nine miles we camped in the bottom opposite La Joya de Cebolleta,[409] in a pretty cottonwood grove with plenty of grass. They brought us corn from the town, and for once we have pleasant weather, and wood, water, and grass, with full rations. As yet I cannot procure beef and feel uneasy lest we have to go without meat, except pickled pork and bacon.

DECEMBER 13. We left camp early and in ten miles reached Limitar, where we encamped, nothing of con-

[409] On the east side of the Río Grande, opposite the present town of Lajoya, Socorro county, New Mexico. "Sibilleta is situated on the east side," recorded Pike on March 10, 1807, "and is a regular square, appearing like a large mud wall on the outside, the doors, windows, etc., facing the square; it is the neatest and most regular village I have yet seen, and is governed by a sergeant, at whose quarters I put up." *The Expeditions of Zebulon Montgomery Pike* (Coues, ed.), II, 628-629.

sequence having transpired. The weather has moderated, and we are evidently in a much warmer climate than Santa Fé.

DECEMBER 14. Today we reached Luis López, and I shall be forced to press beef as we are near the borders of the settlements and have none except two, which I purchased today at fifteen dollars each and had slaughtered immediately. Here we found one instance of liberality in a Mexican, having wood and the use of a corral given us. The people generally have hostile feelings and would be able to render efficient aid to any force sent against us from below. Mesquite bushes and chamiso have made their appearance, and, except the valleys, the country is a barren waste. The timber on the river bottom is low and dwarfish, as it is in fact throughout all New Mexico, except in the region where pine grows. And the river bottoms look more like an old apple orchard in "the States" than cottonwood groves, this being the only growth. We have almost lost sight of the mountains from our low position. The bottoms are wider and in some places appear more fertile than higher up. Grass is abundant, and grama plentiful on the hills and almost green. We have daily met men on their way to Santa Fé and have learned that Major Gilpin is on his march to Doña Ana to secure the provisions and forage at that place. With the exception of a few sand hills, the road is good, the river in view all the time. We camped immediately above the last settlement, and soon will be out of the settlements after a march of about ten miles.

DECEMBER 15. Today we passed . . . Luis López, where I bought corn and in the face of the citizens drove off seven fat cattle, being compelled to press them into the service.[410] We told them we should do so and that

410 See *Journal of William H. Richardson*, 43.

the owners might come to camp if they wanted pay; which they did, and I gave them $93 for the seven. These forced venders of cattle made but little complaint and when paid appeared satisfied, it being more than Mexican troops would have done for them. They have generally driven their stock into the mountains to avoid such things, and solely, I believe, because there is no money in any quartermaster's or commissary's hands except mine; and they do not know the value of drafts, checks, etc. The bottoms are not unlike the Arkansas, and our camp is in a pretty grove on the bank of the river, with wood, water, and grass plentiful. Yesterday an extra mule was left behind by the men who had charge of it, and I have not been able to recover it. We are now beyond the settlements in New Mexico, and the next town we see will be Doña Ana in the department of Chihuahua.

DECEMBER 16. We passed over a pretty bottom with good road and in seven miles came to the river, where we learned that Colonel Doniphan was moving his camp; in fact, we saw several of his wagons on the hills several miles off. We crossed the river,[411] though, having some trouble with one of our ox teams, and in two miles reached Valverde, where we encamped, making our day's march about nine miles. Here we found Colonel Doniphan's commissary train, and he himself paid us a visit in the evening and stayed all night with Colonel Mitchell. He told us many things about the Navajo country, and we were highly entertained until bedtime. All apprehensions that he would order us back, having yet the command in New Mexico, are quieted, and we shall now go on with him. He is glad to have this acces-

[411] They crossed to the east side of the Río Grande near the present Elmendorf, Socorro county, New Mexico.

sion, as I expected he would be, and still thinks his force full small, but he will go ahead. The Copper Mine mountains have been in full view, distant fifty or sixty miles, covered with snow, also another mountain on our right in the Navajo country and the Sierra Blanca on our left.

Our camp is in a pretty grove like an old orchard, the trees about as close, near the base of a pretty mesa which has a singular appearance. Here we found many marks of the traders' encampment which they recently abandoned, with their huts made of rushes, and of all sorts and kinds. The ruins of Valverde [412] are close by, the walls nearly level with the ground, and no other mark of its existence except an old *acequia*. A covey of mountain quails were seen, with their green topknots, their plumage in other respects similar to ours. However, they are a much shier bird than ours, with a more tapering neck and wilder look, and we failed to kill any. Here I lost a *serape,* a pair of spurs, and knife, which I valued highly – stolen of course.

DECEMBER 17. We took an early start, our road leading us around the mesa (near which we encamped) to the high ground east of it, when it [*i.e.,* the road] turned west around its [*i.e.,* the mesa's] southern base. And after a march of six miles we came to the bottom on the other side, where we found Colonel Doniphan's regiment. We spent a pleasant evening with our old friends and acquaintances, first sending all of our animals with a guard to the grama grass on the hills until evening.

---

412 On November 18, 1846, Lieutenant Abert wrote: "During the morning, we walked over the ruins of Valverde. They were inhabited in 1820 and 1825, but constant depredations of the Apaches and Navajoes forced the people to desert their village. Nothing now remains but the ruins of some adobe walls, over which stillness reigns." *House Ex. Docs.,* 30 cong., 1 sess., no. 41, p. 499.

The Table mountain around which we have marched is volcanic, its top level and flat except one little elevation, as if artificial, and its sides very steep, regular, and nothing but volcanic rock. Water is half a mile distant, which puts us to some inconvenience. But we have wood and grass and do pretty well. When we first came up we found Colonel Doniphan's commissary in possession of a flock of 4,000 sheep and goats pressed into the service, from which they were selecting the best. They belonged to one of the Lunas, the same whose corn I pressed the ninth, and I expect he will consider himself an injured man. Mr. Lee obtained about 1,000 head out of the flock, and I contracted with him for 50 head, which, with my beef, makes me pretty well off. We spent a pleasant evening, having Colonel Owens in camp with us, the evening being warm and pleasant. According to my estimates we are now about one hundred and seventy-five [miles] from Santa Fé, but it is generally estimated at more than this. There was once a settlement here known as the "Cantarecio," but not a vestige of it remains that I saw.

DECEMBER 18. We had considerable trouble before we left camp this morning, hunting mules, fat cattle, etc., which the sentinels permitted to escape last night, and I had some uneasiness lest some of our beef cattle never would be recovered. All, however, came up with the details, and we broke up camp. In nine miles we reached Fray Cristóbal [413] and camped in the bottom, and all is

[413] Fray Cristóbal was a camping place and not a settlement. Writing on August 1, 1846, Wislizenus stated: "Travelled this morning about five miles, and camped between one and two miles off the river. This camping place is known as *Fray Cristóbal;* but as there is neither house nor settlement here, and one may fix his camp close on or some distance from the river, the limits of Fray Cristóbal are not so distinctly defined as those of a city, and generally the last camping place on or near the Río del Norte before entering

bustle to prepare for the long march through the Jornada del Muerto,[414] the men being ordered to cook three days' provisions, as there is neither wood nor water. About four o'clock, just as we reached camp, the traders were breaking up and entering this dreary waste, a line of wagons *en route* extending at least a mile. Having a prospect of getting some animals from Colonel Owens, I went to see him and had a hard ride of six or seven miles in the *jornada* before I overtook him, as he was at the head of the line. I failed to procure any, and it was dark before I reached camp, my mule being considerably worsted by the hard ride. The day has been pleasant, with wood, water, and grass plentiful, and our camp is in a pretty bottom, with mountains in all directions.

DECEMBER 19. About eleven o'clock on the nineteenth we undertook this famous road. Volcanic rock[415] is scattered in abundance along the first two miles, and you ascend considerably above the river bottoms when you find yourself upon an elevated valley almost perfectly level, and the mountains at no great distance on each hand. The road is like a turnpike, without timber or even mesquite, the aloe [amole?], or soap plant, and grama grass being the only things to break the sameness – the first unusually large and the latter better than any we

the *Jornada del Muerto* is understood by it." Wislizenus, *Memoir of a Tour to Northern Mexico*, 38. See also *The Expeditions of Zebulon Montgomery Pike* (Coues, ed.), II, 634-636.

414 The distance from Fray Cristóbal to Robledo, the northern and southern limits of the trail across the Jornada del Muerto, was about eighty or ninety miles. *Santa Fé Republican*, Sept. 17, 1847; Wislizenus, *Memoir of a Tour to Northern Mexico*, 38-39; *Journal of William H. Richardson*, 44-45.

415 For information regarding the geologic structure of this desert, see Charles Rollin Keyes, *Geology and Underground Water Conditions of the Jornada del Muerto, New Mexico* (U.S. Geological Survey, Water-Supply and Irrigation Paper No. 123, Washington, 1905), pp. 9-39.

have found. The mountain chains on each side are totally barren except [for] a little short grass, and appear to be piles of volcanic rock of the trap species. The Copper Mine mountains were visible through the gap where the river flows, distant fifty miles, and the snowy mountains, near which is the Salt lake and rock salt, [were] on our left about fifty or sixty miles, both white with snow. Some of my oxen gave out, good as the road was, and were abandoned. And we marched until about nine o'clock at night, when we camped on the open prairie at Siereta [?], sixteen miles from Fray Cristóbal (in the open prairie), and had to use the aloe [amole?] for fuel. These night marches are always bad, as we have great confusion in camping, and it was so tonight, as well as cold and chilly. But having such a long road before us without wood or water, we are compelled to march more or less every night.

DECEMBER 20. We left the Siereta [?] early in the morning and about eleven o'clock, after a march of about ten miles, arrived at the Laguna del Muerto, which we found perfectly dry. Here we camped and sent all of our animals to the Ojo del Muerto in the mountains, three miles distant.[416] After they returned, we remained until about three o'clock, when we continued on the road until nine o'clock at night, having reached the Alemán, where we encamped, with a little low mesquite. It is fourteen miles from the *laguna*. The weather is more pleasant, and all so far get along well. We find no game except a few rabbits and a few antelopes we saw yesterday.

DECEMBER 21. We made an early start and in ten

[416] About five or six miles west of the main trail. Wislizenus, *Memoir of a Tour to Northern Mexico*, 38; *Journal of William H. Richardson*, 45; Gregg, *op. cit.*, XX, 153.

miles came to the Perilla, an isolated mountain in the valley, which here expands, giving the appearance of two valleys. Our road bears considerably to the right and is not so level as it has been, yet very good. Here I was forced to press into the service two yoke of cattle from Mr. Glasgow's train, which his major-domo peaceably submitted to. With them I was enabled to get along my ox teams. And after marching about ten miles farther, we encamped after night at San Diego,[417] where we found many of the traders. Our animals were all sent to the river for water, and we ourselves are tolerably comfortable. This place is off the direct road but very often is passed on account of water, though it is inconvenient, being two miles from where you have to encamp.

DECEMBER 22. We made an early start and in fourteen miles came to Robledo,[418] where we found the remainder of the traders. And they now swell our numbers and add greatly to our display of strength. This place is the terminus of this long stretch, and [during] the last two miles there is a very rapid descent and sandy road, showing clearly the elevation of the valley. We now find ourselves in a new climate, being so warm that we all have our coats off, and the whole camp is shaving, washing, and putting on clean clothes. Our camp is in a pretty place on the bank of the river, with wood, water, and grass plentiful, and all are in fine spirits. Here the valley of the Río Grande is wide and covered generally with low cottonwood and willow, and seems to be rich, with a climate much milder than in New Mexico. We are now

417 A camping place not far from the present town of Rincon, Doña Ana county, New Mexico.

418 Robledo was a camping place near the present Fort Selden, Doña Ana county, New Mexico.

in the department of Chihuahua, as the line is said to cross a mile or two back, and for the first time feel ourselves entirely without the limits of the United States. All we see hereafter will be in a foreign country and in one of its best provinces, for this state is reckoned the third in Mexico in wealth and resources.

DECEMBER 23. We made an early start and in ten miles came to Doña Ana,[419] a small place, but well stored with corn and other things. We found the place filled with men from Major Gilpin's command, who was encamped in the bottom, all noisy and drinking. And being old acquaintances, we could scarcely find time to procure what we wanted. *Aguardiente,* dried fruit, pumpkins, corn, and a few other things are its productions. After purchasing as much of these different things as were required, we moved on to camp, and for the first time our force is together, except stragglers and the various details. From what we learn, there are troops at El Paso, and we shall have a fight. But as yet we have not been able to learn their strength or situation. Our men are in fine spirits and confidently expect to be the victors. Nor could a spectator suppose we were a war party about to measure our strength with the enemy, from the joyous and noisy crowds around camp, the little fear they possess, and the total indifference manifested. On the road today we passed a variety of cacti, new to us and pretty. It grows up as large as a flour barrel, with the

[419] Ruxton, who passed through Doña Ana during the latter part of November, 1846, described it as follows: "Doñana is a very recent settlement of ten or fifteen families, who, tempted by the richness of the soil, abandoned their farms in the valley of El Paso, and have here attempted to cultivate a small tract in the very midst of the Apaches, who have already paid them several visits and carried off or destroyed their stock of cattle. The huts are built of logs and mud, and situated on the top of a tabular bluff which looks down upon the river-bottom." Ruxton, *Adventures in Mexico and the Rocky Mountains,* 171. See also *Southwest Historical Series,* I, 190.

blossoms on top. Now they are not in bloom, but must be beautiful, and from their size are curious. The melons and pumpkins are large and fine, and would be no discredit to "the States."

DECEMBER 24. All things being ready, we broke up camp this morning and after a march of twelve miles camped in the bottom on the river at what we called "The Dead Man's Camp," as we found here the bodies of two Mexicans and, as we supposed, one American.[420] Who they were or how they came by their death is a mystery, as we cannot obtain the least clue to their murder. It is most probable, though, that they fell into the hands of the Apache who infest this country, a nomadic tribe of Indians, real Arabs, who have neither dwellings nor villages, but wander from place to place, their hand against every man, and every man's hand against them. They inhabit the mountains [on] both sides of the river for a great distance, and make incursions upon the settlements as their wants require, generally dashing amongst the herdsmen, killing them, and as speedily driving off their stock. To follow them into their fastnesses is impossible, and the poor ranchero contents himself by making a cross and counting his beads for his lost cattle.

As we are drawing close to the Pass, all things have been made ready for a fight. The arms are regularly inspected, ammunition distributed, a picket guard kept out at night and an advance through the day, and nearly every man seems anxious it [*i.e.,* a fight] should come. We can get nothing from the Mexicans at Doña Ana, and all is anxiety to unravel the mystery and to break the barriers which cut us off from El Paso.

---

[420] Edwards stated that the soldiers found the bodies of two Americans and one Mexican. Edwards, *A Campaign in New Mexico with Colonel Doniphan,* 80-81.

DECEMBER 25. Our road was down an extensive and open bottom, except [for] a little timber and mesquite along the banks of the river; and after a march of fourteen miles we struck another bend in the river, where it was intended to camp, and where we found our advance guard. The men and wagons were scattered along the road for many miles, but a few marching in the ranks, as it was not expected to meet the enemy this side of the crossing, nine miles above El Paso.

Battle of Bracito. Just before reaching camp, Lieutenant Sproul and several others went in pursuit of some spies who were seen, and after following about three miles and not being able to overtake them, returned. Had they pursued them a little farther over the top of a hill, they would have found themselves in their whole army and either have been taken or killed. We had selected our camping ground, and some were engaged getting wood, some were after water, and all were scattered through the brush and bottom, when the alarm was given that the enemy were upon us. My mule being picketed close to me, I soon caught it and was one of the first to mount. But finding it a poor animal for a battlefield, [I] dismounted and gave it to my servant (who had returned from the river) with instructions to take it to the rear, as he had no arms. An order had been given to "Boots and Saddles," but was soon countermanded, the enemy being in sight at this time. We were formed in single rank, the escort on the right. But the cavalry of the enemy evidently intending to charge on our left, we were ordered to strengthen that flank, and moved along the line to that flank and formed on the extreme left.

Having no special command or duty assigned me, I

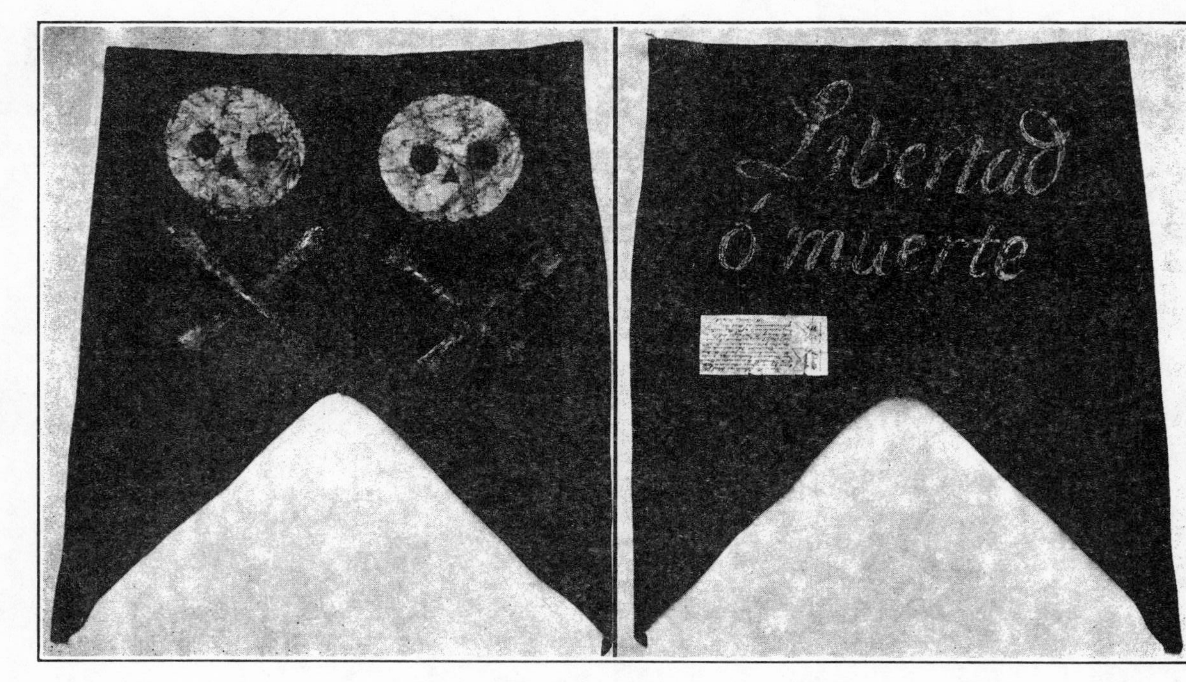

THE BLACK FLAG

The explanatory text attached to the flag reads: "This is the identical black flag borne by an officer who demanded of Col. Doniphan to surrender at Bracito, New Mexico, on Christmas, 1846, and also the same borne in front of the Mexican troops at Sacramento in the state of Chihuahua on the 28th Feby., 1847, and was captured by one of the men of Mr. Mc. light artillery in my command after the victory of Sacramento on that day.—M. Lewis Clark"

took post with Lieutenant Kribben[421] and told him I

[421] On December 26, 1846, Lieutenant Kribben, of the Chihuahua Rangers, made the following report of the Battle of Bracito to Major Clark: "I can only write to you a few lines, being upon the point of breaking up camp. . . Yesterday (Christmas day), when we had just arrived in camp here, with about 600 men, had unsaddled our animals, and most of the men were engaged in carrying wood and water, the news was brought into camp of the enemy's being in sight and advancing. It was about two o'clock, P.M., and the day was very pleasant. Our horses grazing some distance from the camp at the time, we formed a single line, and determined to meet the enemy as infantry. Their attack being evidently designed on the left flank, near which was our wagon train, our detachment was ordered from the extreme right to the left, where we soon took up our position. One piece of artillery, 490 regular lancers and cavalry, and 100 regular infantry, besides some 500 militia troops from El Paso, composed the enemy's force, according to the best information that I can obtain from reports of prisoners, and from papers found amongst the baggage on the field of battle. The enemy ranged themselves on the east within half a mile of our line, the mountains in their rear. In our rear was the river, with a little brushwood on its banks. Previous to the encounter a lieutenant from their ranks came forward, waving a black flag in his hand, but halted when within an hundred steps of our line. Thos. Caldwell, our interpreter, rode out to meet him. The messenger with the black flag of defiance demanded that the commander should come into camp and speak to their General. The reply was: 'If your General wants to see our commander let him come here.' 'We shall break your ranks, then, and take him there!' was the retort of the Mexican. 'Come and take him,' said our interpreter, unwittingly using the phrase of the Spartan at Thermopylae. 'A curse on you; prepare for a charge!' cried the Mexican – 'we give no quarters, and ask none'; and, waving his black flag gracefully over his head, galloped back towards the enemy's line. Their charge was made by the dragoons from their right, directed upon our left flank, bringing our detachment into the closest fire. Their infantry, with one howitzer with them, at the same time attacked our right flank. Their charge was a handsome one, but was too well, too coolly met to break our ranks. After their fire had been spent, their front column being about an hundred steps from the front of our flank, our line poured a volley into them, which, being a few times repeated, created such a havoc in their columns that their forces wheeled to the left, retreating from our fire, and in their flight made an attack on the provision train. Here they met a very warm reception, and were soon compelled to fly in all directions, and in the utmost confusion. Their infantry having been put to flight, the Howard Company, under the command of Lieut. N. Wright, taking advantage of the panic, charged upon them and took their cannon from them. This was soon manned by the artillery detachment, under Lieut. Kribben, in Col. Mitchell's escort. The enemy had by this time fled, leaving their arms, baggage,

would remain by his side, which I occupied throughout the engagement. After the line was formed and dressed, the left wing was found too far advanced, and we were ordered to fall back, which was done in some confusion and with a good deal of noise. We had just accomplished this when a horseman with a flag dashed forward from their line, now about six hundred yards distant, and Colonel Doniphan's interpreter, Mr. Caldwell, and Adjutant DeCourcy went forward to meet him. He said our general must come to their general and see him, when Mr. Caldwell told him to come and take him. He then cried out: "*Carajo!* We will neither give nor ask quarter; prepare for a charge!" And with a flourish of his flag, which proved to be a black one on a lance, he wheeled his horse and rode back. It was as gracefully done as could be, and we since learn it was Lieutenant Lara. But the black flag by no means served to intimidate or cool the ardor of our men, but rather, with the bloody threat, nerved them for any emergency. About this time three or four of our wagons came up in charge of my quartermaster-sergeant, F. S. Edwards, and Sergeant Hart, and formed at the river in our rear.[422] Our animals were scattered over the bottom, the larger portion in the open ground in our front and rear.

The enemy made a handsome appearance from an elevation half a mile or three-quarters distant, where we first saw them, and which they occupied to reconnoiter, and where they formed in order of battle. They

provisions and other stores on the field of battle. A small body of mounted men, under the command of Capt. Reid, had by this time gathered together in a line and charged upon the enemy, pursuing them into the mountains, where they sought refuge." *Weekly Reveille,* Mar. 1, 1847. For a slightly different version of Kribben's report, see *Täglicher Anzeiger des Westens,* Feb. 26, 1847.

[422] See Edwards, *A Campaign in New Mexico with Colonel Doniphan,* 82-88.

marched up in good order but did not approach rapidly, as parts of the intermediate ground is a dense chaparral, low but thick on the ground, and impeded their movements. Their infantry met our right, the howitzer was in their center, and the cavalry on our left. A few mesquite bushes are along our right wing, and many between it and the river and in its rear, with occasionally, all over the field, little hillocks of sand, or rather irregularities in the ground. By this time Captain Reid had collected about fourteen mounted men,[423] who took post behind our center. And all others were afoot, except Colonel Doniphan, Colonel Mitchell, Captain Thompson, and the adjutant and [the] guide.

A battle being unavoidable, we held ourselves ready and suffered them to fire five rounds and to approach within 150 yards, when the order was given to let them have it, our men standing previous to this with their guns cocked, and the officers telling them to hold on until they were close enough for our fire to have great effect. At the word, number one fired, and then number two, our line being told off into files. And it was well done and had a fine effect, their cavalry reeling under it, and [their] whole line giving. Before another [round] could be fired, the cavalry passed around our left and charged on the wagons, where they met a warm reception, [the teamsters] having also held up their fire until every shot told, as they were close. At this time Captain Reid charged upon them, and being unable to cut off our baggage and provisions they retreated in confusion, Captain Reid and his squad giving a hot pursuit. Several lay dead upon this part of the field. When they charged our wagons, our right advanced, and they were driven

423 Doniphan stated that Captain Reid was in command of twenty mounted men. *Senate Ex. Docs.*, 30 cong., 1 sess., no. 1, p. 498.

from every position, their howitzer being handsomely taken with a shout and put in charge of Lieutenant Kribben and the artillery in our escort. Our whole line now advanced until we reached the high ground where we first saw them, where a halt was ordered, as they were out of sight and Captain Reid had gone in pursuit. He finally returned and reported that he followed them four miles into the mountains and could not overtake them, that the road was marked by streams of blood, and that, from their movements, they evidently carried off many wounded.

Our victory being complete and the enemy dispersed, we marched back to camp, the spoils and trophies scattered over the ground and taken being brought to Colonel Mitchell's tent – also two wounded Mexicans, for one of whom we were sorry. He was young, married, and of respectable parentage, and said he was trying to join us when shot and that he had been forced to fight by his father. He told us to save him if we could, and our surgeon, Doctor Moore, examined the wound and pronounced it fatal, as he was shot in the abdomen, and he died that night. As Captain Reid charged, Sergeant Hart came up, being back with the wagons, and made an effort to charge amongst them. But his mule, a very fine one, refused to obey and sheered off to one side in spite of his exertions. Colonel Mitchell rode a white horse, which he valued highly, and [which] really was a fine one and made a pretty appearance. He, of course, was a conspicuous object and most probably taken for our commander, as their fire was directed at him particularly. Once I thought his horse was shot, seeing him flinch or give, and the colonel told me in the evening he thought so [too] but could find no mark about him. Captain Hudson was in front of me, and the colonel almost immediately in my rear at one time, and this was probably the warmest place on the field on account of the white horse.

Captain Thompson [424] aided us materially in the formation of our line, and for his judgment and coolness received our thanks. He was consulted upon all occasions, and his opinion followed throughout. Lieutenant Sproul had a shot which cut his cap; Kribben's servant one which just touched the top of his head, enough to bring blood. Davis was the only one of the escort wounded, being shot through the leg. No one was dangerously wounded. They always overshot us, both with their howitzer and small arms, and Colonel Doniphan says he thought about a bushel of copper ore passed over his head at least ten feet from the howitzer, which they fired several times. We had many narrow escapes, and it seems that Providence was on our side as we did not lose a single man nor one even dangerously wounded. We took but two or three prisoners for the want of cavalry, and because they were greatly terrified and ran for life; and we could not pursue them far, as our animals

[424] Philip Roots Thompson was born in Georgia about 1812. Graduating from the United States Military academy in 1835, he was promoted in the army to brevet second lieutenant in the First dragoons. Before the Mexican war he was on frontier duty at Fort Leavenworth and Fort Atkinson. He was made first lieutenant in the First dragoons, June 30, 1837, and captain, June 30, 1846. Leaving Fort Leavenworth with a small detachment of dragoons on September 29, 1846, he arrived in Santa Fé on October 31. He acted as Doniphan's aid and adviser in the battles of Bracito and Sacramento, rendering valuable service during both engagements. He was breveted major for "gallant and meritorious conduct in the Battle of Sacramento." During the fifties he served at various western posts, including Fort Scott, Fort Laramie, Fort Leavenworth, Fort Union, Fort Massachusetts, and Camp Burgwin. On September 4, 1855, he was cashiered "for disrespect to a court-martial, before which he appeared as a witness in a state of intoxication." He died on June 24, 1857. *Daily Missouri Republican,* Oct. 6, 13, 24, Nov. 7, 1846, Mar. 18, 1847; Cullum, *Biographical Register,* I, 481; Heitman, *Historical Register,* I, 957; *Senate Ex. Docs.,* 30 cong., 1 sess., no. 1, pp. 498, 501.

were tired by the march, theirs fresh. We could not ascertain the loss of the enemy, as they are scattered over several miles, many fleeing into the mountains and carrying off their wounded. Some, though mortally wounded, continued on horseback until they fell off. Our estimate was thirty or forty killed and perhaps five times this number wounded. Only a few lay near our camp, which was where we first selected.

We found considerable spoils on the field: wine (which the men drank immediately), bread, *pinole,* trinkets, beads, crosses, clothes, etc., all of which was collected at Colonel Mitchell's tent, when it made a considerable showing, with the arms taken. I lost one mule, which no doubt ran off when the firing commenced, our animals fleeing in all directions, and had another shot but not killed. The camp was in fine spirits at the Christmas frolic and were reminded of Okechobee fought on the same day.

Our men behaved like veterans and exhibited a coolness and obedience to orders worthy of any troops. Two old mountain men, T. Forsythe and another, dressed in their peculiar buckskin shirts, made themselves conspicuous by advancing before the line and firing with great deliberation, the sharp crack of their rifles announcing that some one had received a shot. Forsythe is an old and experienced Indian fighter, and has already rendered great service as a spy and to carry expresses. When they fired, our men gave a shout and advanced upon the howitzer, which they took, the enemy fleeing in great precipitation. It was late at night before all was quiet in camp, being greatly exhilarated by our victory without the loss of a man.

The ground was well selected by the enemy and is a pretty place for a battlefield. They had the advantage, and if their howitzer had been properly managed, might have done us great injury, as our artillery has not yet been heard from. We immediately called it the "Battle of Bracito," that being the name of the bend just above us where there was once a settlement, scarcely a vestige of which now remains. The Mexicans call it "Temascalitos." *Bracito* means "little arm," and as we are a small part of the western army, the name is appropriate. The number we had engaged is uncertain, not more than 400 or 500, as many were detailed to drive up cattle and sheep, etc., and to aid the wagons, guard them, etc., and many were behind on the road with lame and broken-down animals and did not get up in time. The strength of the enemy was variously estimated from 800 to 1,000, and we since learn they had 1,200, according to their own account. Colonel Ponce de León commanded them, and it is reported was wounded – supposed to have been shot by Forsythe.[425]

DECEMBER 26. Our camp was in motion early in the morning, and the captured plunder being divided, many presented a unique appearance. One had on a Mexican dragoon cap, another a blanket, some beads and crosses, and almost every one something, the best of the arms being given to those who had none. I tied the howitzer behind one of my wagons, as the mule belonging to it [*i.e.,* the howitzer] was killed, and we had no other to supply its place. And we soon took up our line of march, all anxious for another brush. Nothing of consequence occurred until we reached the *lagunita,* except that we passed by their camp, some of the fires still burning, and that some men who were off the road reported three

[425] Writing from Chihuahua on March 4, 1847, Colonel Doniphan made a report of the Battle of Bracito to Adjutant-general Jones. This report is printed in *Senate Ex. Docs.,* 30 cong., 1 sess., no. 1, pp. 497-498.

Mexicans lying dead in the mesquite, which is here very thick and at least two or three miles below the battle ground. We found the water very brackish in the *lagunita,* and we could not even make coffee fit to drink. But after our late success we were all in too good spirits to mind it, and thought only of reaching El Paso and solving the problem whether we shall have another fight or not.

After we had all retired to our blankets, the night being still, there was an alarm, and our whole force was called out ready for action. Lieutenant Kribben being on the picket guard, I took charge of the howitzer and wished for a fight to see what it could do. The alarm having proved to be false, we retired to our blankets, when our picket guard was heard to fire a gun, and instantly we were all out again, there being no mistake this time about the gun. Presently we heard horses at full speed and supposed our guard were driven in, when up came Lieutenant Kribben and reported that a sentinel's gun had gone off by mishap, and that we might retire. It was late before all was quiet, all sleeping on our arms, ready for battle at a moment's notice.[426]

DECEMBER 27. We made an early start, intending to give battle or reach El Paso, fifteen miles off yet, and continued without interruption to where the road forks, one crossing the river, the other following it down the east bank to town. When the head of the column reached the river, an alarm was given that a flag was seen on the opposite shore, and all pressed forward for another fight, when some officers who ascended the bluffs ascertained it was a white one instead of black. It turned out to be a deputation from El Paso to surrender the place,

[426] For a description of the occurrences on December 26, see *Journal of William H. Richardson,* 48.

and to inform us that the Mexicans were totally defeated and never stopped but continued on to Chihuahua in squads, dispersing in all directions. They also brought with them the mules and horses stolen from us, and which we supposed were lost, and said a large party of Apache were on the mountains looking at the battle and killed some of their men who fled to them. They told us the enemy were surprised we did not fire until they had shot several times and began to think we intended to surrender. They asked what kind of people we are to stand up and be shot at and not return it. They say we killed and wounded a great many and that one woman was killed at the howitzer, shot in the eye, and carried off, and that another (there being two on the field who would follow the troops) jumped on a mule and went under whip through El Paso to Chihuahua. A Frenchman with the delegation had the usual volubility of that people and rode with us to town, tendering his services for every purpose. I found him accommodating and subsequently took a room in his house, where I was well provided for and had the best accommodations I had seen in the country. I was a favorite, and my room was kept neat, and Santiago was all politeness and accommodation. Here, for the first time, we found a new species of cactus, from which I got a walking stick. It is much used for hedging and is pretty.

The road between the crossing and town on both sides of the river is over very rough ground, the mountains on each side extending to its very margin. We followed the east bank, and the troops made a handsome appearance winding their way over the hills and valleys. We marched on as fast as possible to see the place, take possession, and to compare it with Santa Fé. Early in the afternoon we reached Ponce's Ranch on this side, and passing over a pretty bottom with rows of cottonwoods and vineyards on each side, reached the ford and were soon across the river, passing through town and camping in a vineyard [on] the other side. As we marched through, they offered us grapes, apples, wine, pears, peaches, etc., in great abundance and made presents of them to the men. We found their fruits delicious and the wine of a good quality, pure, and wholesome.

We are now in a climate much milder than [in] New Mexico. However, it is very subject to winds and dust, which annoy us exceedingly as we are camped in a place exposed to their full force. I obtain wood, corn, and fodder without any difficulty, the two latter in great abundance. Beef or fresh meat of any kind is scarce, and instead of purchasing flour I buy wheat and employ the millers to grind it at 50¢ per *fanega.* Wheat is worth $2.50 per *fanega.* The bread in [the] market is good but not in sufficient quantities; so I shall have to procure four or five thousand pounds of flour. Beans, salt, and soap can also be had. My animals are in corrals, and it saves us some guard duties and trouble. My servant, Lang, I found drunk when I joined the command, having stopped to see my wagons across the river, and this being the case in every town we enter and by no means his first offense, I discharged him and employed Evans.

General Remarks. El Paso. January 1, 1847. We found El Paso different from anything in New Mexico or the United States, with its *acequias,* which are almost of the magnitude of canals, its fruit trees and shrubbery, [and] its vineyards and orchards handsomely arranged and affording arbors which must be delightful in summer. The houses are on the same plan throughout Mexico, but the workmanship and finish, the superior arrangements within, and the greater style of the occupants in this department make it very different from anything we have seen. We found many of the interior courts, or corrals, as we called them, ornamented with flowers and evergreens, and fruit trees and shrubs, making a delightful place to sit at all seasons of the year, as you are equally well protected from all kinds of weather. The great body of the population left but are daily returning, and we shall soon have all the dons and señoritas of the place to add to our society. Miranda [427] and Ponce both remained and treated us with great kindness. Colonel Mitchell has quarters in the *casa* of the latter, and the former invited us to his house, where we found some of the choice El Paso wines and had a few hours pleasantly spent. He is a gentleman of no ordinary kind and once was Secretary of State in New Mexico, and is one of the few who, from the records in that state, did anything for it. He is interested with Governor Bent and others, as he tells me, in lands on Red river and the Mora, and both he and Ponce have been our decided friends. The priest, Ortiz, whom Kendall[428] has rendered famous by his book, is also here, but is the head of the anti-American party and failed to satisfy Colonel Doniphan, who talked rather rough to him. He is a young man of fine appearance, decided talent, and more patriotism than the people generally,

427 Guadalupe Miranda was formerly secretary of government of the Department of New Mexico. In 1845 he was an alcalde in El Paso del Norte. Bloom, "New Mexico under Mexican Administration," *Old Santa Fé,* II, 145, 235-237.

428 Ramón Ortiz, who befriended the Texan prisoners in 1841, was described by Kendall as follows: "The young priest could not be more than twenty-five years of age [in 1841], and was of a mild and benevolent countenance – in short, there was an open and ingenuous expression in his really handsome face that at once endeared him to every one." Kendall, *Narrative of an Expedition across the Great South-Western Prairies,* II, 37. See also Falconer, *Letters and Notes on the Texan Santa Fé Expedition 1841-1842* (Hodge, ed.), 98.

which by no means lowers him in my estimation, though very injurious to our interests.

As a general thing the people have more intelligence than exists in Santa Fé, and both men and women present a neater appearance and have more refinement. Yet the lower classes throughout Mexico are pretty much the same. A *fandango* given soon after we came in the place was generally attended by the officers, and I found it much more respectable than they are in New Mexico. The women were all neatly dressed and some fine, and presented as good an appearance as we usually have in "the States." It was well conducted, and [we had] wine, cake, etc., of the American fashion.

The settlement is about twenty-five miles long, varying in width from two to five miles, and is generally known as El Paso, though the lower town is called La Presidio de San Elizario, and the intermediate ones Socorro and Isleta. The population is estimated at 11,000, but I think is not so much. The people are more industrious than I have found them and seem to live better than the New Mexicans.[429] There is a fort at the

[429] In a letter dated February 2, 1847, Lieutenant Kribben wrote: "El Paso is quite a large place, extending twenty-five miles along the Río Grande (here called Bravo), and numbering about 11,000 inhabitants. The soil along the banks of the river is of excellent quality, and the settlement is decidedly the most beautiful that I have yet seen in Mexico. Its inhabitants are a people of altogether different cast from those of New Mexico, possessing more intelligence, industry and patriotism. . . The chief production of the soil here is the grape, which, manufactured into an excellent wine and brandy (*aguardiente*), forms an important article of trafic to the inhabitants. Besides the grape, great quantities of other fruit is raised here, as well as corn, wheat, and a few garden vegetables; and nothing seems wanting to El Paso but wood, for fuel, which cannot, indeed, be found within twenty miles of it. . . The customs of the people differ little from those of the New Mexicans. Their houses are built of clay, but are large and comfortable. Glass windows are much more scarce than at Santa Fé, and the use of knife, fork or spoon, in eating, seems to be generally abolished here – the inhabitants of El Paso having returned to the ancient and primitive mode of drinking their soup,

presidio [430] capable of accommodating a large force, probably several thousand men, and it is in a tolerable state of repair. Should this country be included in our boundary, it might be occupied at once by our troops. The elder trees were quite green [on] the eighteenth [of] January, and the birds singing as if it was spring. Yet we had some cold weather this month and considerable ice, and the old citizens tell me it is the coldest winter they have had for some years. It is warm through the day, but the nights are cold enough to require fire for comfort.

After boarding awhile with Pedro Jacques, one of the best families, I took a comfortable room at the Frenchman's, eating with my mess as I could not stand Mexican fashions or dishes, the latter all being too highly seasoned with *chile colorado*. On the eighteenth Mr. Ross arrived with the sutler's goods, and we obtained several things not to be found in a Mexican store. He brought us no news nor any letters for me but a few for the regiment. The health of the army continues very good notwithstanding the dissipation, which is carried to a great excess, wine particularly being very abundant and cheap. On the nineteenth some letters were taken with a prisoner from Chihuahua, by which we learn a little of what is going on below. It seems they estimate their force at Bracito at 1,200 men and regard themselves as badly whipped.

Leandro Gómez, a miller in my employment who lives five miles below, brought me a present of wine, grapes, apples, etc., and has taken a great fancy to me.

and of carrying their meat to the mouth by means of the *tortilla* in their right, assisted by the thumb, and the fore and middle finger of their left hand. Tables are a rare commodity with them." *Daily Missouri Republican*, Apr. 9, 1847. See also *Southwest Historical Series*, I, 191.

430 La Presidio de San Elizario.

Juan Spinosa, from the same place, brought me presents and entertained us with a curious Spanish dance, or I should rather think Indian. It was well performed, the music being a guitar. The latter has taken such a fancy to me that he brought all his women up to see me, and I returned his civilities with little presents of *cigarrillos,* tobacco, and beads. His sister is a pretty girl with dark eyes, black hair, and a brunette complexion, and, like all women in the country, has a fine form and pretty hands and feet. Generally the women have small hands and tapering fingers, and altogether are superior in form to the American, probably because lacing and such things are unknown. I, of course, embraced her when she left, according to the fashion of the country, and had no objection to repeat the ceremony at another visit which she subsequently paid me. They told me they would put up and prepare some things for the road to Chihuahua, but my sudden departure prevented me from getting them, about which I was sorry, as I always found everything coming from them nice and good.

Ponce's son also brought me some handsome presents, and I have daily as much wine, fruits, and bread sent me as our whole mess can consume. On all occasions I have been well treated by the people, and find them ready to return civilities or good treatment. We found melons abundant in [the] market, and they have them almost the year round. Gaming of all kinds is carried to an excess, and the streets are crowded with monte banks, etc. Finally it became such a nuisance and such crowds were collected on the sidewalks that Colonel Doniphan issued an order to prohibit it on the street, and the houses are now all converted into gambling concerns where the troops resort in crowds. I frequently met the priest Ortiz at the *casa* of Don Pedro Jacques and dined with him upon several occasions. He is the same person Kendall speaks so highly of, and I found him an intelligent and gentlemanly man. But he is regarded as very much opposed to us, and the troops look upon him as our most dangerous enemy. . .

THE CONQUEST OF CHIHUAHUA

THE CONQUEST OF CHIHUAHUA

El Paso del Norte.[431] At an early day after the declaration of war the attention of the government was directed to the state of Chihuahua, which is regarded as the third in wealth and resources in the republic of Mexico. General Wool was first ordered to march against it, and when the western army reached Santa Fé, General Kearny, finding he had more troops than was necessary for the occupation of this territory, ordered Colonel Doniphan first to march against the Navajo and then to proceed to join General Wool, who it was supposed in the meantime would penetrate to the city of Chihuahua. Having no intelligence at Santa Fé either from Colonel Doniphan, El Paso del Norte, General Wool, or Chihuahua, Colonel Price, on his assuming the command in New Mexico, ordered Lieutenant-colonel Mitchell with an escort of 100 men to proceed south and open a communication, the order for which will be found in the march to El Paso. Being selected as one of the escort, I accompanied the expedition as A.A.C.S. and A.A.Q.M., and in the month of December joined Colonel Doniphan at Valverde in the lower part of the territory, he having just returned from the Navajo country, which he had penetrated to the distance of 300 miles, marching through the snows and over rugged

[431] The fourth section of Gibson's manuscript, which covers the period from January to April, 1847, is entitled: "Recollections of the State of Chihuahua by Geo. R. Gibson, Second Lieutenant Infantry Co. B, Mo. Vols. including the march of Col. Doniphan from El Passo del Norte to the City of Chihuahua in the Winter of 1847."

mountains to the waters of the Gila, where he met the Indians in council and concluded a peace of a very doubtful character. We marched from Valverde to El Paso in company with Colonel Doniphan, fighting the Battle of Bracito, in which the enemy were completely routed after a short action, all of which will be found in the journal of the march.

After reaching El Paso we had necessarily to be detained awhile to procure provisions [and] to recruit our animals, especially the commissary, which were much worsted. But above all we were detained for one month waiting for Captain Weightman's company of artillery, without which it was not deemed safe to advance farther, as we had information that the enemy were well provided in this respect and were using extraordinary efforts to collect a large force. We also were well satisfied that General Wool was not advancing upon Chihuahua and that we would have to make the conquest of it with about 1,000 men, which was all the force we could calculate upon being able to bring into the field. The traders were all with us, having goods to a large amount, probably one million dollars' worth; so that we had a large pecuniary interest at stake, as well as our reputation and the honor of the country. Had the goods fallen into the enemy's hands it would have enabled them to raise fresh and additional troops and [to obtain] all the munitions of war for the whole Mexican army for a summer campaign; and the war, instead of being terminated as was expected, would have been carried on with increased energy by the enemy. We also knew that without artillery we would have to fight (if they remained in their towns) under great disadvantages. And our force being originally too small, it was a matter of great interest to increase it, and especially by the addition of an artillery arm. Colonel Doniphan, previous to leaving New Mexico and while he was still in command in that territory, had ordered it to join him, but various things conspired to create some doubts in our minds whether it would be permitted to leave. And until we knew it was on the road we were kept in constant excitement, as well by rumors that a large force was marching against us as by the doubts and uncertainties of our movements, which depended upon so many things.

As soon as we entered El Paso, we took possession of all the mills, and men were detailed to attend to them. But I preferred purchasing wheat and employing the owners to grind it, which I found much the better plan. In a short time we procured a sufficiency of flour, and for the escort I obtained beans, salt, soap, vinegar, beef, and as much of other things as we usually have had. But Colonel Doniphan's regiment, being larger, were often short in rations of fresh meat; nor was it of a good quality. Yet we all got along tolerably well, the men retaining their health, and their animals improving as fast as they possibly could. The army was composed of men of a restless and roving disposition, and the little discipline which prevailed was totally insufficient to prevent rioting and dissipation,[432] which endangered the

[432] Some of this dissipation is noted in the following entries in Hughes's diary during January, 1847: "Wednesday, 6th . . . the Square like a market place, & the scene of perpetual gambling, monte-dealing, chuck-luck &c – Spaniards & American soldiers block up the streets at monte-dealing. . . Saturday, 9th. Pleasant & fair – nothing of interest occurred except the officers had a rich *Fandango*. . . Wednesday, 13th. . . Three men to be court-martialed for ravishing a Mexican woman. The three men belong to Hudson's Company. . . Friday, 15th. . . The sport of gambling run so high that Col. Doniphan had to put a stop to it. . . Wednesday, 27th. . . Col. Doniphan by order put a stop to horse & mule racing & *Fandangoes*." Connelley, *Doniphan's Expedition,* 90, 92, 94-95.

health of the troops as well as their efficiency. And as a consequence they soon became wearied of any place and were urgent to be led against the enemy or any other place, so that they were in camp or on the march. This made our stay at El Paso very disagreeable; and when the news reached us that Major Clark and the artillery were near, it was hailed as glad tidings, and all was bustle and anxiety to leave. Our animals were in fine condition, [and] the men in good health and full of confidence that they could whip any number of the enemy brought against us. And all this was greatly increased by the stories we had heard of the wealth, the resources, the beauty, and the magnitude of Chihuahua, which we were determined to take before other troops could be sent against it. While we remained here, the weather in general was pleasant, but part of the time it was very cold and nearly always dusty and windy, the last two annoying us very much.

The very day we entered El Paso, Colonel Doniphan and the padre Ortiz, of whom Kendall speaks so well, had an altercation, which continued down to the time we left. It was through his influence that the people rose in arms and met us at Bracito, and having more than an ordinary share of capacity, he was regarded as a dangerous enemy. We also had reliable information that he kept up a constant communication with Chihuahua and had given the governor information of our strength and resources; and fearing that he would cause the people to raise an insurrection when we left, Colonel Doniphan concluded to take him and two others prisoners to Chihuahua for greater security, they having violated the promises which they first made upon the capture of the place. This, of course, created some excitement, and Miranda, who was friendly to us throughout, tried to procure his release but all to no purpose, as our safety to some extent depended upon it.

While at El Paso we were cut off for nearly a month from all news either in front or rear, and at no time could we obtain information beyond the *presidio* except of a scanty and doubtful character. Consequently we had to be on our guard all the time. And numerous camp rumors which were set afloat daily kept the army in a feverish and excited state, and several times produced alarms which put our forces in motion, once calling us all out and inducing a line of battle preparatory to action which was said to be certain. So soon as Major Clark arrived, which was the latter part of February,[433] we made preparations to leave, but grass being scarce it was thought best we should move in detachments. But the traders being scattered all along the settlements, and news having been communicated to Colonel Doniphan that some of them were leaving for the city of Chihuahua, thus furnishing the enemy with the munitions of war which they stood in need of, Lieutenant-colonel Mitchell was ordered to pursue and stop them, as well for this as other reasons; and he and his escort left on February 3 in a few hours' preparation. In fact it was determined upon at nine o'clock at night, and the next morning they were upon the march, although my animals and drivers were some distance below town not expecting to leave for several days.

After seeing them all away, I remained one day to settle with several merchants with whom I had dealt largely, it being necessary now to close our accounts as

[433] This is an error. Major Meriwether Lewis Clark and his company of artillery, under the immediate command of Captain Weightman, arrived at El Paso del Norte on February 1, 1847, having left Santa Fé early in January. *Ibid.*, 395; Edwards, *A Campaign in New Mexico with Colonel Doniphan*, 99; *Daily Missouri Republican*, Mar. 3, 1847.

they wished to make remittances to the United States, Mr. Smith of Santa Fé and others going that way. Colonel Doniphan, being not yet ready to march, remained behind intending to follow us [as] speedily as possible, the escort intending to remain below the *presidio* for him, that being the farthest point to which the traders had ventured. Late on the night of the second, Colonel Mitchell sent for me and inquired if I could furnish transportation and have everything ready to leave the next morning. I told him I could; and he then determined to leave, after remaining in El Paso from December 27, and on the morning of the third bid goodbye to a place where they had recruited and [had] seen both some pleasure and pain. In the meantime the weather had moderated but was still cool enough to form ice every night, and this in a country so scarce of timber caused the men to suffer often for the want of sufficient fuel.

La Presidio de San Elizario. The escort encamped the first night in the fort[434] at this place, twenty-five miles below El Paso, and had to purchase provisions and subsistence of all kinds, the wagons not getting up. The town has nothing about it different from other small places except a fort, [which is] capable of accommodating a large force and is really a strong place, the walls being both high and thick. The church is in the inside and is rather better furnished than similar buildings, but is on the gold and tinsel order. Like all the hangers-on of armies and troops, the people are a low and vile set addicted to dissipation, extravagance, and vice in all their shapes. And the army which met us at

[434] "This fort," wrote Edwards, "has, evidently, been once very strong; and covers more than eight acres of ground. It incloses, within its walls, a pretty church." Edwards, *A Campaign in New Mexico with Colonel Doniphan,* 99. For a plan of the fort, see Connelley, *Doniphan's Expedition,* 96.

Bracito having occupied it, their feelings are much against us, and they receive us coldly and with evident marks of what they would do if they could. We found the padre a very large, fat, and stupid-looking fellow, who cared for nothing but plenty to eat and good pay for the souls he saved.[435] On my return I met him a second time, returning from above, where he had been to purchase eatables and drinkables, and he made me a present of several little rolls of a preparation of meal, butter, and *chile colorado,* which is a great dish throughout Mexico. It is cooked by boiling, and we found them palatable and better than many other things on the tables of the country. The priest wished to be very friendly with Colonel Mitchell and offered to embrace him, but he [*i.e.,* Colonel Mitchell] refused to let him and said he had no objection to be treated so by the women, but as he was a man he must excuse him. The traders are scattered along the road from El Paso down, some being even below this in the bottoms, where they can find the best of grass.

Upon reaching the *presidio,* Colonel Mitchell learned that Kerford and Gentry had left for Chihuahua, contrary to the orders of Colonel Doniphan, and that Elguea [436] with others was also on the road. And with his escort he immediately left in pursuit, intending to make them return,[437] and proceeded some fifteen miles

435 Edwards had a similar opinion of the priest. Edwards, *A Campaign in New Mexico with Colonel Doniphan,* 100-101.

436 Francisco Elguea, a merchant of Chihuahua. *House Reports,* 30 cong., 1 sess., no. 458, p. 48; W. H. H. Allison, "Santa Fé in 1846," *Old Santa Fé,* II, 392.

437 In a letter written from St. Louis on January 26, 1848, Mitchell stated: "The objects we had in view, in compelling the traders to accompany the army from El Paso to Chihuahua, were these: 1st. We wished to make use of the wagons and bales of goods to form a field work, in the event of our being attacked by an overwhelming force in the open field; 2d. We wished to avail ourselves of the services of the American teamsters, whom we had armed and organized as an infantry battalion, numbering nearly 300 men;

on the road, where he found Elguea. But Kerford and Gentry had escaped and reached the city in safety, as we afterwards learned, disposing readily of many of their goods to the Mexicans for the army.[438] Elguea returned and camped on the river, where he remained until our forces left, and in the event proved to be a sensible and decent man. His major-domo was Mr. Skillman, who, a few days after, was elected captain of one of the companies made up of traders and their employees.

On the fourth, after employing a Mexican to take three extra mules which had been left belonging to our teams, I set out to join the escort and had a pleasant day's ride, stopping at the different camps of the traders, at one of which I found one man afoot belonging to the escort, having been drunk and lost his mule. I took him along, and though large and fleshy he proved himself capable of the foot service by keeping up. Opposite the *presidio,* having followed the road down the west bank, we came to Don Porras's [439] camp and inquired for the escort, but could find nothing of them, this being the place where they expected to encamp. After following the road a few miles, and neither being able to procure information of their whereabouts nor see any indication of a camp from the hills, we concluded it was best to return to Mr. Porras's camp and remain all night, as it was sundown and cold. Mr. Porras himself was at town, and all his men proved to be Mexicans who could speak

3d. We wished to prevent this large amount of property from falling into the hands of the enemy, because it would have aided him in paying and equipping his troops." *House Reports,* 30 cong., 1 sess., no. 458, p. 44.

438 Kerford and Gentry, merchants of Zacatecas, left La Presidio de San Elizario for Chihuahua about February 5, arriving in the latter city shortly before the Battle of Sacramento. *Ibid.,* pp. 29, 43; *Southwest Historical Series,* I, 145; Connelley, *Doniphan's Expedition,* 97, 398.

439 J. Calistro Porras, a merchant of Chihuahua. *Daily Missouri Republican,* Sept. 3, 1846; *House Reports,* 30 cong., 1 sess., no. 458, p. 48.

no English; and as I knew but little Spanish, I could not obtain the information which I desired. But they treated us well, gave us a full share of their supper, which we very much needed, and appeared to desire that we should be made as comfortable as their limited supplies and means would admit of. This we returned by distributing a bottle of *aguardiente,* which I had put up for emergencies and hard times, and we soon were quite at home. The night was cold enough to form ice half an inch thick, and we had only green mesquite for wood; so that in regard to warmth we were but poorly off. I had my great coat and saddle blanket, the one to lie on and the other to wrap myself up in. And at an early hour I selected a place with a little tuft of grass on each side, and with my saddle for a pillow, soon forgot everything in the arms of the sleepy god. To say I had wakeful moments might be deemed superfluous, but they came at such short intervals, both from the cold and [from the] noise made by a hundred mules in the corral at my head, that I by no means felt the usual benefits of rest in the morning. And we could scarcely make enough fire to cook, much less to [get] warm.

After a cup of good strong coffee, and bread and meat, I saddled up and started on the hunt of the escort, not knowing what had become of them or how we could learn where they were, and in three or four miles found them on the bank of the river, in a bend with cottonwoods scattered over it and mesquite in abundance. They had pursued Elguea and stopped him and returned to this camp late the previous evening, which they selected as strong ground against cavalry and Indians; for here the Apache are constantly prowling about, to cut off a single individual [and to] steal horses, mules, and cattle and run them into the mountains, which are not far off.

When we reached camp they told us [that] that morning an Indian arrow was found in the bedclothes of my mess, having just missed my servant Evans (who had accompanied the escort) and stuck in the blanket. No doubt it was shot across the river in the night, and was pronounced to be a poisoned arrow by some old men experienced in such things.

The guard having lost the beef cattle I sent with them, I immediately left for the *presidio* to procure some, as well as forage and other things, and to settle accounts contracted the night they were there. Beef I found very scarce, but the alcalde on whom I called said he would use every exertion to procure it; and forage I obtained in sufficient quantities, especially corn. When you arrive at a place in Mexico and wish anything, by all means call on the alcalde first, tell him your wants, give him a dollar or two, and if to be had, he will procure it. It makes him an important personage. And on the whole march I have always gone to him, and whatever is called for he orders to be produced, designating the person who is to furnish it. I dined with him here and had some things which I have not seen on any other table, especially nice preserves, and must say that he manifested every disposition to treat me well. He is a sharp, quick, and shrewd man, but one I would be afraid to trust. Before I left camp it was determined to move back to the camp of Mr. Porras, where I had stayed all night, partly to watch him, as his father is in Chihuahua and he himself is strongly suspected of aiding and furnishing the enemy with information, and partly for other reasons of convenience and defense in case troops from below should come against us before Colonel Doniphan arrived.

We remained in camp until about February 12, when

Colonel Doniphan and the artillery having come up we started once more, the weather being mild but windy, and disagreeable on account of the dust.[440] While awaiting the arrival of the army, nothing of consequence occurred. Nor were we sorry to leave, though the day was spent in town providing for a long march, as there is no place on the road where anything can be obtained. Our road was down the valley of the Río Grande, and early in the evening we encamped at a pretty place, with wood in great abundance and grass sufficient to answer all purposes. This morning Mr. Houck,[441] Ewing, Bray & Company lost a large number of oxen driven off by the Apache after daylight, while out on the hills feeding. They were pursued, and the next day, just before stopping to encamp, we met them [*i.e.,* Houck and his companions] returning, having recaptured nearly all and [having] killed one Indian. Mr. Houck rode up with his scalp on a lance, which he took from him [*i.e.,* the Indian], and all were highly pleased that for once these Arabs had been caught. They [*i.e.,* Houck and his companions] pursued them into the mountains, and had their animals not given out would probably have killed others.

Our camp was a pretty one on the bank of the river, with cottonwoods and willows interspersed, and we expect to lay by here tomorrow to regulate everything and [to wait] for Colonel Doniphan's commissary train

440 Colonel Doniphan with the main body of troops left El Paso del Norte on the evening of February 8. His total force, according to his own statement, "consisted of 924 effective men: 117 officers and privates of the artillery; 93 of Lieut. Col. Mitchell's escort; and the remainder, the 1st regiment of Missouri mounted volunteers." *Senate Ex. Docs.,* 30 cong., 1 sess., no. 1, pp. 498-499.

441 Solomon Houck, a trader from Boonville, Missouri. *Southwest Historical Series,* I, 129; Magoffin, *Down the Santa Fé Trail and into Mexico* (Drumm, ed.), 82-83.

to come up, the wagons being overloaded by the addition of the ammunition and arms taken at El Paso and Bracito. All the next day was spent in destroying ammunition which was not good, and some of the two-pounders [were] thrown in the river after ineffectually trying to burst them. An election was also held for the officers of the two companies formed out of the traders, and Messrs. Glasgow and Skillman [were] elected captains and Colonel Owens major of the battalion, all good and efficient men who can render valuable services by their knowledge of the country and people.[442] The day was very warm and pleasant, and the whole camp busy, having also to provide for the Jornada Cantarecio of sixty-five miles without wood or water, as we here leave the river.[443] Camps of troops and traders are scattered for several miles over the bottoms, and as we are now twenty-five miles below the settlements and fifty from

442 On February 9, 1847, Colonel Doniphan issued the following order: "The colonel commanding orders the mercantile train now on the route to Chihuahua, and with the United States forces, be numbered according to their advance position, and that they move as directed in the rear of the army. And further, that the citizens of the United States, (and no others, unless voluntarily,) belonging to said trains, shall organize two companies of infantry, and report the same to the colonel commanding." On February 11, in accordance with this order, about one hundred and fifty traders and teamsters organized themselves into two companies of infantry. The officers of company A were: Edward James Glasgow, captain; William Henry Glasgow, first lieutenant; C. Huston, senior second lieutenant; and H. C. Harrison, junior second lieutenant. The officers of company B were: Henry Skillman, captain; M. F. Barnham [Branham?], first lieutenant; John Howard, senior second lieutenant; and A. F. Francisco, junior second lieutenant. The two companies formed a battalion, electing Samuel C. Owens major. Doniphan then issued the following order: "The above companies having been, according to orders, duly organized, the above named officers, according to their respective [ranks], will be obeyed and respected as such." *House Reports,* 30 cong., 1 sess., no. 458, pp. 31-32; *Daily Missouri Republican,* May 18, 1847; Connelley, *Doniphan's Expedition,* 98, 397-398.

443 The army left the Río Grande near the present town of Colonia Guadalupe, Chihuahua.

El Paso we all move on together, as well to guard against Apache who inhabit both sides of the road, as to be ready with our whole force for battle in case we should meet the enemy coming up. A spy company of twelve men under Kirker, Forsythe, and others left us a few days ago [444] and have not yet returned, and Lieutenant Gordon with twelve more went ahead from this place to secure all the provisions he could find; so that we are better guarded against surprise than we have been at any time, and we shall be most likely to have information of the whereabouts of the enemy. There is some game about camp, but the moccasin tracks are also thick, and we get none.

Cantarecio Jornada. We broke up camp at ten o'clock and for the first eight miles found the road broken and sandy, and after stopping a few hours in the middle of the day to rest our animals, continued our march until ten o'clock at night, when we encamped within four miles of the Cantarecio, the night cloudy [and] very dark, and occasionally sprinkling rain. Here a mail from Santa Fé overtook us, and we once more have the pleasure of reading letters from our friends and picking up a few scraps of news in the papers. Having no water and but little wood, we made an early start next morning and nooned it at the gap in the mountains, the roads being exceedingly dusty and dry. As the day before, we continued our march in the evening until about ten o'clock, when we camped without water again and scarcely a particle of wood, having to spend an unpleasant night. The third day we resumed our march and about two o'clock came to the Ojo Lucero,[445] which we

[444] February 9, 1847. Connelley, *Doniphan's Expedition,* 98.

[445] Not far from the present Lucero, Chihuahua. On August 18, 1846, when Wislizenus passed Ojo Lucero, he noted that it was a fine spring. He wrote:

found a mudhole, and which our animals refused to drink; and we were forced to continue our march to the Laguna de los Patos, four miles farther, where we found wood, water, and grass in abundance. Two miles from the *laguna,* there is a singular spring coming out of the top of a pretty and regularly-shaped sand hill, and one cannot help but wonder how it happens, as the hill is small, not over ten feet high,[446] and so completely made up of sand that the water does not even reach its base before it sinks. The *laguna*[447] is a pretty sheet of water and is now fuller than usual. And our camp is of singular beauty, being in the center of a valley entirely surrounded by mountains, some of which are high, and of all possible forms and shapes which can be imagined. It looks like an amphitheater on a large scale.

Laguna de los Patos. Soon after encamping, a severe storm of rain and hail blew up, which lasted nearly until night and was of great benefit, as the commissary train was behind in the *jornada* and so much worsted for the want of water that it was deemed almost impossible to get the oxen and wagons through. The rain was hard enough to make large pools, and the men dipped it up by the bucketful. But notwithstanding this, many oxen were so worn out that they had to be left on the road; and at one time it was intended to abandon some of the wagons, but the rain enabled the train to get through. This Cantarecio Jornada is the worst part of the road

"The water comes out of a small, sandy basin in the prairie, but with considerable force; it is clear and soft of taste; the temperature of the spring was 77.5° Fah., while the atmosphere in the shade was 81° Fah. A little creek, formed by it, crossed the road, and spread to the right of it into a small lake." Wislizenus, *Memoir of a Tour to Northern Mexico,* 44.

446 Wislizenus described the hill as "a square mound, some 20 feet high, and on its level top a warm spring boils up in the very centre." *Ibid.,* 45.

447 The trail ran west of the lake, passing a point near the present village of San José, Chihuahua.

to Chihuahua, being sixty-five miles long, sandy and broken nearly half the distance, and the balance very dusty, which injures animals exceedingly when they cannot procure water. About one mile from the *laguna,* there is a large and pretty *ojo caliente,* the water as clear as crystal, and the white sand bottom in constant motion by the boiling up over the bottom. It is not used; nor is it good for horses, on account of the great number of leeches in it, some of which are of gigantic size, swimming and crawling through it. Quite a branch runs from it, and it is of an agreeable temperature and would make a most delightful bathing place. As yet we have no news from beyond Carrizal. But some of our men returned to camp and informed us that they had taken this place and were quartered in the ruins of an old fort, awaiting our arrival, Kirker,[448] Forsythe, and all the spies being there with Lieutenant Gordon and the men who left us at our last camp on the river.

Carrizal. This town is miserably poor, and the people all of the lowest class, the Apache driving off yearly all the stock worth having and committing depredations of every kind upon the poor and cowardly population. In fact they seem to despair of a better state of things, and, strange as it may seem, care as little about improving their condition as the wildest tribe of Indians on our frontier. It is just as much as they can do to procure enough to live upon, though possessed of advantages over most small places which I have seen in Mexico. The fort is large and commodious, and, like all similar buildings in the country, is in the heart of the town but is now much dilapidated, and in a few years, unless repaired, will be a ruin. The walls are high, with quar-

[448] In 1847 the *St. Louis Post* published a biographical sketch of James Kirker, which was copied by the *Santa Fé Republican,* November 20, 1847.

ters, a drill ground, and church within, which you enter by a large porta with rooms on each side. In fact in all the forts of the country the whole enclosure is surrounded by quarters and rooms for some purpose, the walls being one side of a building, which, of course, is a formidable place to enter, as the best of artillery has no effect upon them except to make portholes for the enemy. I went in to town in advance of the army to procure forage and beef, and found both scarce, but procured enough corn, and no beef worth having. The road from the *laguna* here was filled with water and hail, the worst of the storm being between our camp and town, and the hail lying several inches deep where it had drifted the next day. Our camp is on the *acequia,* without any grass whatever. And the evening has been one of our most unpleasant, on account of the wind which blew hard enough to blow all our tents down, and [on account of] the clouds of dust which blinded us. The whole army is now together, and our trains of quartermaster and commissary stores are kept close to our rear, as it might be cut off if permitted to fall too far behind. The traders also keep with us, both on account of the Mexicans and Indians, the latter in large bodies hanging around us, and the former, as we are informed, collecting troops in the settlements west of us for this purpose. As we were on the road we noticed signal fires in the mountains, no doubt communicating our whereabouts to the enemy and advising them of our approach.

It was late next day before we left camp, as here we have to provide ourselves with forage until we get almost to Chihuahua. At length we broke up camp and moved seven miles to a branch, the water of which is very brackish, but the grass around good and abundant. Ducks and a few geese are abundant in the low grounds along the bottom, where it is swampy with occasional pools of water, and some were killed. But we had to put up with fresh pork which I bought at Carrizal, our camp being almost as near town as it was yesterday, but on the other side. We can see plenty of snow on the mountains directly in our front, and at night the air which blows from them is of course cold and chilly. Yet the days are warm and very pleasant – so much so, that we require no fire to be comfortable. We are now getting so far down that we expect the riddle soon to be solved whether we shall have a fight or not, as the next inhabited place we strike is the only one this side of the city of Chihuahua and belongs to the governor.

Ojo Caliente. When we resumed our march the next day, instead of going with the column, I, with my guide, took a road which led us to the right and in a few miles came to the celebrated spring, Ojo Caliente, which we found to be all it had been represented. It is a large, bold stream, clear, and almost tasteless when cool, with a beautiful sandy bottom, which is kept in constant agitation by the water boiling up. At an early day the Spaniards who explored and settled the country built a wall about eighty feet long, making, at its very source, a pool of that length by thirty feet wide and waist-deep to bathe in, which is of a delightful temperature and can scarcely be muddied even when you try. Parts of the wall are now in decay, but a little work would restore it to its original magnitude and beauty; and should this country become ours it no doubt would become a half-way house and stopping place to rest and recruit animals, as the grass on the hills is abundant and good. The spring is at the base of a hill of volcanic origin, as, in fact, all in the country are. And a level plain extends entirely across the country to the mountains on the opposite side, watered by the little stream which runs through Carrizal, the Ojo Caliente, and several others which are now arroyos. We, of course, took a bath and found ourselves considerably refreshed, and many from the army which encamped two miles below to noon it, where the water was not so warm, came up and indulged in a luxury which but seldom occurs either in this or any other country. We found in it many small fish of the trout species but different from any I ever saw, and some large enough to eat. But we had no time to spend angling, and our curiosity being satisfied, as well as our personal comforts greatly increased after dining with Mr. Harmony, who came this road and encamped here, we left and followed the stream down until we joined our forces again.

The day was very warm, and all in camp in fine spirits. And having another *jornada* of fifty-five miles to pass through, we here had all of our casks and canteens filled, and our provisions cooked, as there is neither wood nor water for a long distance. All things being ready, we left in the evening and soon crossed an arroyo where we had to repair the road for our wagons, and found ourselves once more upon an even, smooth road, better than any turnpike. Soon after crossing this dry stream, there was an alarm in front, and the army formed in order of battle. But the troops seen proved to be some of our advance guard, and we continued our march without interruption until eleven o'clock at night, the air in the meantime becoming very chilly and disagreeable, when we stopped without wood or water but [with] grama grass in great abundance and of a fine quality. Early the next morning we continued our march, the road being good and directly to the snowy mountains we had seen at the Laguna de los Patos and Carrizal, and after dark encamped at [ ],[449] where we found a pool of water sufficient to quench the thirst of the men but none for our animals, nor any grass. The night was also cold as we lay at the foot of the mountains, and we repaired to our blankets as soon as possible for comfort and repose. Having no water nor wood, we left next morning without breakfast, intending to stop at the Gallego spring, and about ten o'clock reached it but passed on to the Gaigeta, two miles [on] the other side. There we found a sufficiency for all purposes but not of a good quality, and about noon made our breakfast, which we all stood much in need of.

Gaigeta spring. After procuring something to eat, the men generally collected in squads to spend the day as best they could. And a few clambered over the mountains in search of game and adventures, having seen many antelopes when we first came up, a few of which were killed. Amongst others it fell to our lot to have a quarter, and we were all prepared to do justice to fresh meat, our supply of this article being very limited indeed. Colonel Doniphan and his adjutant dined with us, and we spent a few hours pleasantly, our camp being a mile from the road, in a gorge of the mountains, which protected us from all quarters except in front, as they are very rugged and almost inaccessible to troops of any kind. In the evening a fire broke out in Major Gilpin's camp, and spread with such rapidity that all of his force could not stop it; and it soon extended itself over the mountains, presenting a magnificent spectacle after night. Some men who had ascended the mountains said it had extended to the ranches on the other side, and at no time throughout the night was it out of our view. Yet we lay in perfect security as the wind was from the

449 A blank in the manuscript.

west. The next morning we still found it in the mountains, and throughout the whole day could see it. At noon we struck our tents and continued our march until sometime after night, when we encamped without wood or water, the wind high, cold, and very disagreeable after dark. However, we managed to procure enough to eat and as soon as possible took to our blankets, which we found comfortable.

Lake Encinillas. Throughout the night we could see fire in the mountains, and I thought of the old song: "Fire in the mountains! Run, boys, run!" And it appeared to follow us on our march, and did, as subsequent events proved. The next day we continued our march, having learned in the meantime from some of our spies that a considerable body of men supposed to be 1,000 strong had come up one side of the lake and gone down the other. We also learned from the same source that some of the spies of the Mexicans had been around our camp at the Gaigeta spring, as the fresh prints of their horses clearly showed. What was the cause of these troops coming up to the head of the lake and returning was left entirely to conjecture, and the general opinion was they were retreating upon our approach.

Early in the day we reached the lake, where we thought it possible the enemy would make a stand, but we found no opposition and encamped, intending to remain here, as we had wood, water, and grass. But the fire in the mountains pursued us and soon made it evident we should be compelled to leave or have our wagons and stores of all kinds destroyed. An order was accordingly given to move, and all was bustle and activity, as the wind blew a gale, and the fire approached rapidly. We moved on down the lake, and the men barely had time to make a camping ground by setting fire to the grass in front before it was upon us. The troops rode backwards and forwards from the road to the lake and by doing so beat down the grass, and a large section was then burnt, which we occupied. The grass in the valley being bottom grass, thick and tall and very dry, the flames came crackling with a fearful rapidity, which I had read of but never before saw. It was quite an exciting scene: the teamsters urging their animals to the utmost speed; the rear, composed of commissary teams and traders, narrowly escaping; [and] the smoke, noise, and confusion being very great. The fire no doubt having spread over such an extent of country by the rarification of the atmosphere greatly increased the wind, and it was traveling with a rapidity in the lake bottom which it was no easy matter to avoid, presenting a rolling flame ten feet high. Finally all were safe in the burnt spot. And to us in our security, the spectacle was a magnificent one, the country enveloped in a dense smoke, and the fire visible for many miles in the mountains.

The night previous to this I had a slight chill from cold, exposure, and hunger, and I rode to the upper end of the lake to water my mule, a very fine American animal, when it took a notion to go its own way and finally ran off. Thinking it best to turn it to the lake, where it would have to stop, I let it go. But as it jumped in, the saddle turned, and we all went in together, pistols, sabre, gun, and self, all of which I recovered except my pistols. But the worst of it was I got wet, and before I could reach camp the cold wind brought on another chill, which made me very sick, two in one day being rather a large share, especially in this climate. It caused me to have chills for some time, but believing it was from other than a settled ague I let it alone and finally got well without taking medicine.

A very small detachment went to Governor Trias's ranch [450] on the other side of the lake, where they levied contributions and returned with corn, pork, chickens, etc., though there were men enough to have cut them off. It is quite a village, and a large business is done by the rancheros in the manufacture of coarse blankets and the common woolen fabrics of the country. The lake is a fine sheet of water about fifteen miles long and two broad, and twenty years ago was one of the richest parts of Chihuahua in stock. The pasturage is very fine, and Captain Waldo tells me that when he made his first trip here in 1830 that the whole valley was filled with cattle and horses as wild as the buffaloes on the plains. Now we saw but a very few, and they were so wild that the men on our best horses could not even get close enough to obtain a shot, much less to drive them up. The great decrease is by the Indians, who make annual incursions upon the country and kill and drive off all they want. The population has also diminished, and scarcely any attention is now paid to the cultivation either of stock or the ground. As an evidence of the decline of the country, there was once a large settlement at the Gaigeta spring, a single piece of wall now alone remaining to testify to its existence, and the country having relapsed into its pristine wildness. Ducks, geese, and all aquatic birds are in abundance around the lake, but the water near the shore is very shallow, and it is difficult to obtain access to them, as they keep out in the middle of the lake.

Piñón. The following day we encamped at the Peñol, with good water and plenty of mesquite but no grass. There is a poor ranch near camp, deserted by the inhabitants, and the stock has all been driven off. On the next day we made a short march and camped at the

[450] Encinillas.

Piñón, a small lake of muddy water, which is also brackish. We found ducks and geese abundant, but none were killed as we are too nigh the enemy to pay much attention to such things, and we are all too anxious to know what will be the result. Just as we reached camp Captain Skillman and some others belonging to the advance guard and spy company were seen several miles ahead in pursuit of some of the spies of the enemy. Captain Skillman being well mounted, pursued one so warmly that he had to abandon his horse, saddle, and cloak, and take to the mountains afoot, and he brought in these trophies when he came back. The men, though, all escaped, having taken to the rocks and inaccessible parts of the mountain. There is a high butte six miles in front of us and Colonel Mitchell and some others ascended it to make a reconnaissance. A report which receives credit, being general in camp, [is] that the enemy in force were posted at the Sacramento. And when they [*i.e.,* Colonel Mitchell and others] returned, they confirmed this intelligence, and all are now busy preparing for a conflict which is expected to come off tomorrow. We have in the army, including the traders, about 300 wagons, which are formed into four lines with a considerable interval between; and they make a considerable showing, as well as greatly add to our strength, by enabling us to form a corral immediately if necessity should require us to resort to such a defense.

Sacramento. In the morning all was bustle about camp, and there was much said about who would be missed from the ranks on the morrow. But there was not the least hesitancy, nor the slightest evidence that fears prevailed or that we should meet with defeat. On the contrary, all appeared to have the fullest confidence of success and were glad the time had come when the question would be settled about our capture of Chihuahua. As we left camp, Major Clark's band struck up *Yankee Doodle,* and the scene was animating, as we shall in a few hours be engaged with the enemy. We continued our march as speedily as possible, to arrive at the Sacramento in time to drive the enemy from their position, as we are cut off from the water until this is done. Two miles from the battlefield, there is a small elevation, or hill, from which we could see them and the fieldworks they had thrown up, but I could not perceive the least change in our men unless it was a still greater anxiety to get at them.

Battle of Sacramento.[451] The battle we were about to have not only gave increased reputation to our arms but was one of the most important which occurred during the war in its results and effects. It was the means of keeping down the disturbances which had broken out in New Mexico a short time previous and secured peace in our newly-acquired possessions in that quarter. It made the Indian tribes look upon us as a race far superior to the Mexican and overawed them. It prevented a large amount of property in the hands of the traders from falling into their [*i.e.,* Mexican] hands – property which was sufficient to have supported the whole Mexican army for several months, and at that particular time would have been of the utmost value to Santa Anna and

[451] Colonel Doniphan's official report of the Battle of Sacramento, as well as the reports of Lieutenant-colonel Mitchell and Majors Gilpin and Clark, is printed in *Senate Ex. Docs.,* 30 cong., 1 sess., no. 1, pp. 498-513. These reports have been reprinted in Connelley, *Doniphan's Expedition,* 423-438. Additional accounts of the battle by participants may be found in *Täglicher Anzeiger des Westens,* May 18, 19, 1847; *Daily Missouri Republican,* May 18, 1847; Connelley, *Doniphan's Expedition,* 103-104, 408-421; Robinson, *A Journal of the Santa Fé Expedition* (Cannon, ed.), 74-76; *Journal of William H. Richardson,* 61-64; Edwards, *A Campaign in New Mexico with Colonel Doniphan,* 110-120.

the government. It was an evidence to the northern part of Mexico, where no resistance had been made, of what they might expect if they undertook to resist again, and will be the means of securing to our fellow citizens in [the] future better treatment in their trade and intercourse with them. These are all positive advantages acquired over and above the fruits of victory, which we obtained on the field and in the city. Our troops were all well aware of its importance and felt themselves called on for the utmost energy and activity which they could display. Besides, the black flag at Bracito and the known character of the enemy gave us no room to expect even decent treatment in case of defeat, and every man seemed to feel himself called on to have victory or death. All these things had been duly considered beforehand, which, with the disparity in numbers, made us regard it as no ordinary action.

The battlefield itself was as well selected and as pretty a place for such a scene as I ever saw, and has to be seen to comprehend fully their and our positions, as it is different from all others. Their redoubts lined the road, and to put ourselves on an equal footing we left it and took to the right to reach the high ground they occupied between the Sacramento and an arroyo, which we found very bad to cross with the wagons, one at last having to be left until after night. Just as we reached the arroyo a column of about 1,000 mounted men came out in front of their position, intending no doubt to charge on our rear and the wagons while crossing in confusion. But the drivers and men urged the animals through, and it proved to be only a demonstration which in the end turned to our advantage.

As soon as we reached the high ground with the long train of wagons, Captain Weightman opened a fire upon the body of mounted troops that came out, and so well directed was it that a few shots served to drive them back upon the fortifications and produced a panic from which they never recovered. When we opened our fire, they returned it, their balls being well directed and killing several of our animals and striking the wagons. Just about this time, also, Captain Skillman's horse was shot under him and Lieutenant Dorus when we were about a thousand yards from the redoubts. The wagons, troops, and all continued to march up as speedily as possible, it being intended to use the wagons for defense if any disaster occurred to us, and we all kept together. The two mounted companies, Captain Reid's and Parson's, and about half of the escort who had good horses, charged boldly up to their works and the remainder as speedily as possible, all pushing forward with the utmost speed. There was but one order [452] – to charge – and each man fought as he best could, some riding and dismounting to fire, and again remounting and continuing the pursuit. They [*i.e.,* the Mexicans] really made no stand at any place, being driven from every position as fast as we could come up.

[452] Lieutenant Wooster, of the Fourth artillery, one of Doniphan's aids and advisers, claimed considerable credit for the orders issued by Doniphan during the Battle of Sacramento. In a letter to Adjutant-general Jones on March 7, 1847, Wooster stated: "Col. Doniphan, as most men unaccustomed to military matters would have been under the circumstances, was rather at a loss what to do during the action, and readily assented to any advice given by myself or by Capt. Thompson of the Dragoons who was present. In fact, I may say, without assuming too much to myself, that the movements generally during the engagement were made at my suggestion." Wooster to Jones, Mar. 7, 1847, Letters Received, MSS., O.F.S., A.G.O. Sergeant William Clark Kennerly, of the St. Louis light artillery, wrote: "Doniphan was an excellent attorney, though untutored in the art of war, not even knowing the words of command. In the heat of battle his orders were not the dignified 'Up guards, and at them,' of Wellington, but, 'Give'm hell, boys,' which answered the purpose quite as well and ended in a Waterloo for the Mexicans." Kennerly, Recollections, MS., M.H.S.

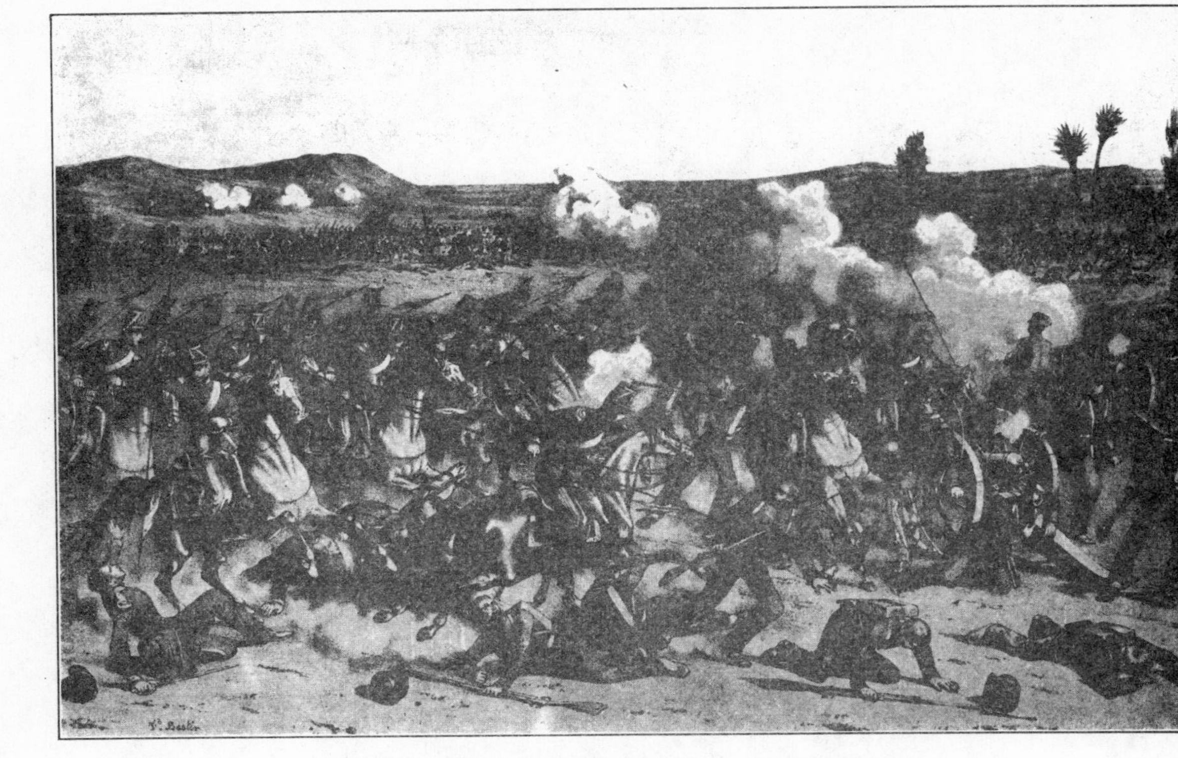

Battle of Sacramento, February 28, 1847

Major Owens was shot at the first redoubt and expired instantly. He had been with me but a few minutes before in the finest spirits and sure of a victory, and never stopped when he left my side until both him and his horse fell. He was a great loss, for we could perhaps have spared any other man better, his influence being great and his judgment sound. With him to lead, we should have obtained much more in the city. Sergeant Kirkpatrick was also shot early in the action and suffered a great deal of pain on the field, though he lived several days.

The enemy fled in all directions, and for miles around, horses, mules, oxen, and men could be seen either wounded or dead. As we came up our troops looked small compared with the crowds of them which covered the hills, and had they [*i.e.,* the Mexicans] only fought coolly and directed their musketry well we must have suffered a heavy loss. But they kept themselves concealed behind the breastworks and in the ditches, and held their guns out so as to shoot without aim and hardly even in our direction. The whole field was strewn with lances, arms, provisions, dead men, etc., and our men raised a shout which almost made the dead awaken when they carefully examined and saw how strong a place they had taken with such odds on their side. Some of their best officers and most distinguished men were present – Conde, Heredia,[453] Trias, Ugarte, Cordero, Olivares, and many others, with about 4,000 men,[454] and we had only about 1,000. Of their 4,000, twenty-two hundred

[453] General José A. Heredia was commander of the Mexican forces in the Battle of Sacramento.

[454] Colonel Doniphan estimated that the Mexican army consisted of about 4,000 men, though General Heredia stated that his forces numbered about 1,600. *Senate Ex. Docs.,* 30 cong., 1 sess., no. 1, p. 501; *Daily Picayune,* Apr. 10, 1847.

were regulars, well drilled in all things except the use of arms and the conduct becoming a soldier. Hardly a man of ours came in without bringing something, some trophy or memento – flags, clothing, money, and provisions of various kinds; and articles which they threw away in their fright filled our camp, with relations of occurrences in different places. They tried to get their artillery on the hill on the west side of the Sacramento, and had nearly succeeded when a few shots from our eight-pounders and Colonel Jackson charging up at the same time put them all to flight, one piece being dismounted by our first shot.

The ten pieces of artillery which we took [and] the wagons of ammunition and provisions were all brought into camp, and there was but little sleep that night; the very fact that we had lost but two men and several badly wounded in achieving the victory being alone sufficient to create a hilarity which but seldom exists. Our transportation is greatly added to, and it takes all the extra animals we have, as well as the captured ones, to get the wagons and artillery to the city. Every man is loaded down with spoil, and the greatest difficulty is to get along with the plunder of all kinds. Many of the prisoners died, and the spectacle next morning was such that no man could help but feel that war was an evil of the worst kind and one which should be avoided if possible. Had politicians who spent so carelessly in these matters been able to look upon it they would have used more precaution in their acts, and many a private and public calamity would have been averted which they brought on. Some were awfully mangled by our artillery. One very decent and respectable officer had both legs shot off, and the little care which the wounded must from necessity receive blunts and hardens men's feelings until they become perfectly indifferent. One of their surgeons was brought into camp a prisoner, taken in the mountains, and immediately released and sent to administer to our wounded enemies, so that they perhaps fared better than usual. But the few accommodations which belong to an army always make a bed of sickness one of great suffering, and of course more generally fatal than a man who has his friends and home around him.

A large quantity of powder and cartridges of all kinds fell into our hands, and I had one ten-mule team of the latter for artillery, which I took to the city and there turned over to Major Clark. We also captured the black flag [455] which cut such a conspicuous figure at Bracito, but the bearer of it made his escape; and it was well he did, for our men would have made mincemeat of him. We found in a trunk $3,000 in copper coin, which appeared to be their military chest. But the men made large acquisitions of silver, and one, I understand, got 100 doubloons. However, they never turned them over and took good care to say but little about it. The next day we also found a great many cattle, mules, and horses between the battlefield and city, all of which were driven up as legal spoils and came very seasonably to supply the quartermaster's and commissary's departments, besides furnishing the men who were afoot and had lost their animals either on the road or in the battle. It was dark before the men all got in camp, having pursued them [*i.e.,* the Mexicans] several miles into the mountains and captured some artillery which they tried to get off.

The next day we only marched about six miles, except a part of the artillery and Colonel Mitchell who took

455 The black flag was brought back to St. Louis by Major Clark, whose nephew, William Clark Kennerly, later loaned it to the Missouri Historical Society. V. M. Porter, "A History of Battery 'A' of St. Louis," Missouri Historical Society, *Collections,* vol. II, no. 4, p. 14.

possession of the city to secure the public property, the army being encumbered with the spoils taken on the field. The weather was delightful, and nothing was talked about in camp but the fight and hairbreadth escapes, and the consternation of the enemy, and a thousand little incidents, each one having something to tell, some incident to relate in which he was a party. We never got close enough to the main body for our small arms to have effect, and consequently we neither killed in proportion to the numbers nor took many prisoners, their animals being fresh and ours jaded by the long march.

All the foreigners friendly to us came out and met us the next day, and were greatly relieved at our victory. Had we been whipped, they would all have been murdered, making a narrow escape as it was, and having to lock themselves up to keep off a mob which raised. So confident were they [*i.e.,* the Mexicans] of success that they had made arrangements to dispose of all the goods of the traders, and we were to be tied and led captives into the city. Every now and then we found dead or wounded horses on the road, one just outside of the city, which had carried its rider that far and fallen dead. The French and Spanish consul came out with his flag to meet Colonel Mitchell and treated us throughout as well as he could.

It appeared miraculous that we all escaped as we did, the balls passing either over us, under us, or just between us, and all admitted that Providence seemed to have some agency in our preservation. Many escaped by dismounting from their horses as a cannon ball came bounding along; some stepped to one side, let it pass, and again pushed forward; and as much perhaps was owing to the watchfulness of our men who kept an eye to their safety, as well as manifested a courage and resolution which none except the best of troops could withstand.[456]

Chihuahua. When we approached the city with its churches and aqueduct and *alameda,* all were struck with astonishment that a mere handful of men should be suffered to capture such a city, and we began to think that against this people nothing was impossible. When we entered the plaza, our astonishment was still increased, this place being really pretty.

The church is one of the finest in Mexico, the architectural work being more perfect than anything we have in "the States." It is about 180 feet long and 80 wide, with two steeples 100 feet high, the front and sides of the building ornamented by statues in niches as large as life. The twelve apostles are in front, surmounted by the Savior, all well executed and giving a finished appearance to the whole. Of course, there is a great deal of carved work, the whole being out of a white rock, which makes a beautiful building material. The church was built from the proceeds of the silver mine about fifteen miles east of town and cost $1,000,000, which, in this country where labor is so cheap, would perhaps equal $5,000,000 with us. The interior is gaudy but by no means in the good taste of the architecture. Yet is has an imposing appearance when you first enter it, every corner

456 On February 28, 1847, Richardson recorded the following in his journal: "It is a fact, worthy of note, that the atmosphere here in this mountainous region is so perfectly pure and clear that a cannon shot can be seen coming, when it is a considerable distance off, by leaving a blue streak in the air. Many a soldier saved his life in the battle by dodging the balls as they came forward. When a flash would be seen from the enemy's battery, you could hear the soldiers cry out – 'watch the ball boys! – here comes a ball boys,' and they invariably avoided them, or the slaughter must have been very great. I saw a ball coming in the direction where I was, when immediately falling off my mule, it passed just over my saddle without injury." *Journal of William H. Richardson,* 63-64.

being occupied by paintings or some scriptural representation. Captain Waldo and myself spent several hours in the steeples, from which we had a fine view of the city and country around. Like all similar buildings in the country, it is well supplied with bells, one steeple having fourteen large ones, some of which are connected with the city clock. Major Owens being a member of the Church,[457] the funeral ceremonies took place in it and were to some imposing. They said every prayer, performed every genuflection, and tried every trick they knew to get him safe into Heaven, but the most potent charm was six hundred dollars which they charged, and which his administrator paid. This took him through Purgatory at once and no doubt landed him safe. His body was interred in a cemetery near the Bull Pen, escorted by Major Gilpin's battalion, who buried him with military honors.

The public fountain is in the center of the plaza, [is] of stonework, and furnishes abundance of water, which the women dip up in their earthen jars and carry by balancing on the head. It is surrounded by trees, and stone seats carved out of the same white rock, with a broad pavement in front, making a pleasant place to lounge, the dons and señoritas frequenting it when lit up at night. Many of the squares are paved and have the finest sidewalks I know, and the private and public buildings are finished off in a style which shows the place once to have been very prosperous and wealthy. There are ruins of a Jesuit church in the lower part of the city, which show it was intended to be the finest in Mexico. But they [*i.e.,* the Jesuits] were expelled [from] the country before it was finished, and it was

[457] Samuel C. Owens was not a Catholic. Sue Adair Owens, Statement to the editor, Nov. 5, 1928.

used to cast the cannon we took from them. We found a great quantity of tobacco in the mint, and corn and grain of all kinds in the public granary. Colonel Mitchell estimated the tobacco as worth $80,000. But not half the amount was realized from the public property taken which should have been under a more experienced commander. The aqueduct is a work worthy of a great people. It is constructed of stone and conveys the water about seven miles from the mountains, and supplies the whole city with abundance. Many of the arches are fifty feet high, the whole being very substantial.

The country is rocky and poor all around the city, it having been built principally on account of the rich mines which are all around it in every direction. The rich silver mine east, though, is not now worked, the water having broken in on them just as they came to almost the solid metal. No doubt in our hands this would be remedied, though it has yielded altogether nearly $200,000,000. The mountains near the city are amongst the prettiest I have met with in the country, but their nudity gives a dreary and desolate appearance to them, as if an avenging hand had passed over the land.

The *alameda* so often spoken of affords a delightful ride or promenade, and extends nearly around the city. It is rows of shade trees, principally cottonwoods, with seats interspersed, and lounges for the lazy population. In the lower end of the city one square is very pretty, having, in addition to the trees and fountains, a plain but neat monument to Hidalgo, the priest who headed the rebellion against Old Spain which terminated in the liberation of Mexico from the Spanish scepter. It has on each face appropriate inscriptions relating to him and the country. The population of the city is now 9,000 and is said to have had in its prosperity 30,000 inhabitants, but I doubt if it ever was so much. The Bull Pen, where they have their bullfights, is a fine building which cost $30,000, and is really a Roman amphitheater constructed of the best and most durable materials. Some idea may be formed of its magnitude when it is known that Colonel Jackson's whole battalion was quartered in it without being in the least crowded.

Many of the private dwellings are finished off in a style which would be no discredit to "the States," and all are comfortable. One of the most luxurious places I ever saw was the French and Spanish consulate. It reminded one of palaces and castles of an eastern court and the "Sunny South" all combined. The furniture and everything pertaining to it was not only upon a large scale but of the richest character. The public houses of all kinds are also creditable but not equal to what one meets with in our cities. And for the first time in Mexico we found shops of the different artisans opened and regularly kept. Some of the work which they turn off is good, but most usually is inferior to that from our best mechanics. We found almost everything to sell which we usually have in our small towns, and grain and provisions in abundance and cheap. Even pork in large quantities was bought at eight cents per pound, the hogs weighing three and four hundred [pounds]. The governor and all the other state officers left the night after the battle. The rooms in the house of representatives were filled with public documents and the archives of state, which were boxed up and generally left untouched.

Everywhere you see marks of the mineral resources of the country, ruined furnaces, immense piles of scoria and ashes, and old smelting houses. A considerable business is still done in the precious metals, even washing for gold and silver. But now the greatest source of revenue to the city is the mint, which manufactures all the copper and silver and gold coins of the state. It is in the hands of an English house who trade for the crude mineral, both here and about eighty miles west in Durango, and coin it. Should the country at any time be annexed to ours, the enterprise of our citizens would again put it in a flourishing condition. In fact its decline now is principally owing to the Apache and Comanche, who make inroads almost to the city and carry off everything valuable. Mexico – at least this entire frontier – seems to be in the same situation Rome was with regard to the northern hordes which overran her territory, only that the Indians are more completely savage than the Goths, Vandals, or Huns. The mines are abandoned on account of them, their ranches are permitted to go to decay, and the immense herds which once covered the land no longer exist; and everything, even the people, are in a state of decline and degeneracy. Generally the population is of pure Castilian descent, with very fair complexions and dark eyes. The women are of good size, well made, and some very beautiful and fascinating, having all the ease and gracefulness of our best and most accomplished ladies. The lower classes, however, are like those in New Mexico. But here there is an upper circle which belong to the exclusives, and [also] a respectable middle class.

Throughout all Mexico there is a want of virtue, even in the upper ten thousand, but there is not that low-flung exhibition of it which you meet with daily and almost hourly in New Mexico. On the streets and in the face of the public, all is decency. One thing in particular shows the bad state of society in a country where living is so cheap, and that is the immense number of beggars you see at every corner, many who look too robust not to be capable of doing something. They are a great nuisance, and consist of men, women, and children in filth and rags. Tuesdays and Fridays are set apart for alms, and you see them out early in the morning, dunning every passer-by, "For the love of God," to give only a *cuarto*.

Like all Mexicans they [*i.e.,* the inhabitants of Chihuahua] are addicted to gaming, and become passionately fond of it, both the men and women. In fact, bull baiting, cockfighting, and gaming are their only amusements, which they resort to daily, from the highest to the lowest classes. Some idea of the stakes played for may be formed when it is known that one man wins or loses $10,000 when he goes to a monte bank. He has great wealth, and when I was there, there was no bank large enough for him to bet at. They also have a cockpit, and many appeared to understand fully all the tricks which can be played off at this old-fashioned sport. The people but seldom visit one another, all meeting at the monte bank. Nor have they any taste for evening parties to spend a few hours with their friends, the women usually never entering where there are visitors. The people seemed to feel they were badly whipped and made no pretensions against us. Neither did they show any disposition to associate, except the most intelligent, who, I really believe, would be glad if we retained the country. They said they fought lions and tigers and not men, which was about all the excuse they had for being badly whipped.

We entered the city on March 1, and vegetation of all kinds was then forward, beans, peas, corn, etc., being up, and the trees getting green; yet the coldest weather they had throughout the winter was after this time.

However, [it was] not severe enough to prevent us from going without fire except to cook, their houses being too thick and close for the little cold to penetrate. The last week in March the thermometer stood at 85° and even above that, and the glare of the sun was so intense that scarcely a man could be seen on the streets from twelve to three o'clock. During this time the stores are all shut up, and it is like Sunday in "the States." The *feria,* or market, is a pretty place but does not compare with ours in the abundance and variety of things to sell. Nor have they the neat appearance which our market people know how to give to everything. We found eggs, chickens, lettuce, asparagus, and beans and peas, with mutton and pork plentiful but generally not good. Ice creams of an indifferent character are offered you about the streets, and upon one occasion I even saw mint juleps, but they were at the house of an officer. The *fonda* is kept by Americans, and we have turkeys for dinner every day, and many other things which remind us of home.

The first [week] of April was the Holy Week, the Church heretofore always celebrating it with great pomp and parade, marching around the streets with images and crosses. But they did not have their usual celebrations this time, though Colonel Doniphan gave them permission. Probably they thought our men would pay too little respect to the ridiculous custom and infuse their feelings into some of their credulous followers. Captain Waldo and myself visited Guadalupe church in the upper part of the city, which is said to be the richest in it, though small and not more than a common building. We found many large and fine paintings, and the altar plainly but neatly finished, and everything in better taste than I have seen in Mexico. From the church we took a stroll around the aqueduct, every few steps meeting ruins of some kind, showing the city to have been very prosperous once. The gardens and yards now are all green and pretty, and we stopped to examine several, in which we found plum trees, apricots, quinces, etc. Flowers of all kinds were in bloom in February, nasturtiums in particular, and several which are alone found in a warm climate. The fig trees are forward, and [also] a pretty species of elder, which is very green and has a very thick foliage. Summer is evidently here. Nor is it to be wondered at when it is known that Chihuahua is farther south than the mouth of the Mississippi.

On the [13th] [458] day of March we had the first number of *The Anglo-Saxon,* a little paper edited by Lieutenant Kribben,[459] which has served us some purpose

458 *The Anglo-Saxon,* the first American newspaper published in Chihuahua, made its initial appearance on March 13, 1847. It was printed half in English and half in Spanish, and its size was about eight by twelve inches. Lieutenant Christian Kribben, of the Missouri light artillery, was the editor, and Sergeant John S. Webb, of the Jackson county volunteers, was the publisher. In 1843, Webb had been one of the publishers of the *Western Expositor,* a weekly newspaper of Independence, Missouri. The press, type, and paper used by *The Anglo-Saxon* were found in the city of Chihuahua. "The fonts of type," according to a contemporary account, "were as barren of *ws* as a cockney's pronunciation, and the publisher is forced into the double cockneyism of using two *vs* as a substitute." *Daily Picayune,* May 11, 1847. See also *Täglicher Anzeiger des Westens,* May 17, 1847; *Daily Missouri Republican,* June 21, 1847; *Jefferson Inquirer,* Sept. 7, 1843; Connelley, *Doniphan's Expedition,* 531.

459 Christian Kribben was born near Cologne, Prussia, March 5, 1821. In 1835 his parents migrated to the United States and settled near Manchester, St. Louis county, Missouri. Three years later the family moved to St. Charles, Missouri, where Kribben studied law and was admitted to the bar. Coming to St. Louis in 1846, he enlisted in company B, light artillery, Missouri volunteers, which was composed entirely of Germans from St. Louis and vicinity, and on June 9 was elected first lieutenant. During the Mexican war he was a regular correspondent of the *Täglicher Anzeiger des Westens* and the *Daily Missouri Republican,* contributing numerous articles on the campaigns of Kearny and Doniphan. Upon his return to St. Louis in 1847, he resumed the practice of law. He was a linguist and a capable speaker. During the later fifties he became interested in politics and was elected to the state

and was continued until the troops left. Major Campbell, with an express for Washington, left about March 12 for Fort Towson, having thirty or forty men with him. We heard of him near the Presidio, and learned that Mr. Barnes, who came down as my interpreter and guide and accompanied him, died about that place, and that if he met with no accident Major Campbell would go through in thirty days.[460] A week before, an express had left for Santa Fé; so that the news of our conquest will spread soon. Though so far south the climate of Chihuahua is delightful, on account of its elevation and situation in the mountains, being warmer in the winter and more equable the year round than the Pass or any part of the upper country. It is also very dry, rain scarcely ever falling except in the summer months, which tempers the atmosphere. Snow is almost unknown, and figs, oranges, and lemons are common about the houses.

A few days before I left we had a specimen of Mexican sport at the Bull Pen. Five bulls were brought in, and four matadors, two on foot and two mounted, besides a sort of clown who tried to amuse the public. There were probably several thousand persons present, with Major Clark's band to assist in their amusements, and

legislature. He died in St. Louis, June 15, 1865. Two days later Doniphan delivered a eulogy of Kribben at a special meeting of the St. Louis Bar Association. *Daily Missouri Republican,* June 16, 18, 1865; *Täglicher Anzeiger des Westens,* June 9, 1846, May 17, 1847; W. V. N. Bay, *Reminiscences of the Bench and Bar of Missouri* (St. Louis, 1878), 352-353; *The History of the Bench and Bar of Missouri* (A. J. D. Stewart, ed., St. Louis, 1898), 100.

[460] John P. Campbell, of Springfield, Missouri, accompanied by about thirty-two men, left Chihuahua on March 14 or 15, 1847, carrying dispatches to Washington, D.C. Crossing the Río Grande at Presidio del Norte, he traveled eastward through Texas and Louisiana, arriving in New Orleans on May 10. Six days later he came to St. Louis. *Daily Picayune,* May 11, 1847; *Weekly Reveille,* May 24, 1847; Connelley, *Doniphan's Expedition,* 107, 451-452.

all went off very well. But except in the adroitness and skill manifested in the use of the lariat, the bullfight scarcely came up to our notions. The bulls, however, were only tolerable, and it was inferior to many similar exhibitions which they have. Only one was brought in at a time, and when completely worn out was turned back and another introduced, which had to go through the same ceremony.

Colonel Doniphan, in order to accomplish the opening of a communication with General Wool or Taylor, dispatched Mr. Collins with twelve men on express to report to either or both of them, and finally, on his [*i.e.*, Collins's] return, received orders to march to Saltillo.[461] In the meantime, having heard that public property of a large amount still remained in the little town of San Geronimo and some other places, he left Chihuahua on April 4 with all of the army except Colonel Jackson's battalion, intending to go as far, perhaps, as Parral, where it was said some kind of a government was kept up. A report that a large force was coming up to attack him, though, drove him back after going about seventy miles; and he then remained in Chihuahua until he received orders from General Taylor, which was about May 28.[462] We had heard the Mexican account of the Battle of Saltillo soon after we entered the city, but it was of such a character that we all felt sure that "Old

[461] James L. Collins, a Santa Fé trader from Boonville, Missouri, had been appointed interpreter in January, 1847. On March 20, accompanied by an escort of thirteen men, he left Chihuahua for Saltillo, carrying dispatches from Colonel Doniphan to General Wool. He arrived at Saltillo on April 2. Starting on his return trip with an enlarged escort of about forty men, he came back to Chihuahua on April 23, bringing orders from General Taylor for Doniphan to march to Saltillo. *House Ex. Docs.*, 30 cong., 1 sess., no. 56, pp. 317-319; Connelley, *Doniphan's Expedition*, 91, 99, 108, 453-463.

[462] April 23.

Rough and Ready" had whipped them badly, and this we since found to be the truth.

The same day that Colonel Doniphan left for San Geronimo, I left on my return for Santa Fé, the weather being very warm and oppressive. And [I] had a pleasant trip up, it being the first time for nearly twelve months that I had not been on active duty, and seven out of the twelve months in the field.[463]

---

[463] The fifth and sixth sections of the journal have not been published because they contain little material of primary historical importance. They tell the story of Gibson's return to Santa Fé in 1847 and of his journey from Santa Fé to Fort Leavenworth in 1848.

APPENDIX

APPENDIX[464]

Muster Roll of Captain Murphy's Company

[*Officers*]

1.	William S. Murphy	Captain. Resigned.
2.	V. R. Van Valkenburgh	First Lieutenant. Killed at Taos.
3.	George R. Gibson	Second Lieutenant.
4.	A. B. Aull	First Sergeant and Sergeant Major. Diseased [?].
5.	M. L. Hardin	Second Sergeant. Discharged, September 17.
6.	James Dougherty	Third Sergeant. Died.
7.	T. J. Wood	Fourth Sergeant.
8.	John Thurman	First Corporal. Detached, October 7.
9.	John McGuire	Second Corporal.
10.	Samuel Doyle	Third Corporal.
11.	Alexander McFarland	Fourth Corporal.

Privates

1.	Allcorn [?], Bransford	
2.	Brooks, Martin D.	
3.	Bennigher, Frederick	
4.	Campbell, Charles E.	
5.	Campbell, Hugh L.	
6.	Chambers, John	
7.	Cowan, James	
8.	Carter, James W.	
9.	Curry, John S.	
10.	Clark, William N.	
11.	Drummond, William P.	
12.	Drummond, L. D.	
13.	Doyle, John	
14.	Dawson, Francis M.	Died.

[464] Scattered throughout Gibson's journal are various lists and copies of documents, the most important of which have been gathered together and published in this appendix.

15. Ellison, John
16. Finch, Franklin
17. Funderburgh, Bleuford [?]
18. Fox, John S.
19. Gibbons, John
20. Groomes, John — Died.
21. Groomes, Robert
22. Griffith, William
23. Graham, John B. — Killed at Cañada.
24. Gladden, Green
25. Hartwell, Benjamin B.
26. Haddick, Lewis
27. Harpst, John
28. Harris, Richard
29. Hubble, Ezra
30. Isaacs, Raileigh
31. Isaacs, Amos
32. Jenkins, Richard H.
33. Kuychenthal, Albert
34. Leary, Henry A.
35. Larison, Ezekiel
36. McCormack, Andrew
37. Morgan, Samuel
38. Morgan, Jonathan
39. Mulkey, Thomas — Died.
40. Pearce, Andrew J.
41. Pearce, Elijah P.
42. Perie, Robert — Died of consumption, October 14. Aged 24.
43. Patten, Joseph
44. Riley, James B.
45. Riley, George
46. Richardson, Samuel
47. Ramey, William R.
48. Snodderly, LeRoy
49. Smith, James — Died October 31, with the measles.
50. Sharp, William
51. Sharp, Jacob
52. Shearer, Joel
53. Surrat, James H.
54. Short, Addison

55.	Swan, Israel	
56.	Skaggs, William	
57.	Ussery, John	
58.	Wooten, Ward	Died.
59.	Wilcoxen, Isaac N.	
60.	West, Henry	
61.	Wiley, Edward	
62.	Wiley, John	
63.	Waldon, Robert	
64.	Wells, John	
65.	Seafert, Gustavus	Discharged, July 16.
66.	Eastborn, Thomas	Musician, drummer.

Of the above, one or two are specimens of American character. H. A. Leary served as a private in the last war with England, subsequently enlisted as a marine and made an expedition to the Mediterranean, and the next place we find him is in New Mexico, able to undergo all the fatigues of a long campaign. Sergeant Dougherty served a long time in the First dragoons, afterwards in the infantry in Florida, and the next place we find him is at Santa Fé. He also served in the navy as a marine.

Ugarte to Armijo
(translation)

Most Excellent Sir: Since the month of March last, in which I was named general commandant of this department, I received orders from the supreme government to place myself equally in communication and relations with the commandant general of Durango and with yourself, to give us power to resist the pretensions of the United States in case of invasion. The scarcity of mails for one cause, and for another the constant movement to which I have been forced, have prevented me [from] communicating with you sooner. Now that the advances of the United States leaves us without doubts, and the results of the last events at Matamoras having arrived in this department, I hurry to assure you that you *may count upon me.* I hope we may place ourselves in frequent communication, and in fine that you may know I am ready to move in defense of my country. I have 500 cavalry and could raise as many more infantry, and at the first advice from you they will be ready to march.

Receive my most considerable considerations of appreciation, friendship, etc.

God and Liberty. July 1, 1846

Manuel Ugarte

ORDER NUMBER 13

Headquarters, Army of the West
Camp near Old Pecos, on Pecos River
August 17, 1846

1. By the annexation of Texas, the Río Grande from its mouth to its source has become the boundary between the United States and Mexico. Consequently all persons living on the east side of that river are to be regarded as citizens of the former and are to be treated accordingly. Assurances have been given that such citizens as remain at home in pursuit of their peaceful avocations shall not be molested by anyone of the army, but shall be respected and protected in their rights, both civil and religious. It is now enjoined on each and all of this army to make good these assurances, and anyone who may so far forget his duty to his country and to himself as to violate them will be guilty of an act deserving the severest punishment, which he may expect to receive. We are taking possession of a country and extending the laws of the United States over a population who have hitherto lived under widely different ones, and humanity as well as policy requires that we should conciliate the inhabitants by kind and courteous treatment. This order, also the fifty-fourth and fifty-fifth articles of war, will be read at the head of each company of the army at two successive parades, that all may be made sensible of the responsibility imposed upon them. And it is hereby made the duty of each one to report at this office any violation of the spirit or purport of it that may come to his knowledge.

2. Captain A. R. Johnston, First dragoons, is hereby appointed the aid-de-camp to Brigadier-general Kearny. He will be respected accordingly.

By order of Brigadier-general S. W. Kearny

H. S. Turner
A. A. A. General

Extract from Order Number [30]

Headquarters, Army of the West
Santa Fé, New Mexico
September 23, 1846

Colonel Price will remain in command of the troops in this territory, which will consist of his own regiment; Major Clark's battalion of two companies of horse artillery, having a part of Captain Hudson's company of Laclede Rangers with it; and Captain Angney's battalion of two companies of infantry. Should any more troops be sent here, they must, unless otherwise directed by higher authority, continue on to Chihuahua and report to Brigadier-general Wool.

By order of Brigadier-general S. W. Kearny

Order Number 71

Headquarters, Army in New Mexico
Santa Fé
November 17, 1846

1. As it is desirable to open a communication between this army and the army commanded by Brigadier-general Wool (now supposed to be in the vicinity of Chihuahua) and to establish a reconnoitering party along the route to that city from this place, Lieutenant-colonel Mitchell, Second regiment, Missouri mounted volunteers, will select from the army present an escort of 100 men for this city.

2. The object to be accomplished by this detachment being of an important character, Lieutenant-colonel Mitchell will be careful to select both officers and men with reference to their efficiency, intellectual and physical, and to see that their horses are in a condition to perform the service required of them.

The assistant quartermaster and the assistant commissary of subsistence at this post will furnish Colonel Mitchell's detachment with necessary means of transportation and subsistence for this march. Lieutenant-colonel Mitchell will receive and be guided by a letter of instructions from the colonel commanding.

By order of Colonel Sterling Price

R. Walker, Adjutant

